Praise for Unleashing the Power of Respect: The I-M Approach

"What if the challenges of your life and the problems of the world became suddenly solvable? Not solved, but solvable. To me that is the premise behind this book. By using Dr. Shrand's I-M Approach and unleashing the power of respect for others and yourself you can team up to first see then enact the solution to most anything. So come out of your foxhole, emerge from your echo chamber and after a good look in the mirror take that first step toward partnering up with people to get things done!" —Steve Aveson, multiple Emmy winning news journalist who has traveled the world as a correspondent and Circus performer telling stories in all 50 states.

"This intimate and powerful work is not only a compelling look at the value of psychiatrist Dr. Joseph Shrand's professional I-M Approach, but it also is about the value of simple respect in building personal contact between people. While the fascinating detail of his practice makes for a rich read, the important broad lesson is about how respect allows our minds and brains to build relationships between all people, not just patients and their doctors. [*Unleashing the Power of Respect*] is a must read for the curious and for those who care about the future in our modern world that seems all too often about what divides us rather than how to unite us. I highly recommend it." —James R. Stellar, Behavioral Neuroscience Professor and past Provost and Interim President at the University at Albany, SUNY

"*Unleashing the Power of Respect* is not just a great title, but more, it is a paradigm shift. Dr. Joseph Shrand challenges all of us to look at people not as problems to be solved but rather to see the goodness and value inherent in all people. A must read!!" —Norm Townsend LMHC/LMFT, Director of Clinical Initiatives, Riverside Community Care

"Dr. Shrand's respect for and understanding of human nature is beautifully genuine. The time has come to look beyond the broken places and listen, connect, and see the value in each other. Reading his perspectives in *Unleashing the Power of Respect* has been like putting salve on my wounds." —Val Comerford, woman in long term addiction and mental health recovery

"This is one of those books that feels applicable as soon as you start reading. Dr. Shrand illustrates his concepts of the I-M Approach beautifully with stories from his career, sharing the experiences, successes, and failures that have led him to put this infinitely valuable approach into writing. Within a few hours of closing the book, I found myself in conversations asking whether or not others were doing the best they could at that moment based upon their domains of influence, rather than jumping to conclusions about their motivations or intentions. This book is a must-read for anyone who wants to reframe their relationships or better navigate the stress that can come with working and living alongside others." —Blake Reichenbach, Senior Product Expert for CMS Publishing and Search Optimization at HubSpot Richmond, Kentucky, United States

"For years, Dr. Joseph Shrand has written and spoken about the importance of appreciating all people in their own rights and validating people in ways that give others a palpable sense of worth. This approach to improving the human condition has proven very successful and inspiring. In his newest book, *Unleashing the Power of Respect*, Dr. Joe masterfully focuses his light on the importance of demonstrating genuine respect for others as an important feature of effective growth at the individual and community levels. Dr. Joe's writing is elegant, captivating, authentic, and accessible. I always feel like a better person after listening to his deeply informed and optimistic take on what it means to be human. Read this book, and you will too." —Glenn Geher, PhD, Professor of Psychology, State University of New York at New Paltz, author of *Positive Evolutionary Psychology: Darwin's Guide to Living a Richer Life*

"With a keen eye and a compassionate heart, Dr. Shrand uses engaging stories to reveal how mutual respect is central to sustaining human dignity. He shows us that even within the constraints of society and biology we still have an empowering choice—the choice to treat ourselves and others with kindness, consideration, and respect." — Jonathan Kahn, JD PhD, Professor of Law and Biology at Northeastern University, author of *Race on the Brain: What Implicit Bias Gets Wrong About the Struggle for Racial Justice*

"This approach has worked so well with the people whom I counsel in my work with inmates or former inmates, but it has an even more far-reaching effect in how it works when I use it on how I treat my own responsibilities. I tend to double task and lump two or more errands together. Since reading and applying the I-M Approach to my everyday work, I have learned not to deny myself the joy of the finished product. When it comes to my artwork, time does not matter, it is in my everyday needs that I now use the Power of Respect lesson which the book unleashed in me. Respect of my daily tasks not only makes me happy, but it makes me respect myself. Thank you, Dr. Joe, you make me happy." — Hedy Pagremanski Page, Artist, Facebook "Mondays with Hedy"

"Dr. Joseph Shrand, child psychiatrist, is a brilliant storyteller. In this page-turner of a book, he presents us with stories of a dozen or so of his patients with humor and empathy. He describes how, as a psychiatrist, instead of 'curing their disorders', he analyzes the four Domains of his patients' ever-evolving I-Ms and helps them change their behaviors through trust and respect. And he shows us how we can use I-M in our own lives. Well-worth reading." —Christopher Sarson, former public TV producer, multiple Emmy Award winner, and mediator

"In his latest book, *Unleashing the Power of Respect: The I-M Approach,* Dr. Joseph Shrand provides a clear, concise explanation of his I-M Approach, which represents an important perspective towards treating and working with others. He then masterfully weaves in real-life examples of how the I-M perspective inherently generates clear respect of the Individual, which in turn creates an interpersonal environment that promotes health and defuses problematic situations. He also shows how the I-M Approach can impact critical social issues in today's society. This is a "must-read" for clinicians, people interested in public policy and anyone who is thoughtful about their relationships." —Christopher T. S. White, Ed. D. President/CEO Road To Responsibility, Inc. Licensed Psychologist

"Dr. Joseph Shrand has produced an excellent book. A text that acknowledges the challenges generated to all of us by mental health conditions . . . but a book that relies, not only on training and clinical wisdom, but, above all, on the need to really understand the person behind the condition. To go beyond conditions is the fundamental step taken by Dr. Joe. He gives terrific examples of how he establishes an alliance with the person he supports; an alliance based on trust, respect and mutual pride. I am persuaded that his approach is easily adapted to universal situations. He was invited to present his work at the Spanish Child and Adolescent National Annual Congress, in my hometown (the very first time the American Academy of Child and Adolescent Psychiatry held a joint meeting in Europe) . . . and I was able to witness that his human and technical approach transcends cultures. Something that it is essential for our global world. ¡Felicidades, Dr. Joe!" —Joaquin Fuentes, MD Chief of Child and Adolescent Psychiatry, Policlinica Gipuzkoa Research Consultant, GAUTENA Autism Community Program Donostia / San Sebastian, Spain

"As a diversity and inclusion practitioner, respect is a fundamental principal that I teach regularly. Respect me. See me. Value me. That's what we all want. The I-M Approach applied appropriately will result in the respect we all desire and deserve. I think [Unleashing the Power of Respect] is such a needed resource for such a time as this. From my lens, Dr. Shrand provides a thought-provoking perspective on two key factors so important today, the power we have to change and the importance of respect. We have the power of choice; the ability to shift our perspective to impact our life experiences. Do the best we can at that time. Love that! That is the I-M. If I were to rate this book, I would give a five-star rating, with much respect to you, Dr. Joe!" —Angela M. Crutchfield, D.M., CEO/Senior Consultant, Crutchfield Group LLC, Vice President for Diversity & Inclusion, Riverside Community Care

"Dr. Shrand is a sage for Western sensibilities: more Star Wars Yoda than Japanese poet or Buddhist monk. Yet I think of all three in the same league. We could use each one at this particular moment, when internecine conflict and international strife appear at all-time highs. Now more than ever we have an opportunity to *Unleashing the Power of Respect* it is high time to start seeing the value in all of us." —Andrés Martin, Riva Ariella Ritvo Professor, Child Study Center, Yale School of Medicine, Editor-emeritus, *Journal of the American Academy of Child and Adolescent Psychiatry*

"Dr. Shrand teaches us through his insightful and humane approach to have profound respect for people's behavior—that they are doing the best they can. He shares a model for understanding why people choose seemingly dysfunctional behaviors and then allows us to experience this model with him as he treats quite difficult patients. Warm, engaging, and readable. Very much appreciated your high-quality therapy approaches . . . Yoda would say, 'Wise he is!'" —Michael S. Jellinek, Professor of Psychiatry and of Pediatrics, Harvard Medical School

"This book is a gift for our troubled times. In our current era of blaming, insults, and overwhelming levels of negative judgments, Dr. Joseph Shrand offers us a framework based on respect and empathy that can help bring out the best of both others and ourselves, while reminding us that transformation can begin with small adjustments. Full of both humanity and wisdom, *Unleashing the Power of Respect* is a valuable resource not just for clinicians but basically anyone who interacts with other people." —David Rettew MD, author of *Parenting Made Complicated: What Science Really Knows about the Greatest Debates of Early Childhood*

"Dr. Shrand takes a careful humanistic approach to a field that at times borders on the mechanical. Through the development of carefully choreographed stories and anecdotes, Dr. Shrand provides the reader with a concise grasp of not only how to treat patients, but how to interact with those in your life. This introspective dive allows the reader to comprehend the impact of their own experiences and behaviors as they relate to the potential of those around them in order to truly *Unleashing the Power of Respect.*" —Matt Anderson, Executive Director. Kids4Peace, Boston, MA

"Animosity. Disrespect. Anger. These fraught emotions are timeless, seemingly embedded in the human condition. Yet they also feel particularly raw and relevant these days. Similarly, with this new edition Joe Shrand has written a book that simultaneously captures and confronts age-old challenges while also giving us fresh, powerful, and practical tools for repairing brokenness in today's society. Joe's book is a must-read for anyone who wants to improve their personal and professional relationships and move through life with renewed hope and joy. Thank you, Dr. Joe." —Mark Bayer, Founder, Bayer Strategic Consulting

"*Unleashing the Power of Respect* provides powerful insights into who we are and why we do what we do, as Dr. Shrand says. As a theater person I appreciate his insights into our human condition and wish we could all apply the power of respect to each other on a daily basis." —Michael J. Bobbitt (he/him/his) Executive Director, Mass Cultural Council, Boston, MA

"In his *Unleashing the Power of Respect*, Dr. Joseph Shrand provides a framework for all of us to build and maintain relationships in a world seemingly overrun with anger, impatience and disrespect. At the core of Dr. Shrand's I-M Approach is the concept that people are doing the best they can at any particular moment. Doing so will help us all pivot from making judgments about others to being more respectful and understanding. He urges us to move away from thinking about behaviors as disorders, but rather as conditions emanating from one or more of our "domains," identified as biological, social, home and interpersonal. Empathy resides firmly inside the heart of Dr. Shrand's book. Don't we all want to feel valued and understood? For the two of us—a family therapist and divorce lawyer—we found this book immensely thought provoking and helpful in our respective professional practices. We urge everyone to "unleash your power of respect" and read Dr. Shrand's book." —David and Julie Bulitt, authors of *The 5 Core Conversations for Couples*

"In his magnum opus, Dr. Joseph Shrand describes his 40-year journey with his patients to find value and respect. Dr. Strand (uh, Shrand) writes in a simple, straightforward style, with exercises for business owners, teachers, clinicians, and individuals to implement that will increase cooperation, respect, and trust, and enable us to become our ever-better selves amidst an ever-changing world." —Jeff Q. Bostic, MD, EdD, Professor of Clinical Psychiatry, MedStar Georgetown University Hospital

"Must admit it: Dr. Joseph Shrand has gotten inside my skeptic's head. True to form (please read this book) he has 'influenced everyone.' Dr. Joe Shrand and I share a 'Social Domain' as friends and neighbors. We are occasional walking companions down the naturally occurring social experiment single lane road to the 'island,' as he describes early on in this book. There is a deep contrast between the stunning wild beauty of the vista, with its intermittently submerged road, necessitating the residents' and visitors' call to do their best in negotiating an ever shifting and challenging environment ('biological domain'). What Dr. Joe does not mention in *Unleashing the Power of Respect: The I-M Approach* is his mastered skills as a playwright. Within that skill set, yet more basic, Dr. Joe is a captivating storyteller, especially for dialogue. I see this as a style with deep roots back to Aesop, who also tried to make sense of human nature. Dr. Joe's dialogues are vivid and engaging, at times devastatingly beautiful. The stories of patients and their families is a rich source of intimate and deep interactions, to which those of us in the medical profession have privileged access. Dr. Joe has given their struggles a voice for good (yes, Joe, works on two levels). I-M and its corollary constructs provide tangible tools to try out. As Dr. Joe nicely acknowledges, these constructs derive from his personal experience and cultural awareness of centuries of others' insights. I will need more time to fully digest all he has written ("Ic"). As with any major theory of human interaction, there may yet remain areas where it does not quite 'fit'. Having said this, I was entranced by the chorus of 'you control no one but influence everyone' and 'small changes can have big effects.' Worthy mantras for this deep agnostic. Looking forward to more walks, Dr. Joe." —Donald S. Marks, M.D., Assistant Clinical Professor of Neurology, Tufts School of Medicine

"Dr. Shrand's new book, *Unleashing the Power of Respect: The I-M Approach*, is profoundly moving and engaging. It is an incredible journey into the human condition and the complexity of our minds. I found myself getting pulled into his stories so much that I lost all track of time. The book's characters come to life and elicit profound feelings of empathy. Dr. Shrand's stories and therapeutic experience opened a window into the long-buried memories I feared facing. I am genuinely grateful for having the privilege of learning from him and beginning the road to growth and recovery due to this great book on the value and power of respect." —J. Carlos Vazquez, DC, Chiropractor, Author, Educator

"In our youth, we were taught to respect our peers, respect authority, and respect the rules. But have we ever been shown what respect can do to transform our lives? In *Unleashing the Power of Respect: The I-M Approach*, Dr. Joseph Shrand shows us that respect isn't simply about acceptable behavior. Instead, he gives us a guide for what respect can do to affect a greater potential in our lives. Beginning with the I-M Approach, Dr. Joe explains through clear, accessible language and inspiring examples from his own experience how respect is a powerful tool in both clinical work and daily life. Respect means that we see each other not merely in terms of our conflicts, problems, or 'disorders,' but as individuals striving to do the best we can at any given point in our lifespan. For clinicians, Dr. Joe demonstrates how every form of psychological treatment, no matter the philosophy or technique, requires respect for a person's I-M without shame or stigma. For all of us, he provides a blueprint on how to treat each other without prejudice and with the understanding that we can influence each other to reach our goals. The I-M Approach is a means to create a deeper understanding of ourselves and each other towards improving the domains of our daily lives and change our potential for greater peace and self-acceptance. With warmth, humility, and wit, Dr. Joe reminds us that though respect can be difficult at times, unleashing its power makes a lasting impression on ourselves and the world around us." —Michael G. Pipich, MS, LMFT, The Colorado Center for Clinical Excellence, author of *Owning Bipolar: How Patients and Families Can Take Control of Bipolar Disorder.*

"Dr. Joseph Shrand has been known to the public over the years, first as a Joe, on the original PBS children's TV show "Zoom", (he's Joe!), and, years later, as the child psychiatrist helping teens get onstage as performers-in-recovery in Drug Story Theatre. His latest book brings us into his clinical work with children and families, promoting a model called "I-M", based on reciprocal respect. He develops the model with unforgettable detail, immersing the reader in the experience of patient and doctor. This kind of work is sorely needed in a field drowning (some would say hopelessly lost) in check-lists and categorical diagnoses, both experience-distant so different from the clinical connection Dr. Shrand describes. Dr. Shrand provides the antidote to that culture, both for doctor and therapist." —Gordon Harper MD, Associate Professor of Psychiatry, Harvard Medical School

"Dr. Shrand has the magic ability to see what is right in front of us and clearly and cleanly and simply give us the tools to use to make life better for all of us." —Craig

Wolfe, Co-host of Veterans Voice Radio Network, Emergency preparedness coordinator for the Town of Hull and the South Shore of Metro Boston

"Dr. Shrand has broken down the basic behavior patterns he has observed over time. His theories on behavior are understood by his peers as well as neophytes in a down to earth fashion understood by all." —Gregg Brasso, Host of Veterans Voice Radio Network, Community Relations Specialist at ITT Technical Institute

"As a decades long recovering opioid addict physician, I interact with hundreds of Methadone Maintenance patients every week, many of them still struggling with fentanyl abuse. Before reading Joe's book, I believed sharing my own history was the best way to earn these patients' trust. I now specifically focus on having them realize their I-M and its potential to improve. Sharing my knowledge of the Biological Domain changes which occur when they continue illicit use makes them more willing to see that recovery is possible. It is very satisfying to see this focus on respect work so well." —Skip Sviokla MD ABAM, Medical Assisted Recovery, Inc, Warwick, Rhode Island, Clinical Assistant Professor, Brown Medical School, author *From Harvard to Hell...and Back*

"*Unleashing the Power of Respect: The I-M Approach* is an excellent learning tool. It's a reminder for the more seasoned and novice practitioner along with the everyday soul about the power of the mind. It echoes the need to maintain the internal belief that no matter how situations and life may seem to be, we all have the ability to persevere and redeem ourselves. Dr. Shrand's use of character situations from his experience base and the consistent application of the I-M Approach model helps maintain an objective analysis of understanding, caring, respect, and solution that can be utilized at all levels and within any situation. The 4 Domains that continually contribute to anyone's I-M reflects the adage 'You can't judge a book by its cover.'" —L. J. Bosco, A.T.R-BC, L.M.HC., D.A.P.A., Group Therapist Adult Mood & Addictive Behavior Unit, McLean Hospital / McLean Southeast

"Dr. Shrand describes in fascinating detail the stories over decades of working as a psychiatrist and the success he has found through his I-M Approach and the power of respect. Through his brilliant work he shows us how easy it can be to incorporate into your life. In the home, in the classroom or any workplace this is a must read for all of us. Simply put, *Unleashing the Power of Respect: The I-M Approach* is life-changing." —Elizabeth Williams, M.Ed

UNLEASHING THE POWER OF RESPECT: THE I-M APPROACH

By

Joseph Aaron Shrand, MD

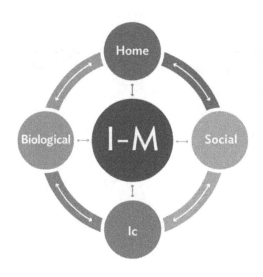

ISBN: 978-1-953865-23-6 (Paperback)
ISBN: 978-1-953865-24-3 (eBook)

Library of Congress Control Number: 2022901151

The names, details, and circumstances may have been changed to protect the privacy of those mentioned in this publication. This publication is not intended as a substitute for the advice of health care professionals.

Books Fluent
3014 Dauphine Street
New Orleans, LA
70117

Table of Contents

DEDICATION

James F. Quine, who understood the power of the I-M Approach when we first spoke about it all those years ago. I miss you very, very much, my brother-from-another-mother.

Linnea Elise Lemasurier Sturdy, taken way too soon from this world, which you left far better than when you entered.

Steven McCann, who had a unique lens on the world, and always said I was his favorite brother-in-law. Be at peace, Steven.

Scott Bock, whose dedication to the power of respect has provided tens of thousands of people the behavioral health care so sorely needed. Your legacy will be eternal.

ACKNOWLEDGMENTS

Unleashing the Power of Respect reflects the convergence of my life experiences, traveling far back into my personal history. It is a synthesis and amalgam of all these experiences and is influenced by all the people I have met or read, by those who lived with me, and by strangers whom I am unlikely to ever meet. By formal teachers and informal teachers, by whose side I simply lived my life. And by the tens of thousands of teacher-patients who I have had the enormous privilege to sit with in their time of need.

My many influences include remarkable thinkers like Charles Darwin, John Bowlby, E.O. Wilson, Alan Watts, Chögyam Trungpa, Lawrence Kohlberg, Konrad Lawrence, Carol Gilligan, Sigmund Freud, Carl Jung, William Shakespeare, David Rubin, F. Scott Peck, Ivan Pavlov, B. F. Skinner, Carl Rogers, James Mann, Habib Davanloo, Daniel Stern, Jerome Kagan, Richard Dawkins, Stephen Jay Gould, Peter Fonagy, Stephen Hawking, Paul Seabright, Gerald Fain, Anna Freud, Jean Piaget, Mary Ainsworth, Erik Erikson, John B. Watson, William James, and every other author I have read over my decades. Behaviorists, psychodynamic psychotherapists, and philosophers like Descartes, Nietzsche, Kant, playwrights like Shakespeare, Sondheim, Sartre, Ibsen, Gershwin, Rogers and Hammerstein, and a myriad of others.

This book in current form could not have been possible without the help of my team from Books Forward and Books Fluent, my developmental editor,

Howard Lovy, my copy editor, Wes J. Bryant, my proofreader, Jana Good, my co-hosts of *The Dr. Joe Show,* Mark Stiles of Stiles Law and Thomas McCoy of Studio B at 892. Erich Engelhardt, my student and friend, who challenges me to expand my thoughts, and Don Marks, an incredible neurologist who does not always agree that we are doing the best we can.

A multitude of people helped in the creation of this book, to whom I have many thanks to extend.

To my team from Drug Story Theater: Kathleen Wright my COO, and Nicole Conlon-McCombe my executive director, along with my interns Aaron and Caleb, my Board of Directors, Steve Aveson, Phil Johnston, Brad Lemack, Andres Martin (mentioned again later!), and Professor James Stellar, the many DST performers, and the tens of thousands of students, educators, (especially Gary Maestas), politicians (especially Governor Charlie Baker, Senator Vinny DeMacedo, Senator Patrick O'Conner, and State Representative Patrick Kearney), and parents who have seen the shows. Drug Story Theater is the application of how respect can influence a person troubled by addiction.

To my team and friends from WATD 95.9 FM in Marshfield and Ed Perry its creator, Benjamin Rabinowitz, my in-studio producer, and Kevin Chase, my other producer, as well as Rob Hakala and the entire listenership of this remarkable radio station that hosts *The Dr. Joe Show: Exploring who we are and why we do what we do.* As well as all the guests who have honored me with their presence on the show, in which we apply the principles outlined in this book on a weekly basis. To my friends from Veterans Voice, led by Gregg Brasso and his accomplices Chuck and Wolfie, whose work to save the lives of those who have served is a true example of how you control no one, but influence everyone.

To my new friends and colleagues at Riverside Community Care including Marsha Medalie, Vicker DiGravio, Kim Fisher, Satya Montgomery, Norm Gorin, Norm Townsend, Kim Fisher (again because she is so cool), Bryan Kohl, Tom Hall, Brandi Ditch, Monica Garlick, Angela Crutchfield, and Val Comerford, Chris, Charley, Manny, Anne, Andrea, Julie, all of my nurse practitioners and prescribers, and all of my Connect2Recovery team and clinical team who embody the power of respect in caring for those in need.

To the people I have worked with at Road to Responsibility, including Chris White, Kesha Garcia, Rich Holbert, and the many dedicated providers who care for and respect some of our most vulnerable population challenged with profound developmental delays.

To my old friends and colleagues including Daniel Mumbauer, Fran Markle, Alfredo Gonzales, Heather Caldera, Mourning Fox, and many others at High Point Treatment Centers.

To my teachers and mentors from Mass General Hospital and McLean Hospital including Gene Beresin, Joseph Biederman, Tim Wilens, Mike Jellinek, Marty Miller, Janet Wozniak, Bruce Cohen, many others, and the departed-too-soon Joe Powers. To my great friend and fellow duckling Andres Martin, who has always supported my efforts, challenged my imposter syndrome, and actually laughed at my puns. Jeff Bostic, who has the same adolescent mind as me. And of course, Ken Duckworth, a leader in psychiatry and public health who has brought enormous change to our system of health care delivery—thank you, Ken.

To my international and local colleagues and often guests on *The Dr. Joe Show* including Sylvester Sviolka, Michael Pipitch, Blake Reichenbach, Mark Bayer, Joaquin Fuentes, Dave and Julie Bullitt, Michael Bobbitt, Ken Davenport, Glenn Geher, Gordon Harper, David Rettew, Hedy Pagremanski, Elizabeth Williams, Larry Bosco, Jonathan Kahn, Matt Anderson, J. Carlos Vazquez, my birthday buddy Kathleen Howland, my new Marshfield Marshes team of Mark, Jen, Joel, and Jackie, my almost sister Lisa Volpe, and a score of other thinkers, artists, and influencers.

To Dan Rosen, MD, who helped me to begin understanding theory of mind and its remarkable application, along with the Asperger's Association of New England who supported our family when we needed it most.

To my legal friends and companions David Llewellyn and Eric Parker, who have helped scores of injured find justice.

To Andy Thom, a man of infinite patience who has been my yearly friend since my mother introduced us in 1993. Andy, I could not have done this without you! You have always had my number and held me accounatable.

To Linda and Philippe Ducrot for being amazing friends, believers in *unleashing*, and who taught Galen how to cook!

To the late Louise Rose, my writing teacher at Sarah Lawrence, who saw in me a skill I did not fully appreciate.

To Jim Cantwell, the most compassionate politician I have ever met, who has travelled with me on my various paths, always with a genuine handshake and support. And to our amazing Chief of Police Phil Tavares, who shows how community policing is a breathing example of the power of respect.

To my high school friends from all those years ago: Biorn, Larry, Stanley, Emily.

To my college friends Lisa (and her husband Paul) Susan (and her husband Greg), and Adam (and his wife Beth)—who was best man at my wedding as I was best man at his.

To my surrogate uncles who took me in when I was a teen and needed some guidance: George, Gerry (rest in peace my friend), and Rodney—the music we wrote back when I was a teen still plays in my mind today.

To my early writing team of Leigh Devine, Julie Silver, and my previous editors, as well as my agent Linda Konner and my former publicist Janet Appel. This book rests on the foundation of those first four.

To Christopher Sarson, my *Zoom*-papa, and my entire *Zoom* family approaching fifty years of friendship (although Kenny only wants to acknowledge forty years). *Zoom* is where my recognition of respect all started.

To Dorothy and Richard McCann, without whom I would not have the joy I have today of loving going to work and loving going home. Along with my in-laws Liz (sorry, Elizabeth), Kathy, Paul, and Elsa who accepted me right away into their loving family.

To Bella, Lucy, and Dodger, our canine companions, and our amazing cat, Mike Tyson, who have always given me unconditional love and kept me moving on our walks.

To the influences from my parents, my siblings—Susan lost too soon, and Lana Jessica who has always and will always remind me she is still my big sister. Ora and Myron Gelberg (I miss him) my cousins from New York who took me to theater when I was three years old. And my long-lost cousin Darryl Segal: after forty years apart, we picked right up where we left off. The influences of friends, those who were not friends and became them, and those who were friends and turned away. The influences of enormous trends in thought, technology, politics, and economics. The influences of big ideas, small ideas, an inspirational walk alone or with a companion. To each, and all, I owe a debt of gratitude, as many of their ideas are synthesized into the I-M Approach.

And finally, to Carol Marie McCann: That small change when you walked into the room had an influence that still ripples through every aspect of my life. Without you, there would not be our amazing children Sophie, (who married Brendan into our ShrandClam) Jason, (who has brought Liz as close as possible to marrying her into our ShrandClam), Galen, and Becca. I thank you for always being honest with me, telling me when my ideas are great, and absolutely when they are not! I thank you for laughing with me every day. Carol Shrand—I could not have done any of this without you.

FOREWORD

Unleashing the Power of Respect is a book for this time. The benefits and indeed magic of treating people with respect has never been more in need. As a society, we are struggling with many longstanding problems, and the power of respect is grossly underutilized. The isolation, grief, uncertainty, and trauma of the COVID-19 pandemic brought out many mental health and substance use issues. These issues require an approach that is positive and productive. Fortunately, Dr. Joe offers this approach in a readable format.

This book works on the macro, or national, level. Our long history of racial trauma and injustice activates many of us. We continue to allow 30 million Americans to go without health insurance. And our political actors appear to be unable to consistently use respect as a healing agent. I wish every one of our leaders would read this important work, which also works for each of us. I am glad you are reading it, as it will help your life and those around you.

Joe Shrand—an expert in adult, child and adolescent, and addiction psychiatry—makes the clear and affirmative case for how and why we should use respect. It is refreshing to have a translation of intricate ideas into something we can all act upon. He does so without complex jargon or terminology, a common challenge in the mental health field. Dr. Joe uses his experience to lay out a non-clinical, non-technical way to think about improving your life, your relationships, and the world.

Everyone intuitively gets that being respected is important. When I visited prisons during my forensic psychiatry fellowship, I was impressed at how being "dissed" was central to the assaults that happened in the prison setting. Disrespect can be a killer. As the state medical director for the Massachusetts Department of Mental Health, the work our team did showed me that respect can be applied for good in the service system. We wanted to reduce the overuse of restraints in the child and adolescent inpatient psychiatric units, as we knew this was re-activating trauma and not teaching the youth how to manage their own emotions. We focused on the child's experience and needs, attending to what calmed them and knowing what agitated them. We lauded the staff for their work and praised them publicly when they were able to reduce restraints and provide alternatives. We were able to reduce restraints by over 70 percent across Massachusetts. I did not know Dr. Joe's I-M model at the time—but I was seeing results from applying some of his principles.

Dr. Joe reminds us that respect does not just happen—it is a choice. Treating people with respect generates a very different and much better emotional response than anger or confrontation. Dr. Joe lays out a creative way to think about the choice of respect. This framework involves the biological, social, home, and interpersonal levels. The idea of unleashing this power of choice we all have; it is a brilliant way to make this act *active*, and not a result of good luck or a good day. Respect is a choice we can all make. Respect is not passive or unconscious. It is an active, powerful tool in our lives.

"You control no one but influence everyone," is another superb observation within this book. When you really take that truth in, it greatly simplifies where you exert your life force. You are the master of your choices and can make changes within yourself. You *control* no one, though, so that helps re-focus energy on what you do with the opportunities and stresses upon you. Respect generates influence.

There is more than theory at work here. Dr. Joe has created a remarkable teaching vehicle that I was fortunate to see with my own eyes. His program, called Drug Story Theater, takes youth who are in recovery from addiction and has them develop and perform for younger children in school settings. The work is empowering for and respectful of the youth—it is their story that is being affirmed as worthy of teaching others. It is also respectful of the audience, as they are engaged with questions and answers after each performance. I was once at a performance when Dr. Joe asked the middle school children in attendance how many of them knew someone who was addicted to substances. A great many hands were raised. In that moment, they knew they were not alone in this crisis. Reducing isolation is also respect for experience. In a different performance, given to parents, a father asked what he should do if they were worried about their daughter and the possibility that she was using drugs. A sixteen-year-old who had just finished conveying her own story on the stage said, "You know your daughter better than anyone. Trust your instincts and speak to her and listen to her." Dr. Joe creates respect everywhere he goes.

At the National Alliance on Mental Illness (NAMI), where I am the chief medical officer, I have seen the power of listening, empathizing, and supporting family members who are very ill with psychiatric symptoms. The conscious applications of listening and empathy often changes relationships. A father told me, "It took me a long time to realize that my son didn't want to be fixed. He wanted to be *heard*." Their relationship changed for the better as a result of the communication skills the father learned at NAMI. He was, essentially, respecting his son and his experience, and both have benefited greatly from that. The son has come to respect him in turn, and they are in a new phase of what has become a positive relationship. I think Dr. Joe's book could have accelerated their transformation, which took many years.

Thank you, Dr. Joe, for putting this important work together. We have never needed it more than now.

Ken Duckworth, MD
CMO, NAMI National
Assistant Professor Psychiatry, Harvard Medical School

INTRODUCTION

My mother, Frances Shrand, was an actress, my father, Hyman Shrand, a pediatrician. They did not have a happy marriage and divorced when I was fourteen. (My mother quipped that she was a divorcee but always wanted to be a widow.)

During the peak of my disrupted home life, I was fortunate enough to audition for and get picked to be a "Zoom Kid" in the original production of *Zoom*. "I'm Joe!" This PBS show became a national success and I found myself temporarily "famous." My mother gave me the best advice on how to handle this fame. She helped me recognize how much courage it must take for a stranger to come up and ask for an autograph. And she told me to always treat people with respect.

I wished my parents could have treated each other that way. During the divorce, I saw how much damage can be done when you see the other person as hateful. The arguing and blaming impacted both my parents' lives for as long as they lived and created in me a determination to have a very different marriage. My home environment had a huge impact on my social environment—then and in the future.

In her field, my mother was incredibly respected as a terrific actress. My father was a much-loved and respected pediatrician. The difference in how people reacted when treated with respect was emblazoned in my mind by these remarkable contrasts. Because, at work, my parents were happy, respectful, and respected. But at home, it appeared a constant battle—rife with allegations and mistrust. The power of *dis*respect was unleashed as a weapon—dangerous and debilitating. When they finally divorced, animosity lingered between them for decades.

After high school, my journey led me to the liberal arts school of Sarah Lawrence College. There, I could pursue the only two things I knew how to do—the two main arenas to which I had been exposed: science and theater.

As an undergraduate at Sarah Lawrence College, I took a course titled, "The Western Discovery of Buddhism." I read works from twentieth-century British spiritual philosopher Alan Watts, ancient classics by the founder of Buddhism, Siddhartha Guatama, modern spiritual classics like Aldous Huxley's *The Doors of Perception* and Trogyam Chumpra's *Cutting Through Spiritual Materialism*, and others. The idea that we are not separate but connected, always, worked its way into my own sense of self; how I saw myself was profoundly influenced by how I thought others saw me. My parents were so full of rage and anger, and treated each other as enemies, which perpetuated their animosity and mistrust. I realized that I could have an influence on how others saw me by the way I treated them.

At the same time I was studying the spiritual side of life I took a course in animal behavior. I became enchanted with wondering why animals do what they do. What is the advantage to their behavior, based on Darwin's theory of natural selection? Although excellent, the courses in this topic at Sarah Lawrence were limited, and there were none on the new and emerging field of sociobiology: the idea that *behaviors* were subject to the same Darwinian evolutionary pressures as any physical component of organisms. I began to realize, however, that just because an animal was trying to survive did not mean they would always get it right.

To study more, I applied as a Visiting Scholar to Harvard University, where people such as E.O. Wilson, Stephen Jay Gould, and Irven Devore were exploring and teaching sociobiology at the time. I was accepted and became immersed, as much as an undergraduate can be, in this fascinating synthesis of human behavior and human biology. The I-M Approach has certainly been influenced by my exposure in the social domain to sociobiology and the genetics of behavior.

I returned to Sarah Lawrence for my senior year of undergraduate school and helped start a psychobiology lab, looking at attachment behaviors in rat mothers and their pups. At the same time, I became a director in the studio theater department. There is an approach in theater to developing one's character: Read what other characters say about your part. You begin to play your role based on how others see you.

Behavior happens in a context, in an environment. A turning point for me was after I graduated college with a Bachelor of Liberal Arts (as a side note: I always thought it ironic that both men and women were awarded "bachelor" degrees!). I was working in New York for CARE, the international aid and development organization, as a grant writer. I helped to win a grant for an educational program in Belize in which village children were taught basic science and economics by learning how to grow their own crops. I was flown there to report firsthand on the project. While there, looking at the children running barefooted through their villages, I realized I was doing medicine wholesale but wanted to do it retail. When I returned to New York, I enrolled at Columbia School of General Studies to take pre-med courses. The small event of winning that grant changed my life—an example of how a small change can have a big effect.

* * *

All of us have been in a situation where we can either remain stuck and conflicted, or cooperative and forward moving. This is not always easy for us as human beings. We are designed to be competitive. To stubbornly stand our ground is practically baked into our DNA.

Here's an example from my life: I walk my dog, Bella, several times a week along an unpaved, single-lane road that stretches across marshes separating the mainland of Marshfield, Massachusetts from the very small Trouant Island. Macombers Way is barely wide enough for a large car, and every day, the island inhabitants must time their comings and goings to the changing tides of the Atlantic Ocean that flood the thin stretch of road. When a car approaches during our walks, my dog and I have to stand in the marshes to let the car go by. If two cars are trying to access the one-lane road at the same time, a sign gives the right-of-way to the car approaching off the mainland.

Last weekend, when Bella and I were about halfway through the marshes, we heard a car approaching from the mainland. As always, Bella and I stepped to the side to let the car drive by. As it passed, the driver waved at me, and I waved back to the island dweller on his way home.

And then I heard another car coming off the island. It did not stop.

The car that had just passed me sped up to try to make it to the island in time.

About a third of the way off the island, toward the mainland, the two cars met.

One of them was going to have to back up across the treacherous path.

The doors to the driver's side of each car opened. I was too far away to hear what they said, but the person who lived on the island was pointing in the direction of the sign indicating who had the right of way. The driver coming off the island shrugged their shoulders and raised then crossed their arms, suggesting they had either not seen or ignored the sign. There was tension. No one could move. I could see the discussion continue.

And then, both parties extended their right arm towards one another, they shook hands, and each got back into their cars.

The person coming from the island began to carefully back up, and the island dweller slowly drove toward him, head out of the car, an arm waving in apparent helpful direction. The car backing up eventually got to the island, reversed into the pull-off space, and waved as the island dweller drove past, also waving in appreciation. If neither car had budged, they would both have been flooded. There was nowhere to go but cooperation. The two drivers managed to move beyond their competitive programming and come to a compromise.

Yet, we are still driven (no pun intended) by some pretty primitive and basic survival instincts that have served us well for millions of years. Animals that overcame other animals survived and passed on the strategy to their offspring. Our own innate "survival of the fittest" is why we spend so much time worrying that we should be doing better, worrying that others see us as "less than," as this could jeopardize our ability to survive. As Herbert Spencer said, "Survival of the fittest, implies multiplication of the fittest." [1]

Human beings often measure their "fitness" in terms of value.

We are desperate to feel valuable and be seen as valuable.

Sometimes, we even try to increase our own value at the expense of someone else's value.

Those two drivers were in just that position. If one of them backed down, would they have less value? They may not have been aware of it, but that consideration was pushing their decisions—a modern manifestation of a primitive survival approach that has determined who we are as human beings for millennia.

Why is this *value* thing so important? This goes back to our evolution.

Millions of years ago, we weren't the biggest animal, the fastest animal, nor the strongest animal. We were isolated mammals scurrying around hoping not to be lunch. We were prey.

And then we formed these small social groups and our survival potential increased so dramatically that human beings are pretty much everywhere on the planet.

But to access the protection of your group you had to contribute something. You had to have value. So, whenever we think we have less value, we can become very angry, anxious, or sad on some deep primitive level worrying we are going to be kicked out of our protective group and be lunch for some predator. Our "fitness" became not just about the individual, but about our group.

---

[1] Herbert Spencer, *The Principles of Biology, Volume 1* (London: William and Norgate, 1864).

Humans evolved a survival strategy still in use today: For millennia we have often increased our own value by decreasing someone else's value. We do this on an individual level, on a racial level, on a societal level, on a national level. And then we are astonished we have mistrust, retaliation, anger, which sometimes propels us into wars between nations. As social animals, an entire *group* would try to diminish the value of another group. This afforded protection, and the opportunity to both retain and enhance your value at the expense of an entire group.

We see this all the time—in allegiance to sports teams, retail stores, brands of beer or favorite yogurt.

But now the stakes are higher.

If we do not outsmart this tendency, we will have war. Or political stalemate. Or riots in the streets. Today, the headlines are filled with what can happen when we do not move beyond our evolutionary programming. When we remain fearful that we will be seen as less valuable if we lose to someone else, we will do whatever it takes to win. The drivers of those cars were in a situation where they were both going to lose unless they found some compromise.

Can our human brain overcome a survival strategy that will ultimately kill us?

Yes, it can.

We have another option.

When we increase someone else's value, we actually increase our *own* value.

How do we accomplish this fundamental shift in an ancient strategy?

There is a powerful element we can unleash called *respect*. When we remind someone of their value, we increase our own value. And then we all feel safer. We can enhance our success when others feel more successful. When they feel more successful, they have less need to block your way on a narrow road.

You are about to meet some remarkable people who had been blocked on that single-lane road, people who were labelled with a "diagnosis:" Schizophrenic Disorder. Attention Deficit Disorder. Bipolar Disorder. Substance Use Disorder. Borderline Personality Disorder. Obsessive Compulsive Disorder. One teenager had Asperger's Syndrome, now called Autistic Spectrum Disorder. Another child witnessed domestic violence. One tween desperately wanted to be valuable to the point of appearing a psychopath.

But rather than isolating them on an island to be flooded-in every day, rather than seeing them through a rear-view mirror of sickness and "disorder," come with me on the road to their island. There is always a wide-enough path for all when we see the value in each other.

Joseph Aaron Shrand, MD

CHAPTER 1
THE I-M APPROACH

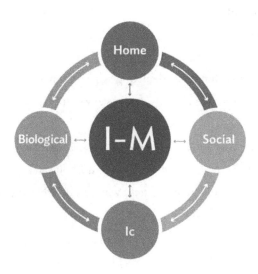

The origin of the I-M Approach

Let me flashback to 1982. I had graduated two years earlier from Sarah Lawrence College with a BA in Liberal Arts. But I decided I wanted to be a physician. I began to pursue my pre-med requirements.

I was taking physics. (Still awake? I find that people suddenly fall asleep when I mention the word *physics*.) Anyway, in ph***cs, the symbol "I" stands for a potential current, for electricity. But I wondered what would happen if we turned the "I" upside-down; still an "I" but now a "current potential." Current—right now—but with the *potential* to change in the very next second to another current potential. Influenced by Charles Darwin and the idea that animals were always trying to succeed, every one of those current potentials was actually a *maximum* current potential. At every moment in time, we are doing the best we can, but with the potential to change in the very next second to another "best we can." I named that current maximum potential an *I-max*, which I have since changed to be represented by I-M.

I-M has several acronym meanings: Is Me; I Matter; I Am; Inner Mind; Inner Me. Many acronyms, but each depicting a paradigm shift. Instead of seeing ourselves as doing "less than," I-M sees us as always doing the "best we can, with the potential to change." *I-M* always changing.

Instead of worrying you have less value, the I-M Approach says you are doing the best you can, but if you don't like what you do, you can change, adapt, evolve. The I-M Approach helps you understand why you do what you do, based on the influence of the Four Domains.

Our I-M is influenced by Four Domains

Your I-M is always changing, adapting, evolving, influenced by, and responding to Four Domains:

➢ Your Home Domain
➢ Your Social Domain
➢ Your Biological Domain (of your brain and body)
➢ Your Ic Domain (how you see yourself, and how you think others see you)

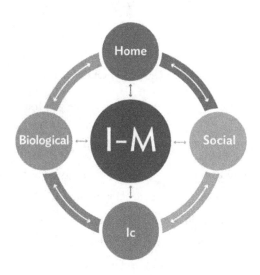

The interaction of the Four Domains is captured in the above graphic. The double-headed arrows convey that the domains influence each other all the time. And the result is your I-M: Dynamic, changing, adapting, and evolving. Responding the best you can, with the potential to respond and change again in the very next second to another I-M.

The Home Domain

No one is going to argue that your home has had an influence on who you are today. The Home Domain is where connections to other people first begins; the importance of our family, and the influences of that environment. The Home Domain is distinguished from the rest of the world—the Social Domain.

The Social Domain

The Social Domain is being at work, or at school, going to a movie, walking down the street; anything other than the Home Domain. Things that happen at home influence the choices you make in the rest of the world. And things that happen in the Social Domain influence the choices you make at home. These two domains of Home and Social are outside of, but connect with, the two internal domains.

The Biological Domain

The Biological Domain is your brain and body. Are you hungry? Are you tired? Are you digesting your lunch? Are you on medicine or fighting off a cold? We are a collection of cells that are always changing, responding to the world inside and out. Sometimes these changes are part of growth and development, like brain-maturation, growing bones, or sexual development.

Sometimes the change in our brain and body may be due to genes that are turned on or off at a this moment in time. Perhaps the changes are in response to what food we eat, how much exercise we get, how much stress we feel, or how happy we are going to work or coming home. Changing the environment of the cell changes its response. No one is sick or broken: we are simply responding the best we can, our I-M.

The Ic Domain

Pronounced "I see," the Ic Domain is our current concept of self: how I see myself and how I think other people see me. Human beings, as social animals, are very interested in what other people think or feel. But we are especially interested in what they think or feel about *us*. In particular: *do they see me as valuable?*

Our Ic Domain is driven by a powerful brain tool called "theory of mind." This clunky scientific term is not like theory of relativity, or theory of evolution. We can't see someone else's mind, so we have to guess, "theorize" what they are thinking or feeling. It is given a separate domain from the Biological Domain, just as the Home Domain is parsed out from the Social Domain. Theory of mind is the foundation of every human social interaction. The root of empathy: our ability to appreciate what other people think and feel, and the brain tool we use to guess what other people think and feel about us. [2]

We use our Ic Domain all the time in every single interaction. Have you ever been to a job interview? Why do you wear certain clothes and not your pajamas during the interview? Because you care what other people think about you. When you are trying to attract someone romantically, do you brush your teeth and comb your hair or dress like a slob? You try to present yourself a certain way so you can influence someone else's response. You want them to like you, to respect you, to value you, to trust you. The Ic Domain is where all these things are happening.

Everyone is at an I-M

Everyone is at an I-M, doing the best they can at this moment in time with the potential to change in the very next second to another best they can, another I-M. The I-M Approach is not saying that your current I-M is the best you will *ever* do. You don't have to like your I-M or condone it. Just because it is the best you can do at that moment does not mean your I-M is a free ride: you will be held responsible for your I-M, because everything you do has a natural consequence. But responsibility is different than blame. Blame is shaming. Responsibility is empowering.

Your I-M doesn't even mean you will win and be successful. For some people, success is when you love going to work and love going home. For some, success is having enough food in the refrigerator. For some, success is just having a home to *have* a refrigerator. And for some, success is merely waking up and getting though the day. We all get to decide what success means to us.

But instead of judging ourselves as "less than" and broken, as not doing as well as we could, as "should be doing better," as sick, diseased, or disordered, let's look again at *why we do what we do* based on the influence of the Four Domains.

---

[2] I explore this domain in-depth in my previous book *Do You Really Get Me?* (Center City, MN: Hazelden Press, 2015).

Think about these words: "look again." Turn them around: "again look." Again—as in to repeat something. Look—as in being a spectator. The I-M Approach says let's *respect* why we do what we do. Without judgement. Simply recognizing the influence of the Four Domains. The I-M Approach is a position of **respect.**

When is the last time you got angry at someone treating you with respect?

Never.

Anger is an emotion designed to change things. We get angry at people when we want someone to do something different: to stop doing something or start doing something.

But being respected feels great, so we do not get angry. Why would we want to change that?

The brain does not activate anger when it feels respected. This principle has the same reliability as gravity: apples don't fall up, and the brain does not activate anger when it feels respected.

Respect leads to value. Think about every person you know. They all want the same thing: simply to feel valued by somebody else. This need for being valued is the common thread that binds us all. And what's cool is, at any and every moment, you can remind someone of their value. And whenever you remind someone of their value, you increase your own value.

Respect leads to value, and value leads to trust. Trust is the antidote to fear, and anger, and sadness, because when you trust someone, you can make a mistake and know you will not be seen as less valuable. The I-M Approach allows you to unleash your unlimited human potential, your wonder, your creativity. It unleashes the power of respect.

The Two Truths of the I-M Approach

Truth #1: SMALL CHANGES CAN HAVE BIG EFFECTS

Because the Four Domains are so connected and interactive, a small change in one domain can have an amplified and ripple effect in the others. You don't need to change everything. If you think you have to change everything, you can become overwhelmed. If you're overwhelmed, your Biological Domain can feel angry, anxious, or sad—which will then affect the other domains. Relax. *Small changes can have big effects.*

Truth #2: YOU CONTROL NO ONE BUT INFLUENCE EVERYONE

The second truth is even more powerful. Everyone has an I-M. We are all interested, through our Ic Domain, about what others think and feel about us. You are part of someone's Home or Social Domain. You have an effect on their Biological Domain, through their Ic Domain, because you know it *feels* different when someone says you are amazing or says you suck—when you are treated with respect or not. This means that *you control no one but influence everyone.* You get to *choose* the kind of influence you want to be.

Applying the I-M Approach

You can use the I-M Approach right now to explore who you are and why you do what you do, based on the influence of the Four Domains. The I-M is a roadmap: What small change can you make in any one of the domains that can have a ripple effect through the entire system, so you can move to another I-M?

If you are a business owner, you can use the I-M to enhance your product: what small change can you make to move your company, and all of your employees, to a different I-M? If you are a teacher, you can use the I-M to structure your classroom: what small change can you make to move your students to a different I-M? If you are a politician, what small change can your constituents make to move your entire district to a different I-M? If you are a clinician, you and your patient can use the I-M to structure a change plan: [3] what small change can they make to move to a different I-M? If you are a parent, what small change

---

[3] Notice I don't say "treatment plan." *Treatment* implies there is something broken. *Change* is adaptation and evolution responding to the Four Domains.

can you make to move your family to a different I-M? Every one of those small changes you make has an influence on someone else.

Everyone wants the same thing: to simply feel valued by somebody else. Using the I-M Approach, seeing ourselves and each other as doing the best we can instead of less than we can, at any and every moment in time you can remind someone of their value. And every time you remind someone of their value, you increase your own value. And everyone wants to feel valuable. You get to *choose the kind of influence you want to be.*

You are at an I-M. When you view yourself this way, you can wonder instead of worry. With this small change in perception, you are already moving yourself to a different I-M.

Practice Respect

Remember a time when you were sad? Had something happened at home or in the Social Domain? Did it have an influence on the way you saw yourself, which then influenced the way you felt? What about a time when you were scared . . . happy . . . angry?

Now use the I-M Domains to reflect on a time you made someone else feel sad, or happy, or angry or scared. Perhaps it was confusing why the person responded the way they did, but the Four Domains are a roadmap to help you tease apart the chaos of life, every time.

The more you use the I-M Approach, the better you become at it. Next time you feel nervous about going on a first date or applying for a job, you can use the I-M Approach. First, you can recognize your Biological Domain response: you feel reflexively anxious and scared. Why? Because your Ic Domain fears you will be seen as less-than, with less value. Even being afraid is an I-M. But if you don't like it, you can change it. You can be more confident, recognizing that everyone has an I-M, and if the best that other person can do is reject you, what's going on in their Four Domains? You can remind yourself of your value, which will lead you to trust yourself, and decide what you want to do from a position of being the best you can instead of being less than you can. You remind yourself of your value by respecting who you are and why you do what you do.

An example of the I-M in action

Here is an example of how the I-M works:

A nine-year-old boy argued with his mother about brushing his teeth. At school, kids made fun of him because he had bad breath. That was his I-M. The bacteria in his mouth, however, also have an I-M and were exuberant, delighted to be safe in their own home domain of their host's mouth!

The nine-year-old looked at the Four Domains, the I-M roadmap to change. What was going on his mom's I-M that she got angry with him? How was his refusal to brush his teeth influencing her Ic, and their Home Domain? How did that influence his day at school, in the Social Domain? How did that influence his Ic Domain and his Biological Domain?

What about the I-M of the bacteria? Everything has an I-M, and the bacteria had made his mouth their new Home Domain. They loved it when he didn't brush his teeth, as they got to thrive. Of course, they gave him bad breath because they were pooping in his mouth, but OK—he still didn't want to brush his teeth. Very nice of him to treat his mouth bacteria so well!

But in his Social Domain, of school, the other kids stayed away from him more, and didn't want to talk with him or play together. Not brushing his teeth influenced their I-Ms as well, and they did not want to have a kid with bad breath in their group or Social Domain. This influenced his Ic Domain, and he felt sad and less valued.

The boy made a small change with a big effect: he brushed his teeth in his Home Domain and therefore changed his Biological Domain before venturing into the Social Domain of school.

No longer influencing his peers with bad breath, he was cheerfully included. The boy's Ic Domain was bolstered, he felt better, his Biological Domain responded by generating oxytocin (a brain chemical of trust), his healing properties increased, and his self-esteem improved. He went home, and his mom, whose I-M had also been influenced because she felt respected and valued by her son (also increasing oxytocin), greeted him warmly. (The bacteria in the boy's mouth, however, were disrupted by an invasion of a toothbrush from the Social Domain, upsetting both their Ic and Biological Domains in their new Home Domain. At least, for a day—they bounce back pretty quick!)

This small change began to expand into other areas, where he would be more thoughtful about the requests made by his parents, teachers, and others in his Home and Social Domains. As he made others feel more valuable through their Ic Domains by treating them with respect, he began to feel more valuable himself. His I-M had moved closer to loving going to school and loving going home.

Small changes can have big effects. You control no one but influence everyone. That's the I-M Approach.

Why now?

If I created this in 1982, and have been applying it all through my training and career as an adult and child and adolescent psychiatrist and an addiction medicine specialist, why would I just now publish this book? Why tell the world about the I-M Approach almost forty years later?

My developmental editor, Howard Lovy, asked similar questions. "What is the reason this book was written?"

Well, I wrote this book to introduce the I-M Approach, and to reframe what we call "mental illness" and "addiction" as people doing the best they can, influenced by the Four Domains of Home, Social, Biological, and Ic. I wanted to use the stories of some of my patients as windows into each of us. I chose to publish this book at a time when our world is going in and out of a pandemic, and where we have had an opportunity to appreciate sadness, anger, anxiety, and isolation on a global level.

Long before the pandemic, I had been saying that there is no such thing as an illness—just an adaptation and response to a change in our environment. The pandemic has been devastating and shown how a small change can have a big effect, and that we as individuals control no one but influence everyone. A virus is a very small change, but with a huge effect on our Biological Domain. That small change gave each of us an opportunity to do something to protect someone else while protecting ourselves.

During the shutdowns and quarantines, many people began to appreciate what they had taken for granted all along: family, friendship, fellowship. The stories in this book reflect people who may have felt isolated long before the pandemic, but our own recent isolation gives us an appreciation, an *empathy* that may have previously been shadowed by stigma and separation. The pandemic revealed how similar we all are, rather than focusing on our differences. This book is a platform to take that understanding and do something, so we can literally make the world a place where we each feel more valuable rather than less valuable.

My editor asked, "How are we supposed to feel after we finish reading this book? What is the call to action? Who is the book for?"

The book is for all of you.

For the professional, I hope you can use the I-M Approach to help your patients explore who they are and why they do what they do. To accomplish this, they have to trust you. To trust you, they have to know you value them and are a therapist, not a judge.

For friends, family, and caregivers, this book is to help you understand why other people do what they do, based on the influence of the Four Domains, and what small changes you can make to help them reach their next success.

And for all of you, it is to help you find a way to say, "This is me, but if I don't like my I-M, I can change it."

The call to action is to remind ourselves and each other of our value. And with that value, create hope. Rather than look at ourselves as not doing well enough, let's assess our current success and use the I-M Approach as a roadmap to take us to our next success. As your I-M changes, your definition of success may also change. When we achieve one success, we can then determine the next.

CHAPTER 2
BUILDING ON THE SCIENCE

What is stress?

The first book I wrote was called *Manage Your Stress* and explored the science behind a very simple and ancient reflex: the stress response. When we perceive a danger through our Ic Domain, our Biological Domain responds reflexively. Under the stress of a potential predator, our body reflexively responds "to the event of being cut off in traffic almost in the same way as if a rhinoceros had charged you. When you experience a stress trigger, your heart beats quickly, your palms and body sweat, blood rushes to your face and your breathing quickens. Some stress makes us just want to run away or hide. Other times, people feel charged, ready to fight after the event has passed. Sometimes people feel exhausted by it, or overwhelmed. Whatever your instinctive feeling may be in those moments, it is what you choose to *do* right after that stress moment that can mean the difference between a ruined or normal day."[4]

These days, that danger may not be a saber-toothed tiger, but our Biological Domain responds in the same way. In our day-to-day lives, the stress is more often a fear of failure. Being late. Not doing well on an upcoming exam or presentation. Not making a sale. Ultimately, anything that diminishes our value can activate that same response. Less valuable means more vulnerable. It's an I-M, but once

---

[4] Dr. Joseph Strand and Leigh Devine, *Manage Your Stress* (New York: St. Martin's Griffin, 2012).

you recognize the reflex is happening, you can step back and again-look at what has changed in any of the Four Domains. You can become *reflective* instead of reflexive.

The best way to manage your stress is to help someone else manage theirs. That small change can have a big effect. When you do, your value increases, as well as the person you are helping—controlling no one but influencing everyone.

EXERCISE: Thank and Connect

Pick a coworker who seems to have a hard time handling stress. You know who they are. Put their name on a piece of paper. Underneath the name, create two categories: Thank and Connect.

In the Thank column write:

1. How does this person help me do my job?
2. How does this person help the company perform better?
3. Acknowledge three things this person does that I or our group appreciates.

In the Connect column write:

1. Their full name.
2. Any details of their life you know.
3. Three questions you could ask to know them better.

Once you jot down the lists, you are going to assign yourself small tasks from #3 of each column. First, when the opportunity presents itself, you are going to go out of your way to make sure that person is thanked for their efforts. You probably already thank them reflexively for ordinary things, such as bringing back a stapler they borrowed. But give them an extra thanks for being the last one to stay the other day, or cleaning off the table in the conference room, or starting a meeting for you when you were running late. Whatever it is, when you offer that extra thanks, you are conveying that you noticed their effort (even if it is part of their job), and that you *value* them.

The same thing goes for the Connect list. You may ask a question that allows you to know them better. This could be about where they went on vacation, how many kids they have, or if they've ever been to Disneyworld. These are not deep, personal questions, but they reveal information about their lives and open the door for follow-up questions and better knowledge. By asking, you are *connecting*. You are conveying that you are interested in them as a human being, and that you value them. Now, do the same for another person, and then another.

You may be wondering, *so what does "Thank and Connect" have to do with minimizing stress?* It's simple: when we make the effort to show others they are valued, we are practicing respect. Of all the human desires and needs, feeling respected is one of the most fundamental. You can relieve someone's stress simply by showing them they are valued and respected for their work and who they are. Stress and anxiety make people feel insecure and unsettled, and in the extreme, very angry. But when people feel valued and respected by others, they relax and let down their guard. Their cortisol levels decrease, and they move in the opposite direction of stress. While you can't remove every stress trigger from your colleagues' lives, you can still influence their stress levels by practicing Thank and Connect.

You can do this in both the Home and Social Domains. By reminding someone of their value you decrease stress and the move to a different I-M. Try it and see what happens.[5]

Outsmarting anger

My second book, *Outsmarting Anger: 7 Strategies for Defusing our Most Dangerous Emotion*, won the 2013 Books for a Better Life award in the Psychology and Self-Help category. It explores the science which underlies the most primitive emotion: the "fight" branch of the fight or flight response. The entire book was

---

[5] Dr. Joseph Strand and Leigh Devine, *Manage Your Stress* (New York: St. Martin's Griffin, 2012).

based on the question: When was the last time you got angry at someone treating you with respect? The answer is you don't.

Outsmarting Anger built on my first book but focused on the fight branch of fight-flight-freeze. Science shows that anger and other emotions come from the limbic system. And we get angry when we want someone to do something different. The book laid the foundation for the I-M and respect.

Fear is worrying you are less valuable

My third book, *The Fear Reflex*, was on the flight branch of fight-flight-freeze and introduced the I-M theory—at that time called *I-maximum*. The book further explores the science behind our fear of failure: small things that can diminish our value. Tiny terrors start in the Biological Domain. Our Rapid Response is our Ic Domain, assessing the danger and the threat to our value. I explore the influence of the Home Domain, as well as how we look to groups for safety, and talk about traversing our Home and Social Domains together in order to counter these fears of being seen as less than by reminding each other of our value. The chapter titles spell out the word TRUST, the antidote to fear. The I-M Approach transforms fear into trust.

We all want the same thing: to feel valued by someone else

My fourth book is being repurposed with a new title, *The Empathy Revolution: Conquering our need to Divide*. This book focuses on the Ic Domain, or theory of mind. This is how the Biological and Ic Domains interact, again reacting to whether we are seen as valuable or not.

This book, *Unleashing the Power of Respect: The I-M Approach*, ties the previous four together, building on the science translated into the I-M Approach. Here is the basic idea: rather than worry that we have less value, let's recognize that the very worry itself is the best we can do based on our ancient survival brain. But now that we know this, we can shift our perspective and decrease our stress by always seeing ourselves as being at an I-M. But there is more: this small change can have a big effect, including a healthier life with lower cortisol secretions.

Enacting the second truth, we can further increase our value by reminding someone else of theirs. This goes against a lot of political and social pressures, in which one person competes against another trying to get something for themselves at the expense of someone else. Rather than compete, we can connect—and unleash the power of respect. Respect leads to value and value leads to trust and trust reduces stress and the fear of being kicked out of our protective group.

In this book, I am going to tell you some stories about people at their I-M. Each story illustrates the I-M Approach in action. Some are at the extreme end of our human spectrum of behavior. Everyone gets sad, but not everyone gets depressed. Everyone gets worried, but not everyone has panic attacks. Everyone has thought someone else was judging them, but not everyone becomes paranoid. We live on a spectrum, each of us at our own I-M: This Is Me. My Inner Mind. This is who I am. I Matter.

I will use the I-M Approach to break down the chaos of some of my patient's stories. After each chapter, I will share my I-M perspective of the story you have just read. Not as a diagnosis, but as a person doing the best they can in response to the Four Domains. Each story is a window into ourselves, who we are, and why we do what we do. Our I-M. I will be ending each I-M perspective by applying the Two Truths:

SMALL CHANGES CAN HAVE BIG EFFECTS

The first small change was to let you know about the I-M Approach. I hope this small change has a big effect.

YOU CONTROL NO ONE BUT INFLUENCE EVERYONE

I hope that in your learning about the I-M Approach, I have demonstrated this second truth!

Let's apply the I-M Approach in the next chapter to Jan in "Lady with a Gun."

CHAPTER 3
LADY WITH A GUN

"I don't think I love her, no."

Jan answered my question with a resigned sadness. She was a thirty-four-year-old single mother of a feisty ten-year-old blonde-haired, blue-eyed little girl named Bridget. Bridget had been brought to my office by her mother Jan, and both of them had been driven to my office by Jan's mother, Ann.

The three were together in the room with me. Jan did not say a single word. The initial history had been given by Ann, who'd told me that Bridget was terrorizing Jan—not listening and being disrespectful and demanding. The story was not unusual, but it was odd that Jan said nothing in response. Nothing. Bridget sat next to her grandmother. Apart, distant, and separated from Jan, fidgeting while she drew with crayons. She didn't look particularly oppositional and had begun drawing her and her family doing something together.

But she was drawing a dog. Then another. And another. The dogs were stick figures, but with large, sharp teeth. They were of different sizes, and the smallest looked the most intimidating. The largest of the dogs had eyes that seemed vacuous and distant. It was also the furthest away from the smallest dog. The middle dog was facing the smallest one, and the two larger dogs were facing away from each other.

"Bridget doesn't listen to her mother, and barely to me," continued Ann. "She has seen two therapists and refuses to take any medication. Jan needs help taking care of her."

Jan, still, had done no more than introduce herself for the session, but only with prompting from her mother. While her mother talked, Jan seemed far, far away; her eyes distant, her mouth drawn down, a void of expression, the epitome of what psychiatrists call a "flat and blunted affect." Even as her mother criticized, declaring Jan unable to rein in her child, Jan expressed only minimal emotion. One could imagine how distant she was with her own daughter, if this was the most connection she could muster. She said nothing.

But I was not sure whether this response was part of the mother-daughter dynamic between Jan and Ann, or if it extended to the dyad between Jan and her own child.

Intuitively, I wanted to talk to Jan alone.

When a psychiatrist has an intuition, it is important to follow it, to check in with one's own feelings. Unlike a GI doc, or a cardiologist, or any other specialty that has an instrument with which to look into the human body, a psychiatrist *is* the instrument. If we have a feeling about a patient, it is often a clue as to who the patient is, what the struggle is—and we are picking up on the unconscious emotions and the effects of them.

Politely, I asked Ann and Bridget to wait in the seats outside my office so I could ask Jan some questions alone. Although Ann bristled, and Bridget complained she had not finished her drawing, the two did leave. I told Bridget she could take the crayons and paper with her, and I would look forward to hearing more about the pictures she had created. Ann glanced at Jan, even as Bridget walked right past her without a look.

The door closed, and Jan and I were alone.

"So, I've heard from your mom. What's *your* take on your kid?"

There was a pause, too long for a simple answer, too long for the thoughts to formulate. It was a silence of a woman whose depression was slowing her thoughts, numbing her feelings. I almost asked the question again when Jan responded. "I don't think I love her."

I listened.

"She's a handful. Too much energy for me."

I listened.

Jan proceeded to tell me the story of her daughter's birth. Jan had met Bridget's father after her first significant suicide attempt, while both were inpatients in a psychiatric hospital. Jan already had a history of multiple minor suicide attempts, most of which she never admitted to anyone. She'd hidden years of self-injurious behaviors, mostly cutting, invisible under the sleeves of her clothes and pants. She never wore dresses. Frequent visits to the bathroom right after a meal disguised difficulties with food, purging the offending material from her body. Food binges were easier to manage, alone, late at night, two boxes of cookies easily evacuated with a finger down the throat.

Although not my patient, I found myself asking the routine questions one asks while taking a psychiatric history. She denied any abuse as a child and denied any drug use. Her father had been a high-ranking military man, and she had an estranged relationship with an older brother. Her father had died a few years before but had left a large house and a substantial estate to her mom as well as a trust fund for both her and her brother.

She had done well in school and in college and had risen to an important position of authority and responsibility in her organization. But her depression continued to torment her, and she would cut herself in attempt to rid herself of "emotional pain." After one of her more significant episodes, her psychiatric team hospitalized her. For the first time.

It changed her life.

Inpatient, behind locked doors, Jan believed she had been abandoned by her team and parents. It is potentially a terrifying experience, being a patient in a locked ward. Imagine—already compromised, afraid, sad beyond measure, perhaps psychotic and delusional, paranoid that the rooms harbor hidden cameras and that the medicine the nurses want you to take is obviously poison. It mandates that a professional staff treat each person with dignity and respect. And that a clear message is sent: We are here to help. We are psychiatrists, nurses, social workers, psychologists, mental health workers, and not judges. Every one of my patients initially walks through the door feeling less valuable. My goal is simply to rekindle their sense of value, by affording them respect. For it is in that small change that the real healing begins.

However, this does not always happen.

Jan may not have been mistreated in the hospital, but she did feel very, very alone. Hopeless, helpless, worthless, unlovable, incapable. Even in the hospital she tried to cut herself, to drown out the unbearable limbic pain that flooded her. She was too young but already too old. Very alone, and unsure if anyone would ever love her.

And then he noticed her. And he became her friend. He was also alone, and his blue eyes and blonde hair in the fluorescent light of the locked ward promised more than companionship. Protection, nurturing, love, acceptance, understanding.

And then he was discharged. Then she was discharged. And then they met, and their tryst seemed unimaginably perfect and fulfilling.

So they married.

No longer out of reach, no longer a prize to be won but a prize too easily conquered, the relationship changed. Nurture turned to neglect. Compassion to indifference. Acceptance to disdain. She described the relationship: volatile, abusive, disrespectful. There was no romance, and the lovemaking was as close to rape as she could imagine. The sadism emerged. Sex was forced upon her no matter her own desire, even once at gunpoint. And Bridget was the result.

He had blonde hair. Bridget had blonde hair. He had blue eyes. Bridget had blue eyes. He had a temper. So did Bridget.

The child reminded Jan every day of the violence and cruelty of her marriage. Her husband soon abandoned her but sent threatening letters for months. Then he stopped writing. Jan thought he may have been killed and was dead. Or, at least, she wished so.

That's when I found myself asking Jan about her feelings towards her daughter. Did she see her ex in Bridget? Did she love her?

"I don't think I love her, no." With her mother and daughter out of the room, this admission fell from her lips with resigned sadness, but also a finality and relief. She no longer needed to pretend, at least not here. Her face did not reveal any remorse, but a resignation and complacency not seen in the vast majority of mothers who had come to my office. "I couldn't say that with her here. And I don't want my mother to know."

Over the next several months, Bridget came in for play-therapy. We spoke about her drawing of the dogs, and how they were her real family. Her mom never played with her, and always seemed depressed. It was all the little girl could do, to get her mother to even shout at her when misbehaving. It seemed that Bridget had no idea she was actually unloved, but felt her mother was distant and uninvolved, too depressed to even move off the couch.

In her play, Bridget would have animals protect and care for little boy and girl dolls. When the doll children were in danger, it was the dog and not the mother doll that would place itself in between the girl doll and the threat. Sometimes the dogs would try to threaten the mother doll, or the little girl doll would pull and push the mother off the furniture. Sometimes the little girl doll would pretend to be sick or in danger, but most of the time the doll would stand angrily in front of the mother, berating. Finally, Bridget would suddenly make the mother doll jump up, angry but energized, and chase the little girl around. The dogs would then come and try to get between the two, but Bridget would shoo them away and let the mother doll catch her. As they touched, the mother doll would become caring, cooing, and loving, telling the little girl how sorry she was for scaring her, and promising to take her out for ice cream.

For many children of depressed parents, sometimes they misbehave in an attempt to mobilize the parent out of their anergic state. *Maybe*, they subconsciously think, *if I am bad enough, my mom or dad will have to take care of me.* Maybe if I put myself in enough danger, it will stimulate their biological need to take care of me, so they can get their genes into the next generation. So, I am going to be really, really a handful—and hope my energy rubs off and activates them.

This strategy did not work with Jan. Indeed, things got so bad that Ann took over as the primary caregiver, but Jan retained guardianship.

Bridget dropped out of therapy.

Jan took her place.

* * *

Every Wednesday at 9:00 a.m., Jan came for her session. At first she spoke about parenting, how difficult it was, how ineffective she was, and how much better her mother was. Bridget was still not listening but was doing well at school. In fact, the school did not see any behavioral problems. Those were all confined to the home.

Jan became more despondent. She was already on medication when she entered my practice and went through a series of antidepressants and antipsychotics. She reported flashbacks of being abused by her ex-husband, sleepless nights, disrupted days, and she began feeling more and more suicidal.

One Wednesday, she came in for her session and showed me the cuts she had made on her arms the night before. She acknowledged this was not the first time, but that she had been afraid to tell me. A secret is not a secret because of what we have done. A secret is a secret because we worry, *how will someone view me differently if they know my secret?* Jan was worried I would not treat her, or that I would hospitalize her. She had been cutting since before we started in therapy six months before. Although I had asked her previously if she ever hurt herself, she rationalized her negative responses because it didn't "hurt." Instead, she felt an enormous relief from her "emotional pain." So, even though I had asked her, in our very first encounter when she acknowledged that she used to cut, if she still hurt herself—she had answered no.

"It doesn't hurt, so I wasn't lying. I deserve it anyway. I'm a lousy person."

But now she was worried. For the first time, she had not stopped at her arms, but went on to her thighs and abdomen. She showed me the cuts on her belly. They needed stitches. We agreed to call her mom and to have her taken to the ER for evaluation. Jan waited in my office and continued the session until Ann arrived.

I received a phone call from the ER later that morning. The ER clinicians were worried because Jan could not guarantee her safety from herself. They were going to admit her to an inpatient psychiatric hospital. Ann was in agreement, and so was Jan. She was admitted in anticipation of a short stay, with treatment involving medication changes and addressing her flashbacks.

The day after her admission, her inpatient team reported that Jan had found a piece of glass and cut herself. A short stay turned into weeks as she continued to regress. Her depression worsened. Medications were adjusted, but she still could not say she would be safe from herself if she went home. During one visit from her mom, Jan asked if she could give up custody of Bridget, at least temporarily. Ann agreed and became Bridget's guardian.

Jan seemed relieved. Her anxiety and depression began to abate, and she was able to go home in safety.

Months passed. Jan came in to see me every Wednesday. She was in a day treatment program and had moved into a small apartment, leaving her mom and Bridget in the family home. Too many memories remained there. Pictures of her father in his military uniform. The bedroom where she grew up. The spidery woodshed hidden behind a small grove of pine trees at the far end of the yard. The dining room. The living room. The attic. The smells. The colors. Her mother caring for her own daughter. Her mother caring at all.

The flashbacks were worse. The cutting no longer satisfied what she described as voices calling her stupid, horrid, useless. In her day program she listened to women talking about being abused, men talking about rage and anger, all of them working, working, working. Healing. Leaving. Moving on. While she stayed, crippled and ashamed. Useless. Unlovable. *Unlovable.*

It was a Tuesday night when my pager went off. The hospital operator told me that my patient Jan had called and asked me to phone her at home. It was an emergency.

Jan had never paged me before. Faithful to her Wednesday appointments, she'd saved her distress until then.

I called her at home.

"This is Dr. Shrand. What's the emergency?"

"I wanted to tell you I won't be at my session tomorrow." Jan had never missed a session. Any other patient cancelling a session would not be a pager-worthy event. They would leave a message on my voice mail, as instructed to do so more than twenty-four hours in advance so the time could be filled by another patient. In Jan's message, there was more than just a cancellation of a visit. These thoughts flew rapid-fire through my head within the few seconds between the end of Jan's last sentence and the start of her next. "I'm going to cancel all the sessions. I just wanted you to know."

This did not sound good.

"What's going on, Jan?" There was a silence, long, but different than that initial silence when I'd first met her. Silences have enormous and varied meanings. Sometimes depression robs one of the ability to rapidly organize thoughts and respond. Sometimes, silence is rageful, aggressive. Sometimes it speaks to the resignation of life's futility. Sometimes it is the terrifying calm of a decision, an answer to haunting questions, doubts, despair. Silent determination. Silent resolve.

With no response, I repeated the question. "Jan. What's up?"

"I'm dropping out of therapy."

"I got that part. How come?"

I could feel my own anxiety increasing. Jan now lived alone in a small apartment two towns over from the hospital. The week before, she had spoken about how she felt her life was useless. She couldn't care for her kid. She *didn't* care for her kid. She couldn't concentrate in the groups; didn't want to concentrate, wanted to sleep all the time, slept through the groups, hated the groups, hated herself, the cutting didn't help, she knew that taking pills would not . . . that she couldn't be sure . . . she needed to be sure.

She had left the session promising to be safe. Another psychiatrist may have hospitalized her, but Jan and I had an agreement built on trust, trust developed over the eighteen months she had been coming to her sessions every Wednesday at 9:00 a.m. I knew she felt suicidal. It had become part of who she was. It was the best she could do right now, but she promised me she would call before she tried anything.

The phrase that I use in these circumstances, I'd said to Jan at that last session: "I can live with it if you can." I know my patients may cut themselves, that they have pills in their cabinets with which they could overdose, that they have razors, knives, glass, "sharps." For some, having access to lethality gives them a sense of comfort; if things get too overwhelming, they can always die. "I can live with it if you can," says to the patient that I, as your therapist, can live with these instruments as long as they do not kill you. If you can live with all the implements of suicide around you—*live* with them—then I can deal with it. But if they are going to kill you, then you come into the hospital.

"I can live with it if you can." If you *can't* live with it, the deal is off and you abdicate your responsibility for safety, temporarily, to me.

Jan knew all this. She had pills, razors, sharps. Things that take time to kill, and a promise to tell me if she was going to use them. A promise is a nebulous agreement between two people. But in therapy, it represents trust: a patient who trusts their therapist is one thing, but when a therapist has trust in a patient, and lets them know of that bond, that connection, remarkable things can happen. From a *theory of mind* point of view, the patient recognizes their own sense of value and self-worth, that this powerful professional sees them as simply doing the best they can; as capable, strong enough to tolerate the anguish, determined enough to come to terms with their distress, and to live.[6]

---

[6] *Theory of mind* is our ability to theorize about another person's mind: what they are thinking or feeling. It is explored more in depth later in the book.

The difference between attachment and connection

A lot has been written about attachment. It is one of the cornerstones of psychology. Attachment theory explores how we attach to others.

There are four basic types of attachment influenced by our early childhood relationships: Secure, Dismissive-Avoidant, Anxious-Preoccupied, and Fearful-Avoidant (a.k.a. disorganized). Very often, attachments can keep us in the past, powerfully taking us away from the present. In therapy, these attachment styles are explored, but the tool used to explore them safely is the connection a patient has with their therapist. Connection allows for the freedom of exploration, uncovering the sources of the often-disrupted attachment that may have brought the person to therapy in the beginning. A safe and I-M connection is the foundation of the vulnerability that people may experience, finally recognizing that they can be vulnerable without being in danger—in danger of being judged as less than. You will see me use the word "connection" in this book, rather than "attachment," to describe our human need to feel part of a group.

There was Jan on the other end of the phone. I heard her breath, choppy, labored, anxious. Cancelling not only tomorrow, but all her appointments. Another silence. Broken.

"I have a gun."

With those four words, Jan changed the rules.

My anxiety rose.

"Guns are too quick. I can't help you if you have a gun."

"I know. I just wanted to tell you."

"Thanks! So now what? What do you think I should do?"

"That's up to you. I just wanted you to know."

"But how come? You didn't have to tell me. I would have been waiting for you to show up tomorrow, and you would be dead. I would send the police to your apartment, but you would be dead. Guns work too quick, Jan."

"I promised. I'm just keeping my promise."

Beginning in the third year of medical school—the true start of one's clinical rotations—the overarching experience is not simply learning how to recognize diseases, or diagnosis the source of fevers, or to learn about broken bits of the human body. It is not just how to read a lab result; how to listen to a patient's words, heart, lungs, bowel; how to decide which medication to use, which antibiotic, which anti-inflammatory. The true learning that occurs, over tens of thousands of hours, is how to rapidly synthesize an enormous amount of information, extract the critical components, assess the situation, make a swift and salient decision, and then apply treatment.

I was faced with a decision now: I could keep Jan talking and find a way to contact the police, have them go to her home, disarm her, and bring her to an emergency room for evaluation and hospitalization. Part of me screamed to just do it.

But Jan had called me. This meant something.

She called to *tell* me she had a gun.

"We had a promise to each other. I can live with it if you can. You can't live with a gun, Jan. It's too quick, too permanent. You changed the rules. I can't live with that either." The next words that came out of my mouth seemed impulsive on my part but were based on the eighteen months of trust Jan and I had built up. Based on my thousands of hours of training, synthesizing information, interpreting the data, making decisions.

I was about to test the strength of the relationship.

The strength of her connection.

The strength of meaningful therapy.

"I can't treat you if you have a gun. You have to give it back if you want to stay my patient."

In retrospect, it was an enormous risk. The gun could have gone off right there. Jan could have said, "Fine, I won't be your patient, I won't be anyone's patient," and pulled the trigger.

Silence . . . Silence. No shot. No explosion.

Silence.

Which one? Was this a silence of defiance, about to be underscored by the crack of a pistol? Was this the silence of despair, a hopelessness so profound the only solution was to pull the trigger? No. I could hear in this silence a contemplation. A consideration. Jan was thinking. I could hear her breathing. The character of her breathing was different. Not abrupt and choppy like before when she waited to tell me of her new possession. She was listening, waiting for how I would respond.

"I'm going to trust you, Jan. I'll call you back in twenty minutes. If you don't answer the phone, I am going to send the police over. Twenty minutes."

"OK."

"I'll call you then." I heard Jan put down the phone, and then did I.

Twenty minutes. Would she pick up?

As I went through medical school, internship, residency, and then fellowship, I'd had many incredible teachers. Over time, I had adopted two rules, which I now teach every resident, nurse, social worker, and staff member. Two rules—one based on a book, and the other from a mentor, supervisor, and friend.

The first rule is from the book *House of God* by Samuel Shem: Never worry alone. If you're worried about something—about a patient, what they said, what they are doing—go and find someone to worry with. Never worry alone.

The second rule was from one of my supervisors, Marty Miller: The therapist must survive. You have to be able to leave work behind so you can do it again the next day. It does not mean you are cold, impassive, or without compassion. But if you go home and worry about your patients . . . then you haven't followed the first rule. You have worried alone.

Jan had a gun. I should worry with someone about it, call a colleague, call the police. I knew what would happen if I did. *Are you out of your mind? Get the police over there right away! She's got a gun.*

I didn't call anyone. I worried alone. One minute. Five minutes. Ten. Eighteen. Nineteen. Twenty.

I dialed Jan's number.

One ring. Two. Three. Answer. The phone stopped.

"I'm here."

"So what are you going to do?"

Jan paused. Without a sigh, flat, blunted, not calm but composed, she replied, "I'll give the gun back tomorrow."

"I'll check my voicemail in the morning. If there is no message by seven a.m. I'll send the police over. See you tomorrow at nine."

Never worry alone. But I did.

Next morning, I checked my voicemail. 7:00 a.m. There was a message from Jan. "You don't need to send the police, but I understand if I can't be your patient anymore. I'm too dangerous. I'll give the gun back today."

I called her. "See you at nine."

Jan was in the waiting room. I went out to meet her. I asked her if she had a gun in her purse. She smiled and said no, opening her bag to show me. We went into my office.

Eighteen months. We had met Wednesday mornings at 9:00 a.m. for eighteen months. I had not hospitalized her the night before, though many therapists probably would have. She began to talk.

Spilling out of her came story after story about how her father sexually abused her. How her brother sexually abused her. How her birthdays, from the age of eight, were terrifying, as her father would come into her room early, before anyone would wake, and give her his special birthday gift. The blood. The smell. The shame. The confusion. How her brother would take her into the spider-infested woodshed, how the cobwebs would penetrate her hair, stick to her clothes, absorb her. How the rooms seemed upside down and backwards, as if she were watching from a far-away corner. How she cried. How her silence grew. How the cutting began, to make her ugly, so no one would want her, no one would want to touch her, no one would come near her. No one would get close. The blood.

But it did not work.

Her body became not her own. And her soul became not her own. And she blamed herself for not fighting, for not resisting, for the confusion of her body that responded despite itself, despite her revulsion. He was meant to love her, after all—her father. Meant to care for her. Meant to protect her. What had she done wrong? What had she done?

And then he died.

And the funeral was big and grotesque, and full of military pomp and full of people who loved him, and full of tears and sorrow at the loss of such a citizen, of such a good, good man.

And did her mother know? And did her mother care? And if she knew . . . And if she didn't.

All of this spilled out of Jan, who had held her secret for so long, a chalice, a shrine, an open wound that could never heal and scar.

And did her mother know?

What sense did her mother make of the tears that never came from her daughter for the loss of Dad? Did Ann see her as too sick already, too absorbed in her own self-pity, mistaking self-absorption for what was truly self-loathing that was truly a mask for a rage that was deep, deep, deep and seething? An emotional pain satisfied only by the sight of blood, drawn under her control this time. Under *her* control.

The most difficult feeling for a human being to tolerate is feeling powerless. It is a deeply biological disease, a fear of vulnerability, of the possibility of being consumed literally and figuratively. Our small mammalian ancestors were always vulnerable, always at risk of having their lives cut short by some larger, sinister predator waiting to hunt them down, kill them, eat them, cut short their reproductive lives and threaten the advance of their biological contribution to the next generation of mammalian genes.

Powerlessness is abhorrent to human beings. So, to defend against it, we sometimes make things up. We pretend. We try to convince ourselves that we were never really powerless, but that we made bad choices. A rape victim may say, "I should have been smarter. I should have been stronger. If only I hadn't gone there, if only I had done this. I should have, if only . . ." As if they had any control at all. But they were powerless. There is no "choice" in being raped or abused or neglected. These things happen to a person. No one *chooses* to be raped. One is powerless.

A little child who is abused does not say, "Why did you hurt me?" They say, "What did I do?" They blame themselves. It can take years for a person to look back and say, "It wasn't me. I didn't do anything wrong. Why did they hurt me?"

Jan had kept her nine o'clock appointment. And she was starting on her road. No more contained, affect flat and blunted.[7] Tears dripped down her face. Words full of life, animated, rhythmic, flowing, kept coming, kept coming, surged and gushed. More memories, broken images, fully formed images, pieces, fragments, sounds, smells, tastes.

And did her mother know? Did she turn her head? Where was she? Did mothers love their daughters? Did she know?

And he had died. And inside, she felt no grief but huge relief. And then enormous guilt. And wanted to die. "She loved him so much she wants to join him," the strangers thought. They were so close. The way he looked at her. His baby. His little girl.

And did her mother know why Jan wanted to die? Why she made such a real attempt, after all those hidden ones, the hidden hacking at her arms and legs? And was she lovable? To anyone? And to herself?

The story continued to spill itself out, purging, vomited, purifying.

And yet, for the next six weeks she continued to feel suicidal. She continued to cut. We kept adjusting and readjusting her medication. She kept going to groups and was able to stay out of the hospital. Each week there was more of the story, and more processing how it had influenced her life. Each week she wondered if her mother knew but had not yet gained the courage to ask her.

The gun never really existed. She had obtained a license to buy a gun and was going to get one the next day. She wanted me to know she had finally decided to die, to see what I would do.

---

[7] "Flat and blunted affect" is a psychiatry description of someone who does not show any emotion.

As I reflected on my decision not to worry *with* someone, I wondered why I had deviated from my first, most sacred rule. I had worried alone. *Alone.* Kept Jan's deadly secret until the next morning.

And then it hit me.

I had kept her secret.

For at least one night, I had experienced what Jan had experienced for years. Living with a secret so outrageous, who would believe it. Tolerating the anxiety along with her, not locking it away in the confines of a psychiatric ward. Wondering if there would be a message, her message, on my voicemail the next morning, or if I would have to send the police to discover, what—blood, brains, the brutal end of a tormented woman.

I had lived, for that one night, with the worry of a secret.

Looking back, I am convinced that was the turning point of her treatment. Part of it was sharing her anguish, the other trusting in the strength of the connection, the relationship forged over the past eighteen months. I had never before broken the first rule and have never broken it since. But for that one night, subconsciously, my instinct as Jan's psychiatrist led me down a path perhaps dangerous, but with an outcome that solidified the *trust* I had that this woman could heal. That whatever secret she had to tell I would not judge her. I am a psychiatrist, not a judge. I am simply interested in why people do what they do, and in trying to help them understand themselves, their choices, why they do what they do.

Jan had called to tell me she had a gun. She did not need to do that. It meant something.

The weeks went on, however, and she still remained torn and sore. We looked at the guilt she felt, the deep wish that her father would die, the magical thinking of a little girl who blamed herself when he did die, the rage she felt towards her brother and how he had hurt her, betrayed her.

And did her mother know?

We explored and explored. She desperately wanted to ask her mother but was terrified of the answer. She could not do it. Her daughter lived with her mother.

Her child, still unruly, feisty, angry, defiant. Jan began to realize that, in some ways, she *wanted* her daughter to be like that: strong, powerful, invincible.

Yes, invincible. No one would be able to hurt Bridget the way Jan had been hurt. Bridget could take care of herself. No man would be able to penetrate her shield. But it had kept her from her daughter, this wish to see her daughter strong and impregnable. How was she to get close to her now? Was it too late?

And always, always, coming back to her own mother.

* * *

Jan came to the Wednesday session. Her face contorted, a different anguish. She sat heavily in her chair and tilted back her head so her eyes gazed up at the ceiling. Her voice directed towards the heavens as she reported.

"My mother has lung cancer. She is going to die."

And yet another silence. This filled with longing, grieving, decision.

At the next session, Jan was accompanied by her mother. I had not seen Ann since she had taken guardianship of Bridget. Ann looked pale, gaunt, the knowledge of cancer already depleting her of resources and energy. She did not know why Jan had asked her to come to the session. But she had come when asked.

I waited with Ann. Jan—cautious, daring—told her.

Silence. Stunned. Stunning.

Jan told her about her father. And about her brother. And she watched her mother's body and face and breathing and skin, and if she flinched or reddened or remained silent, and waited for the words "I know." Or "My God." Or "Impossible." "Liar." "Nonsense."

And Ann, weak from her own body's betrayal, moved her body in her chair, and straightened her back, and poured strength into her shoulders, and reached over to her daughter, just out of reach so she stood from her chair, took one step, and pulled her daughter into her arms, hugging her, holding her, caressing her, letting her cry and cry and cry until the two blended and fused, a mother and daughter—a mother who never knew, a daughter who had never told.

"Get my son on the phone," she instructed me. She told me the number. I dialed. "Put him on speaker." The ringing of the phone filled the office.

An answer.

"What did you do to your sister?"

"Mom?"

"What did you do to her? *What* did you do?"

And his voice carried from far, far away, muffled by spiderwebs that had clung to his hair, an ancient shroud removed. And he cried, and wept, and through his tears flowed apology after apology, regret, repentance, a plea for forgiveness. And then blame. His father. His teacher. The attic, the woodshed. His father. The teacher.

* * *

After Ann succumbed to the cancer, Jan gave Bridget up to the state Department of Social Services. She was yet too unsure of her ability to be a mother, of her ability to love and to accept love. And yet, for the next two years, she did everything asked of her so she could win her daughter back. She went to day treatment, then graduated and began to work in the community, slowly regaining an identity of a capable, competent woman, scarred with the designs of many battles, but with open wounds becoming faded marks of distant wars.

In time she did win back her daughter, sold the family home, left behind the cobwebs of childhood injury, and began a new life in another state. Once a year, she would return for a follow-up session with me, reporting the fear of new relationships, and the joy of new relationships. And she met a man, and was afraid, and then allowed herself to be cherished, loved, married. And she began to trust him, unconditionally.

Bridget had moved out when she reach eighteen, and with that a friendship between mother and daughter began to grow. The young woman gained a greater appreciation of the older, while embroiled in her own and parallel disruptive relationship far from home. She would call her mom, for advice, for comfort, for strength, support, encouragement.

Far away, in another state, an old woodshed collapsed in its rotted heap of unraveled webs. In her new home, Jan kept the door open for her child. Unconditionally.

CHAPTER 4
I-M PERSPECTIVE:
THE POWER OF RESPECT

In Jan's story, and in the stories of each person in this book, we can trace out the Four Domains, elaborate on each, and begin to unravel the complex reciprocity in life. Let's step back for a moment and review the Ic Domain: how I see myself and how I think others see me. We *really* want to know: "What is that person thinking about me? Do they see me as valuable?" Theory of mind is how we *remind* another person of their value through the Ic Domain. This is the power of the I-M Approach and its Ic Domain: in using it to again-look, to respect another person as doing the best they can instead of less than they can, in response to the domains.

One of my favorite cartoons that illustrates the power of the Ic Domain is a *Rose is Rose* set of panels in which a little boy is playing baseball with his dad. The boy can't hit the ball, throw it, or catch it, but his dad leans down to him and says, "You were amazing out there." The dad is not saying "you are great at baseball." That would be a lie, the kid stinks at baseball.

What the dad is saying is "you tried, you didn't give up." This is resilience. This is exactly what we want in our children: to be willing to make a mistake, get up, learn, and try again. The little boy would not be willing to make mistakes if he thought his dad was going to criticize him. But the boy trusts his dad, because his dad values him, and treats him with respect. His dad saw his son at a certain I-M and used the Ic Domain to convey his perception. In the last panel of the cartoon, the little boy walks away smiling. And so does his dad—smiling as he walks next to his son. This is the power of theory of mind.

But theory of mind has a dark side. Human beings are also really good at making someone else feel like a worthless piece of crap. We use theory of mind to make someone else feel less valuable. Charlie Brown, your prototypical depressed kid, is a great example. Why is he depressed? In an incredible cartoon, Charlie Brown is trying to get the attention of kids and Snoopy, saying to them, "Believe in me. Believe in me. Believe in me." None of them stop but walk right by him. In the last panel, Charlie Brown sits alone, dejected, elbows resting on his knees, his head held up by his jaw resting on his hands, and says, "I just can't get people to believe in me." *This* is why Charlie Brown is depressed. Through the eyes of others, he sees himself as a loser. This is the dark side of theory of mind. Human beings are really good at reminding someone of their value. But we are just as good as making them feel they have none.

Jan's Ic was being assaulted in her Home Domain, and she was led to believe that she was worthless, powerless, useless. Jan saw herself as valueless and she became depressed. She would cut herself to relieve the emotional pain, but her Biological Domain would release a brain chemical called an endorphin: a natural form of morphine. That is why she did not feel physical pain but instead a sense of relief. But when others found out that she harmed her body or tried to kill herself, that small change would often get her placed in the Social Domain of a psychiatric hospital for the mentally ill. You control no one but influence everyone. Her Ic knew that other people saw her as broken, and the psychiatric hospitalization would unwittingly reinforce her sense of worthlessness.

Sometimes we are faced with a predator we know we can beat, so we fight it. In humans, this is anger: we want the predator to change and to flee from us. Sometimes we are faced with a predator we know we can't beat, so we want to get the hell out of there. In humans, this is anxiety: we avoid something and run away.

Sometimes we are faced with a predator we know we are not strong enough to beat, and not fast enough to get away from. So, the next best strategy for survival is to freeze, become invisible, and hope the danger passes. Depression is the "freeze" branch of fight-flight-freeze.

Jan was frozen, stuck in a world where she felt she had no value, was useless, and felt she did not deserve to live. The influence of that Home Domain influenced her Social Domain with an abusive husband. Abuse is the antithesis of reminding someone of their value. Jan began to see herself the way her father and brother saw her—without value and to be abused. She responded by decades of self-injury, suicidal feelings, and a profound ambivalence about her own child.

What happened in our session? Jan revealed her secrets the day after I did not hospitalize her, when *she* chose to stay alive, and she recognized I trusted that she would make that choice. I believed in her. I saw her as valuable. I saw her as a person struggling with and responding to the influences of her domains, but at her own current maximum potential.

As I write this so many years later, I wonder, "What the heck was I thinking? She could have killed herself!" As I look back, there were many forces in action at that moment influencing my own I-M. Jan and I had been working together for a few years by then, and she had been out of a hospital for a while. I would not have been so assured if we had not built a relationship, again based on respect and value. We had formed a "therapeutic alliance," worrying together and not alone.

Jan was at an I-M: her Ic and Biological Domains influenced by her Home and Social Domains. She was not broken. She was then, and is now, at *her* I-M.

But small changes can have big effects. By inviting Jan to the Social Domain of her regular appointment instead of admitting her to a psychiatric ward, I reminded her of her value. I believed in her as capable of making her own choices—in this case, a choice to live. This Ic influenced her Biological Domain and she realized that there was at least one person in her Social Domain who respected her as valuable. Respect leads to value, and value leads to trust. The trust to take a chance, take a risk, and disclose the horrible reality of being sexually abused by her father, her brother, and her husband.

Small changes can have big effects. That small change of not hospitalizing her had a huge effect.

You control no one but influence everyone. Jan's Ic was influenced. She began to see herself as more valuable, began to trust, and shared her secrets.

With this change in her Ic, a ripple effect began throughout the other domains. Jan had always thought her mother knew about the abuse, and that she had turned away, reinforcing Jan's self-image of worthlessness. Jan made a small change in her Home Domain and told her mother what had happened. Jan saw her mother's shock and horror at what had happened to her baby girl. Her mother had no idea how much Jan had been abused. Realizing that her mother had been oblivious and not silently complicit further rekindled Jan's sense of value. [8]

As Jan's Ic began to recognize that other people could see her as valuable, she began to recognize the negative influence she was having on her own child by being distant. Jan began to make different choices in her Social Domain and worked hard to get custody back of her daughter. She was able to return to work and manage the stress and demands of an office. Her success in both areas further bolstered her evolving Ic as a capable and valuable human being. She was developing self-worth. She controlled no one but influenced everyone, and she got to *choose* the kind of influence she wanted to be.

She was not powerless.

The sense of powerlessness

From my experience as a psychiatrist, powerlessness is the most difficult feeling for a human being to tolerate. Millions of years ago, if our human ancestors were powerless, they were usually lunch. Today we defend ourselves from this overwhelming response of our Biological Domain by shifting our Ic Domain: We *pretend* we have power.

---

[8] This example reveals how the home environment in which we grow up is not static. Years later, we can reflect on what we thought was going on from our perspective as a *child*, but now from the perspective as an adult. In this way, events that occur in the Home Domain can still be dynamic. Such change in perspective can have an amplified effect on one's I-M.

Victims of abuse—physical, sexual, and emotional—will blame themselves rather than truly experience powerlessness. "I should have been stronger. I could have been smarter. I should have been better. I could have, should have . . ." A "should have, could have" mentality maintains the illusion of power, of having some control over the situation. For example, a patient of mine, a fifteen-year-old girl, had been raped when she was drunk at a beach party. She came into the hospital after trying to kill herself. Ashamed, terrified of how she would be seen if word got out in her school that she had been assaulted, she blamed herself. "I shouldn't have gone to the party. And if I hadn't gotten drunk, I could've kicked him off me."

She sat in the hospital, weeping as she relived the horror of being raped. I discussed with her the idea that it is easier to blame herself than recognize there was nothing she could do, and that the assailant had no right to hurt her in any way. That it was *his* limitations, his culpability—not hers. There was nothing she could have done.

"But I wanted to. I wanted to kill him, to hurt him . . . to hurt him."

"So how does this connect with hurting yourself?"

"Who could love me? I'm useless. No one is going to care about me."

No one is going to care about me. Firmly rooted in the Ic domain, this young woman, at that moment in time, viewed herself as valueless. In the truest sense of the word: an invalid in-valid. Her lack of value was reinforced in the interaction with her rapist. Who could love such a useless person?

No one has the right to violate you—at a party, drunk, sober, anywhere, anytime. But this girl had been violated; a brutal statement that she had no value. That she was prey. Rather than experience the profound sense of powerlessness, this girl blamed herself. She *should have, could have* done something.

This was an I-M. She did not have to like her I-M, nor condone it. Taking responsibility for drinking is not the same as saying it was OK to be raped. But instead of judging herself as less than and broken, she began to apply the I-M Approach, which made it a little easier to say, "My God, there was *nothing* I could do. Nothing." She was able to experience the powerlessness of that situation without seeing herself as worthless and broken. She was resilient.

Every resilient person has had at least one person in their lives who has seen them as valuable. Using the I-M Approach, Jan was able to rekindle her sense of value, and create a loving Home Domain for her own child. The I-M Approach is a reminder that we are *all* valuable. If you don't like your I-M, you can change it— by unleashing the power of respect.

SMALL CHANGES CAN HAVE BIG EFFECTS

When Jan realized that I saw her as valuable, she began to trust. This is a small change we can do for anyone at any time. You can try it today at home or in your Social Domain. See what happens to the other person, and then recognize how that has changed your own Biological Domain.

YOU CONTROL NO ONE BUT INFLUENCE EVERYONE

Lead by example. When you unleash the power of respect you are modelling a way of engaging in the world. Instead of judging, wonder. Use one of our greatest human inventions: language. Instead of acting on a feeling of being disrespected by someone who is not using the I-M Approach, recognize that is the best they can do and do not let them activate your mirror neurons to be disrespectful in return. It will be hard, at first, because our brains are designed to compete and not always cooperate. When you influence the rude person by treating them instead with respect, it will startle them. What were they expecting their influence to be on you? Surprise them with wonder, rather than responding in rage. You really do get to *choose* the influence you want to be. Treat the disrespectful person with respect, remind them that you see them as valuable even as they try to diminish your value, and see what happens. You are both at an I-M, but you can influence the direction the disrespectful person is headed.

CHAPTER 5
DECAF, OK?

"Put down the chair!"

I was walking onto the inpatient unit floor. A nurse was screaming in fear for herself as a very large and psychotic man had a chair raised high over his head, ready to smash it onto the defenseless woman. Staff were already running towards them, about to intervene, about to try to wrestle away the "weapon" and place the man in restraints if needed.

"Put it down!" another voice joined; another person scared and startled. The chair hung weightless in the air, held high by the man's fully extended arms. A metal frame securing a plastic seat and backrest, the gleaming sheen of polished steel ready to crack down on the skull of a nurse who was just doing her job, just trying to keep patients safe . . . just about to have her head cracked open by the man draped in a hospital gown, face red with the flow of adrenaline, breath fast and heavy with the flow of psychotic rage.

Dan was my patient. The one about to assault a nurse. I walked over, a brisk but controlled pace, the ten steps to cross the room. Not running, not giving a hint of urgency or a mote of exigency. I arrived at the side of Dan and the nurse, where they both could see me.

"Hey, Dan. Want a cup of coffee?"

The non sequitur made Dan pause. The nurse startled, a plea in her eye but without a voice. The other staff, ready to take control of the situation, looked at me in astonishment as if to ask, "Who is the crazy one here? This guy is about to beat the crap out of a nurse with a chair!"

Dan looked toward me, the chair still poised high above his head, a feather of ferocity wielded by a very sick and angry man. But he was my patient, so I went on.

"Decaf, OK?"

A grin crossed his face, and he put down the chair. "Cream?"

"Sounds like a plan. Let's go and talk." As the nurse let down her protective arms, and the staff remained within a reasonable distance in case Dan's mood changed again, my patient and I walked to the kitchen area for a cup of decaf.

Dan was thirty-five and had been in a state hospital for sixteen years. He had not responded to a multitude of antipsychotic medications, remaining in a world of delusion and paranoia, fearful and feared—as he was a big, a *very* big and very psychotic man. He had been moved out of the state hospital as the first step towards a transition into the community. Not because he was particularly ready, or better, or more able to manage reality. Throughout the country, financial aid for the mentally ill was drying up. And who did these people, crippled by mental illness, have as their champion? How were these severely incapacitated people meant to organize and lobby for themselves? The societal fear of mental illness continues to place a moral overlay on behavior that is, on occasion, erratic and unpredictable, creating anxiety in a community and resulting in ostracizing rather than an understanding of the inner world of these most remarkable of individuals.

So, Dan had become my patient in a university-based hospital after surviving for two days post-discharge from his sixteen-year sanctuary.

He was my first patient on Clozaril®, a new antipsychotic that had just come out in the early 1990s. I was a second-year resident doing one of my inpatient rotations, and Dan was one of my patient-teachers. By the time of the chair incident, I had known him for a week as tremendously paranoid and just wanting to "go home." He was on a court order to take medication and judged too impaired by his psychiatric condition to make his own decisions about his treatment.

Clozaril® had just been added to the treatment plan, but he had not yet started it. We spoke about it all over coffee—about the need for weekly blood draws to check his white blood cell count, about how fast we could go up on the medicine, about how it was new and worked differently but that it may not work at all, about how grateful I was that he put down the chair and did not need to be restrained or given injections.

Dan nodded gently as he sipped his decaf with cream. He was still paranoid, but being treated with respect and dignity, he calmed. Not until more than a decade later did I recognize that the style of care I was developing as a resident had a calming effect on patients, and staff. By treating them with dignity and respect. By seeing them at their I-M. By letting them know they are valuable, that they matter, and that I have a true interest in who they are and why they do what they do—as a *person* and not a chart nor diagnosis. These people, at their time of greatest need and vulnerability, recognized that I was just trying to help, and so rarely would become enraged.

Even in the throes of psychosis, a patient can usually recognize when they are not in danger, although they can perceive danger where none exists. They still can access their Ic. It was through this domain that I was able to calm Dan down. He did not perceive me as seeing him as a threat, nor did he see me as threatening.

I am convinced that if I had come into the ward and demanded he put down the chair, or addressed it at all, the nurse would have been injured and Dan eventually restrained. By my doing something nonthreatening, even perhaps outrageous and off-topic, Dan was able to withdraw from his aggression and paranoia and put down the chair.

So we sat together and prepared to start yet another new medicine.

Some weeks passed. Slowly, slowly, slowly, Dan began his return to reality. His paranoia abated, his rage receded, and he began to connect to the world in a way he had not done for almost half his life. He had not passed a day without being psychotic or delusional, despite heroic efforts with medication after medication.

And now he was beginning to clear.

And now he began to see his reality without the lens of psychosis obscuring his vision.

And "now" was very, very real.

I sat with Dan after his psychosis had cleared. Together we began to look forward, to a time when he could indeed leave the confines of a psychiatric hospital and start his life in the community.

"What have you done to me?" he asked.

His question took me by surprise.

"What have you done?" he repeated. "I didn't know what I had lost. All those years. Why have you done this to me?"

Dan was no more psychotic, but the enormous grief of sixteen years lost was beginning to overwhelm him. He began to wonder about his friends from high school, how they had gone on with their lives while his had been frozen in a world where his mind betrayed him, where he lived without freedom, locked in the abyss of his mental illness.

Free of those chains, Dan now had to face his world—far, far behind his peers, far, far away from his family who had grown on without him, never giving up but having to go on, having to continue with their lives. His mother had died without him even knowing. His father was now old and infirm. His brothers and sisters had moved to other states, had families, children, jobs.

And he had nothing but his sanity. It was too much to bear. He wondered if he should stop his Clozaril and return to the horror and trauma of psychosis—at least he could escape the despair he now experienced.

No more psychotic, he was now depressed.

Healing has its dark side as some people begin to face the results of rescue. Perhaps infirm, perhaps with handicap, perhaps with anger, deep regret, the grief and loss and outrage of opportunity gone, of facing days upon future days with a body or mind that had betrayed them at the deepest level.

I put Dan on an antidepressant, in retrospect, a small change in his Biological Domain. It would not heal his wounds of lost years but would at least give him a chance to begin his path back to some degree of functionality. He had every right to grieve, but at the same time could not afford a regression back into psychosis, although part of him desperately yearned for this retreat.

In time he rallied. A team was built around Dan, and he was, indeed, able to transition slowly slowly slowly to a group home. A day treatment program, closely monitored, provided job coaching, training, and support. He was not a stupid man, and without the gauze cowl distortion of his psychosis, he quickly learned a skill at which he excelled. With time and help, he rebuilt a life, not as a replacement for his lost years, but rich with potential and a renewed sense of who he was, who he had been, and how he was emerging out of the fearful world of distortion and depression.

Dan taught me a lesson: A break with reality can be a trauma but coming back can sometimes be worse. At first. And it is always good to have someone with whom to share a cup of coffee—even if it is decaf.

CHAPTER 6
I-M PERSPECTIVE: STIGMA

Dan was at an I-M, about to smash the chair down on the nurse's head, but he stopped. Why? When I approached Dan with respect, he de-escalated. Instead of challenging him, I took a position that was nonthreatening. When Dan was offered a cup of coffee, there was a shift in the Social Domain. This small change in one domain had an amplified and ripple effect throughout the system. His aggression de-escalated, as his Ic accommodated to my different approach, shifting his Biological Domain from the reflexive limbic system to his reflective prefrontal cortex.

When Dan appreciated that I saw him at an I-M, he was able to calm down. I did not control him with this small change; I influenced him and shifted his I-M. His Ic Domain recognized I was treating him with respect, which led him to feel valuable, which allowed him to trust. We built that trust between us. Respect leads to value and value leads to trust. Trust decreases aggression. When is the last time you got angry at someone treating you with respect?

Dan did not feel in danger anymore, he was able to put down the chair and have a cup of decaf with me. As this trust evolved over the course of his stay in the hospital, he was able to talk with me about his despair, sense of loss, and to allow himself to be emotionally vulnerable.

Stigma

"Mental illness" still carries an enormous stigma, almost a limbic and irrational fear of the irrational. A diagnosis of a mental illness sends a message to the uniformed: this person is "crazy." In my field, stigma is unintentionally perpetuated by using words like "disorder." As soon as you diagnose someone as having a disorder, you separate and lump people into two groups: one that is ordered and one that is not.

As a result, many people with mental illness are often given short shrift in the community. Outside the profession, or their family, the general population does not understand people with mental illness. While the mentally ill may be tolerated, at best, the unpredictability of these people often leads to fear and mistrust by the other members of the community.

I propose that this *mistrust* is the core belief contributing to the enormous stigma of mental illness. Can a person who is "crazy" be trusted? But trust goes both ways. We do not treat these people with respect; instead seeing them as inadequate and dangerous, needing to be isolated from the rest of the community. Then we are astonished that they often don't trust us and reject treatment.

Early in my career as a psychiatrist, I took over an adolescent unit where all the patients were on a "level" system. They started at red, the most restrictive, and had to earn points to climb up the ladder to yellow and then to green. If they did anything wrong, they were dropped to a lower level, and more restrictions. Imagine being compromised, perhaps impulsive, and trying to figure out the rules to move up a level system in order to get more privileges. No wonder the hospital had so many restraints! It was devaluing and demoralizing.

The medical director at the time refused to allow me to get rid of the level system, believing it was the only leverage his nurses and staff had to keep the patients doing what they were meant to do (whatever that was).

I kept the level system—but everyone in the unit, and then every new admission, started on level green. They did not need to prove anything to me. They could give away (not lose) their level based on unsafe behaviors to themselves or others but could quickly earn them back by treating themselves and others with respect. Working with staff and patients, we painted the I-M logo on the walls of the unit. Everyone learned and applied the approach. Within two weeks, the restraints were practically non-existent.

As a result, I soon was asked to become the medical director of the hospital. I proudly took the position. The state had closed half the beds in the facility because of the number of restraints. When I examined the hiring process and the training new staff received, I found that the *first* thing they learned was how to restrain a patient. They had been taught that the patients were dangerous, unpredictable, and not to be trusted. The level red, which all patients were supposed to start at, implied danger.

I changed the level system throughout the hospital so that every patient then started on green. I changed the staff training program. The first thing new staff learned was the I-M Approach, focusing on the Ic Domain and theory of mind.

Our patients may have temporarily lost their ability to appreciate how other people thought or felt, but they all knew how *they* were being treated.

"When I was a medical student"

I told the new hires, and the entire staff, a story of when I was a medical student working on a locked inpatient psychiatric ward with psychotic patients. All the doors were locked. If a patient wanted to go to the bathroom, to the group room, to the nurse's station, they had to ask a staff member to unlock the door.

Imagine being already paranoid, afraid, compromised, and having to find someone to get a door unlocked to do basic things.

Medical students were not given keys either. I also had to find someone to unlock the door when I had to go to the bathroom, the group room, the nurse's station, and even to depart the locked-down inpatient unit at the end of my day.

I have never forgotten that experience.

When I told the staff about this, I reminded them that they had a key to come and go. They were *valuable*. They mattered. But more importantly—*they* were the key. They were the key to helping their patients move to another I-M.

Within a few weeks, the use of restraints dropped dramatically. Patients began to feel respected, valued, and were able to trust. We had rekindled their sense of value.

I have been able to use this approach in substance use programs, outpatient centers, and individual, group, and family therapy. Couples learn to see each other at an I-M. Parents learn that it is much more rewarding to be amazed at who their child is than disappointed in who they are not. Individual after individual who learns the I-M begins to rekindle their sense of value, moving away from the shroud of stigma.

But more importantly, I use the I-M Approach in my everyday life. It changes the way I see people, and the way I see myself. No one is broken. Everyone is valuable and has the capacity to trust themselves and others.

Beyond the outhouse

Gary Larson drew a cartoon where a chubby boy with glasses was playing a tuba behind an outhouse. In the distance stands a small crowd of people. With flat expressions, they look in the direction of the outhouse. From their perspective they do not see the boy, just the outhouse. They hear an extreme evacuation that they believe is coming from *inside* the outhouse. You probably know what they think they are hearing. And it is not a tuba.

To me, the outhouse represents stigma. Stigma is when we judge someone without really knowing who they are and why they do what they do. It is a stain of disgrace associated with a particular circumstance, quality, or person. Very often, stigma is shaming. Every time, stigma is ostracizing.

It is ostracizing because it pushes a person out of one group and into a less respected group. That push is powered by mistrust. A stigmatized person is less valuable and not as trustworthy.

But that mistrust goes both ways. A person who feels less valued by you is less likely to trust you. Why should they? You don't trust them.

Stigma is the application of labels, bias, and prejudice. We see only what is in front of us, obscured by preconception. We do not see a person for who they are, influenced by their family, their society, their sense of self, and their biology, doing the best they can. We treat each other with *dis*respect. And we even apply stigma to ourselves, often judging ourselves as not doing as well as we should.

When we stigmatize and cannot look behind the outhouse, we miss our own and each other's music. This book asks you to look beyond the outhouse.

Using the I-M Approach, and recognizing you will not be judged, look at how you may be applying stigma in your own world. Some use the term "unconscious bias," but even that term can create a barrier and obstacle to looking at who you are and why you do what you do. Most people do not like to acknowledge that they stigmatize other people, lumping them into categories and tribes outside their own. They don't like to acknowledge it because, on some level, it diminishes their value. That is a good thing. I would much rather people were uncomfortable with being prejudiced and biased because it means, on some level, that they care what other people think about them.

If you don't like it, you can change it, and the first small change is just to acknowledge "you do it, I do it, we *all* do it." Make your list today, in each of the Four Domains. How do you see people in your home? What criticism do you have of their I-M? Do the same for your Social Domain. Then step back and again-look at why they may be doing what you are critical of. Why are some people prejudiced? How is their sense of value being so threatened that they have to diminish someone else to feel more valuable themselves? And how may you be doing that—not only to others, but even to yourself? How are you meant to trust yourself and others if you do not respect or value them?

The importance of trust

Why is trust such an important part of our societies? I suggest it is a product of the enormous evolutionary pressure of a social animal that needed to know what someone else was thinking and feeling about them. Theory of mind had to evolve in concert with our development as a social species.

From an individual level to the affiliation between global powers, it is trust that drives relationships. It is the presence or lack of trust that propels the choices made in those relationships. From the decision to accept or ask for a date, to the resolution to enter into a treaty between nations, it is the willingness to believe that you can trust someone else that ultimately closes the deal.

How do you know who to trust? How do you make that assessment? In order to "trust" someone, you first have to have a sense of what they are thinking or feeling about you. The basic desire and need to trust is not limited to social class or culture. It is pervasive in our species. Indeed, trust versus mistrust is the first stage of psychosocial development in an infant, covering birth to eighteen months.[9]

Trust is the foundation of relationships across cultures. This suggests there must have been an enormous evolutionary pressure for human beings to develop this ability that we now take as so fundamental to the fabric of our society. Knowing what someone else is thinking or feeling about you confers a selective advantage over organisms that do not have this capacity. From an evolutionary perspective, it was much more important to know if someone was looking at you as their lunch than if they were hungry. This, first, is about survival: am I safe? Second, it is about empathy: should I share?

Where in our evolution would we find the roots of a fundamental ability with such enormous implications for our individual survival? I think we can find the beginnings of this in an ancient mechanism we now know as "fight, flight, or freeze."

The vast majority of animals have a fight-flight-freeze mechanism that evolved over millions of years as a way to protect against the real risk of becoming lunch for some other organism. The fight-flight-freeze circuit lives in an ancient part of the brain called the limbic system. The limbic system is, in essence, the seat

---

[9] Erik H. Erikson, *Childhood and Society* (New York: W.W. Norton & Company, 1950).

of emotion, of fear and pleasure, of irrational feelings and impulses, of emotional memory. Even today, the limbic system is active in our emotions, from love to fear to hate to addiction and the vast range of feelings we experience in our daily lives.

The survival-based need to infer what someone else is thinking or feeling about you activates an instantaneous (if unconscious) algorithmic evaluation:

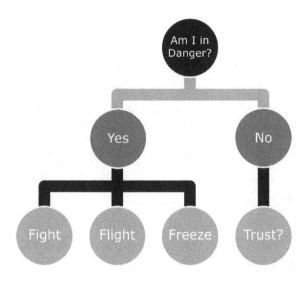

From an evolutionary perspective, there would be a selective advantage to a proto-hominid who could figure out if the animal, or other proto-hominid, across from them was planning on eating them for lunch. It is unlikely that we had many ancestors who did *not* develop this ability, because they would indeed have *been* lunch for that animal and would not have passed down those particular gene-environment complexes to the next generation.

One can extend this idea to the early formation of societies. Imagine a scene, several hundred thousand years ago, in the Social Domain of the savannahs of Africa . . .

You are a small proto-hominid. Somewhat hairy, stooped slightly as bipedal motion is a new and recent adaptation, walking clumsily through the tall amber grasses.

You stop as you see another somewhat hairy proto-hominid clumsily ambling towards you. You think, *Hmm. That is another proto-hominid.* This small change influences your Biological Domain's limbic system. Your Ic Domain begins to assess if the other proto-hominid is seeing you as lunch. *Or will he share his lunch? Or, working together, maybe neither of us need to be lunch for that larger animal over there. Together we could even go and make that animal our lunch!*

The second proto-hominid, its Biological Domain and limbic system already activated as well, thinks, *Hmm, is that proto-hominid thinking that I am lunch? Or will he share his lunch? Or, working together, maybe neither of us need to be lunch for that larger animal over there. Together we could even go and make that animal our lunch!*

Once you figure this one out, you can decide if this other humanoid is someone with whom you want to share your lunch, find lunch together, protect each other from becoming something else's lunch, or if you should just go and find someone else to sacrifice for lunch. You begin to create a relationship built around *trust*.

The fight-flight-freeze instinct had to be assuaged in order to form social groups, but only if there was an advantage to being in a group that outweighed the chance of being eaten by your neighbor.

Try this: Stand back-to-back with someone. Without moving your body, turn your head to the right and left as far as it will go. You can probably see about 180 degrees. Tell your partner what you see directly in front of you and ask them to do the same. You cannot see what they see, nor can they see what you do. Together, you can see all around you—360 degrees. If a predator emerges from behind you, and assuming your companion tells you this, both of you can decide which branch of the fight-flight-freeze response you want to take. You literally have each other's back. Proto-hominids that formed such small social groups were so successful, from a survival perspective, that their ancestors—us humans—are practically everywhere on the planet. We have evolved three new Fs: family, friendship, and fellowship. (And, if you are not very good at spelling: fysician.)

Individuals in societies have evolved a complex system of checking and cross checking the other people in their groups. This social-cognitive behavior is designed to assess the veracity and reliability of the other person, calculating if their actions are predictable and "trustworthy." Following the rubric of Darwinian natural selection, organisms that evolved this ability did better, from a survival "get-your-genes-into-the-next-generation" perspective, than organisms that did not have this ability.

It is this predictability of the other person's response that decreases our anxiety. The limbic system does not activate to a perceived danger, and the fight-flight-freeze mechanism is not activated.

A person with mental illness may not respond the way you expect. Their behavior may be erratic, shifting in emotion and thought, morphing the way they respond to you and the world perhaps from one moment to the next. What happens when you engage with a person whose actions you cannot predict?

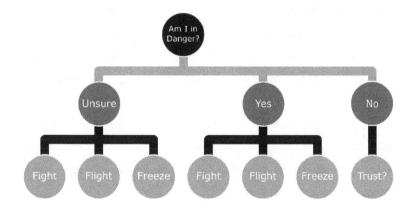

When you cannot answer the first question in the algorithm, the uncertainty triggers the fight-flight-freeze response. When your Ic cannot predict what someone else is thinking or feeling, you are going to get anxious, an indication that you feel in danger and have activated a limbic response.

The majority of people respond to the unpredictability of those with mental illness with fear. They cannot trust what the mentally ill person will do. Placing this thought process in an evolutionary perspective: if you are "crazy," it means you are erratic, unpredictable. If you are erratic and unpredictable, you are not someone with whom I want to go hunting for meat, or foraging for mangos, or rely on to protect me. In fact, you may not be someone I want to have in my social cluster at all. What if you become erratic when we are trying to hide from a larger, more threatening predator? What if you give away our location and *we—I—*become lunch! Such a "threat" poses too great a risk, so if you are unpredictable just stay away.

Dan had been sent to a state hospital for sixteen years. In essence, he was exiled from the community. He could not be trusted due to his mental illness.

The I-M Approach changes the way we see each other, and how others then see us. When you really appreciate that the person in front of you is doing the best they can, responding to the influence of the Four Domains, you don't have to like what they do or condone what they do, you can hold them responsible without blame or shame and you can respect that this is the best they can do at this moment in time—that this is their I-M, their current maximum potential. You use respect to influence, and not control. You use respect to send a message, through that person's Ic, that you value them. That they can trust.

When you feel respected by someone, you do not feel in danger from that person.

Respect is really saying, to that ancient limbic response, "I am not going to eat you for my lunch. You are safe."

Stigma perpetuates mistrust. We can change this today by unleashing the power of respect, just as I did with Dan. But this does not need to be confined to how we treat people with "mental illness." Stigma is not confined to psychiatric conditions. We have racial stigmas, socioeconomic stigmas, political stigmas. We even see people as disordered if they do not share our political views, our religious views, our views about education, or just a different perspective. Why do we mistrust someone who does not share our view? They all come down to a sense that someone is not part of our group, and if not part of our group, they represent a danger. But as I said before, we are all one group—called humanity. Once we recognize that we *all* want the same thing, to feel valued, then we can use the I-M Approach to connect with each other, rather than disconnect.

What happens when you do not feel trusted? You feel less valued and less respected, which will activate your own fight-flight-freeze response. And a vicious cycle begins and is perpetuated. We label people as having a "disorder" and are astonished that there is stigma about mental illness and addiction.

The I-M and politics

I have a friend who does not share my political views. Recently, we were having a discussion about these differences when he began to get very angry, and in his anger became more distant and resistant. But when I used the I-M and saw his views as the best he could do without being condescending or judgmental, I was able to say to him that just because I disagreed with him it did not mean I saw him as less valuable. Practically instantaneously, he calmed down.

Anger is an emotion designed to change a behavior. Respect is a behavior designed to change an emotion. As both our brains calmed, we were able to explore our differences and learn more about each other's I-M.

You can do this in any situation in your Home or Social Domain. When you are really interested in what another person thinks or feels, they know it. That interest alone increases their sense of value. Remember, at any and every moment in time you can remind someone of their value. And whenever you do that, you increase your own value. The results of a conversation like that are far more rewarding than the fights and arguments resulting from feeling less valued, from feeling stigmatized.

EXERCISE: It's all about perception

Look at your index finger and close one eye. Go back and forth, opening and closing one eye after the other. What do you notice? Your finger moves. It moves because each of your eyes has a slightly different geographic location in the world, a slightly different perspective. There are seven billion perspectives in the world, each as valuable and interesting as the next. How do we help someone else share their perspective?

Now try this: Imagine you are in a crowded room of strangers, and all of you are directed to close both eyes and count to three. If you do it, that's trust. Because you don't really know if one of those strangers may jump up and bop you. In a world where every friend was once a stranger, how do you get someone to trust you enough to share their secrets? To negotiate a contract? To share their perspective? To do that, they have to trust—trust that you are not going to judge them.

We spend a lot of time judging ourselves and each other, often concluding that we or other people are not doing as well as we can, that we should be doing better. This judgement works against trust. When I respect and value your perspective as your I-M, it creates a foundation of trust. With trust, we can have difficult conversations, wonder together instead of worry, and share our perspectives.

We have an opportunity to share our perspectives globally, right now. Instead of stigmatizing, we can use the I-M Approach to again-look at the influences of the Four Domains leading to our perception and others' perception.

The I-M counters unpredictability and mistrust, substituting the stigma of "differences" with the recognition that we all want the same thing: to be valued by another person. Respect removes the fight-flight-freeze response and replaces it with family-friendship-fellowship. Instead of anger or anxiety, I can feel trust.

When is the last time you got angry with someone treating *you* with respect? You don't. The brain simply doesn't work that way. Not yours, not mine, and not Dan's.

SMALL CHANGES CAN HAVE BIG EFFECTS

When you use the I-M Approach, you can look at yourself and others without judgement and remove the barrier and obstacle of stigma. We stigmatize ourselves as well—when we think we should be doing better, or that others are doing better than us. Use the I-M Approach to wonder rather than worry; shift your Biological Domain to the prefrontal cortex (PFC), away from the limbic system.

YOU CONTROL NO ONE BUT INFLUENCE EVERYONE

By wondering about other people without stigmatizing them, you remind them of their value. By treating someone else with respect instead of judgement, you create an opportunity for collaboration and connection rather than competition and rejection. You can be honest with yourself without fear of judgement, for if someone else judges you as less than, that is their I-M. It is about their own insecurity rather than your inadequacy. You will be much more powerful and influential when you are not judging others as less than.

CHAPTER 7
THE TWO GIFTS

"I made you something."

Brenda had been passed from psychiatric resident to resident. Now, at twenty-six, she had wound up with me—in my third year of training, yet another psychiatric resident. She had come dutifully to her first appointment six months before and had never missed an appointment until she was hospitalized for cutting herself, being unable to say she did not want to die.

And now she sat across from me, her first visit after being discharged from the locked inpatient ward—offering me a gift.

* * *

Brenda had grown up in a cult. After her mother, Linda, gave birth to her "out of wedlock," as described in Brenda's chart by a long-distant reporter, Linda had found her own family to be less than receptive. Her and Brenda's father were young, naïve, and poor. But they did not separate; they instead found a like-minded group of people who were involved in a community type of living.

This was as much as I had read in Brenda's chart. Usually, my style was to read the first few sentences, then wait to hear the story from the patient. Narrative—storytelling—is an ancient art, long preceding the written word. How a person tells their story is often just as important as the story itself. Their history, their mythology, and their emphasis or dismissal are clues as to where they are, what they believe is important, and what may be simply too difficult to manage.

So that was all I'd read and knew when I first met Brenda.

Other than the words of caution from her previous resident: "Warning. She's a Borderline."

Not, "She carries a diagnosis of Borderline Personality," a diagnostic label that describes a constellation of symptoms including volatility in relationships, often a history of self-harm and mutilation, and the implication of a horribly degrading experience somewhere in life—often sexual abuse by someone, somewhere, for some time.

No. Nothing. So removed from emotion, and even suggesting disdain, irritation, annoyance, perhaps even frank dislike in the resident's warning. Not "has" but "is"—as if this woman's entire existence was *defined* by her diagnosis. I didn't recall anyone saying to me, about another patient, things like, "He's a Major Depression," or "She's a Bipolar Disorder," or "This little boy is an Attention Deficit with Hyperactivity." The diagnosis was not supposed to become a descriptor, densely decorated with ominous overtones. "A Borderline."

So, I waited to see *who* Brenda was.

And read the chart no more.

This may have been a mistake.

In fact, at our first meeting, after our introduction, and after I asked my first question about what had happened to bring her to the clinic, before Brenda started to describe the highlights of experience, she appeared to bristle at the question and asked, "Well, did you read the chart? It's all in there, you know. What happened. I really would rather not go over it again."

I was in trouble. A psychiatry resident-in-training at my first outpatient clinic, facing a seasoned patient who had volatile relationships surely based on something bad that had happened to her in the past. With an idiot for a resident who had not read her chart. Images flashed through my mind in an instant of being stupid, inadequate, and being reported to the board of medicine. My pulse began to go faster, I felt a little anxious, and I found myself feeling a little defensive.

Hell, a lot defensive!

This was in the first sixty seconds, and I was slated to have her as my patient for the next year. My heart sank, and I found myself drifting back to the warning from the prior resident, wondering if that small smile on her face as she'd passed me Brenda's chart had indeed been a smirk, a subtle grin of glee.

"I did skim it, but only glimpsed," I said, trying to regroup. "For me, it's more interesting to get the story from you. I can always read what somebody else wrote, but then I may be reading what *they* think is important." This answer met with silence. "But I am interested," I continued hopefully.

"Read the chart," she replied, unmoved. "Dr. Grendel did."

The previous resident, a woman, had treated Brenda for the past two years then graduated. It was Grendel who had signed Brenda out to me warning, "She's a Borderline."

I had heard about this mysterious and ominous creature, the "Borderline," since my second year as a resident. The label was reserved for patients, usually young women, who had been abused, and as a moniker for the patient who gave you the most trouble, who would alternately idealize and then reject you, agree to be safe, then provocatively tell you they were suicidal, consistently search for support, attachment, then refuse your help. For many residents, "Borderlines" were the bane of their clinic, for nurses, the bane of the inpatient unit, and for the line staff, the bane of their existence—often losing control, or hiding something sharp with which to cut during the watch of staff who felt progressively helpless and worthless, slowly becoming enraged with this, this, *Borderline* who would not let them do the job of keeping them and the unit safe.

Brenda didn't look borderline. She looked perfectly normal, in this case a pleasant-appearing twenty-six-year-old woman, well-groomed, wearing a casual pair of jeans and a simple shirt and light sweater. Although she was bristly at that moment, who could blame her? She had been passed off from resident to resident, in the same way (as I would learn) her mother had passed her off from adult to adult or teenager to teenager in the commune. She'd been passed off so many times that no one knew when the abuse started, or with who, until she began to run away, again and again, until her mother finally asked her why. *Why* would she want to run from this most idyllic of settings? From people who cared for her? Where she had not just one mother but several, not just one father but several, and dozens of brothers and sisters—all who loved her.

And now she had to sit with me, passed off like a child with no recourse, to yet another stranger. So, she did not want to recount her story yet again, but assertively told me to just read it and that I should have read it already and been prepared. After all, that's what Dr. Grendel had done.

I was just learning about this stuff—therapy—and here I had a young woman, a patient, telling me I was already doing it wrong. I felt stupid, inadequate, and started to get angry.

And there was a silence.

And I remembered to breathe.

And I realized I had a feeling, a response to this, the first minute of my time with Brenda—then a stranger to me as was I a stranger to her. It was a sense of danger, or power being bandied back and forth. It was about control.

The first minute.

I found myself hearing all my supervisors shouting all at once in my head, in harmony, deep within the jacket-and-tie-top-button-buttoned model of a psychiatrist that I believed myself to be as a budding therapist. *Hey, is that a feeling you are having? What the heck is that about? Oh yeah—it's about the patient.*

And I responded to Brenda, "Seems like you are thinking about Dr. Grendel."

I said it as an attempt to acknowledge in what I hoped was non-judgmental way, despite being judged myself, that Brenda was comparing me to the other resident. I was not being defensive, but perhaps a bit too elusive. An issue on which I was called on by Brenda immediately.

"No, I'm talking about you, Dr. Strand."

"Shrand."

"Whatever."

By the next session, I had read the chart. The whole thing. Twice. I knew vaguely about her childhood, living in the commune, which was really a cult, how her mother had found out from a disgruntled commune member who had left that her daughter had been passed from adult to adult. How Brenda's mother had trusted these adults to care for her child, never ever imagining they were molesting her. How her mother had then taken her thirteen-year-old daughter and the two escaped. How her father pursued them, allegedly to bring them back, but in reality, making his own escape.

From there, the history was even vaguer, but depicted a teenager in distress, getting into drugs and alcohol, suicidal, cutting, burning, promiscuous, uncaring, uncompromising. She did poorly in school and would stay out for days and nights before returning home.

In desperation, her mother sent her to a convent in Italy. Her hope and wish was that the nuns would help her daughter find "God"—really, some relief from her suffering. And then, Brenda was back in the US, embarking on a long series of hospitalizations, medications, and a steady stream of third-year psychiatric residents.

Back for her second session, I related her story back to Brenda. "Did I miss anything? Is there anything you want to add?"

Brenda continued to seem ready for a confrontation.

"Are you saying I didn't tell you everything?"

"Actually, you didn't tell me anything except to read the chart."

"That's all there is."

"That's it?"

"That's it."

And for the next several weeks, that was it. But there was a big gap missing. The story in the chart seemed to skip over several years in the convent, picking up with the multiple hospitalizations over the next several years. Dr. Grendel had hospitalized Brenda *eight times* during the two years of her treatment, always for the same thing: cutting, usually superficial, and then "provocatively refusing to guarantee she would be safe."

In the hospital, Brenda would continue to regress, trying to cut herself, usually winding up on a close supervision, with a staff member always within arm's length and a foot in the bathroom door—an abdication of her own safety to the control of the staff. She would often need restraints, be given injections of medication and placed on her back with her wrists and ankles bound in cotton-padded leather restraints that were woven through well-designed slits in a wooden bedframe.

So that was all Brenda was going to say about the chart, about her past that had been up until now preserved in the words of others.

"What's on your mind today?"

"I cut myself last night."

Just like that—simple, minimal emotion, a blank acknowledgement of some underlying torment.

"How come?"

"Too much pressure. It's a relief."

"Pressure?"

"Yeah. My job. My boyfriend. My parents. Lots of stuff."

"Did it help?"

"Well, of course it helped, Dr. Strand, or I wouldn't have done it."

"Shrand."

"What?"

"Shrand. My last name is *Shrand*."

"Whatever."

I lost her, and she did not want to talk about her cutting anymore that day. But I went on.

"So, are you safe?"

"If you mean 'am I going to kill myself,' I don't know."

There I was, a psychiatrist-in-training, and a twenty-six-year-old woman—who I'd met maybe five times—is telling me she cannot guarantee her safety. Overcoming the enormous desire to ask her to just wait while I called my supervisor, or while I tried to find Dr. Grendel, while the cold sweat of terror built bead upon bead on my back and I hoped against hope that a visible torrent did not start flowing easily, serenely, and blithely down from my forehead—instead, I pursued her perceived provocation.

"Do you have a plan?"

"A plan? I have pills, razors, knives, ropes, a car. Why do I need a plan?"

On the spot, I made something up, something I have used again and again during suicide assessments.

"On a scale of zero to ten, a suicide scale, with zero being you say to me, 'Dr. *Shrand*, if I walk out of here, I'll be fine,' and ten being, 'Dr. Shrand, if I walk out of here, I know exactly what I'll do, where I'll go, nobody will find me, I'll be dead.' Where are you on that scale of zero to ten?"

Without a pause Brenda said, "Five."

"Why not a six?" I was asking her to consider what needed to be different in her environment, in her world, to make her more suicidal. Now she paused. I worried I had lost her again, but she replied.

"Because my boyfriend and I aren't fighting that much."

"Why not a four?"

Again a pause, and then, "Because I have a project due at work and my boss is being annoying that I haven't finished."

"What's the project?"

Brenda began talking about her work, then about her boyfriend, and a little about her mother who was always calling, worrying. As the session progressed, Brenda began to teach me about her world, and about how the small vagaries of her life manifested in a desire to hurt herself, to relieve herself of the "emotional pain." Toward the end of the session, I asked again how suicidal she was. This time she was a three.

"But that could change."

"And then what?" I asked.

"And then, who knows?"

"But can you at least stay alive until our next visit?" I felt the cold sweat again. Would she take this as a challenge? And if so, what would I do?

"OK, Dr. Strand."

* * *

Over the next several months, Brenda began to attach—keeping her appointments, routinely exploring the suicide scale and the things that influenced her suicidality and self-injury. She would show me the superficial scratches or remark how many pills she still had left over from other therapists. She and I made an agreement: if she was going to overdose, it would not be with any pills that I had prescribed. The silliness of the suggestion appealed to her, and she agreed.

In the same way, in regard to her cutting I would say to her, "I can live with it if you can." It was impractical to think that I could stop her cutting, but if it was going to become lethal, then she would have to come into the hospital where we would temporarily relieve her of the responsibility for her own safety until she could once again maintain it herself.

This also sat well with Brenda, and although she still scratched at herself, I did not hospitalize her. Instead, we began to look at why she scratched, what was her anguish, and we began to see a link between anger and powerlessness and her own self-harm.

Then I went to a conference.

I listened to Dr. Habib Davanloo, the founder of "Intensive Short-Term Dynamic Psychotherapy." This technique, according to Dr. Davanloo, promised a method to "unlock the unconscious." He spoke about assessing a patient's readiness to embark on this "rather confrontational approach," as he said, always addressing and acknowledging the resistance until finally the patient would have a cathartic moment of unparalleled psychic vulnerability, whence forth a hidden memory from the unconscious would blossom and emerge.

One had to choose patients carefully, however, especially those with Borderline Personality Disorder, as the confrontational style may be too much to bear, tipping them into dissociation, a break from the horror of their own deep unconscious murderous rage.

It sounded too cool!

Back with Brenda, back from my conference, back after a week away, which meant Brenda and I had missed one of her weekly sessions while I was immersing myself in this new technique, I sat across from her, ready to try this Intensive Short-Term Dynamic Psychotherapy.

Brenda may have had some feelings about my being away. She had cut superficially during my absence but had attributed one to a fight with her boyfriend, another to a fight with her mother, another a fight with her boss, to drinking at a bar, being tempted to pick up a stranger, and a dozen more reasons.

"I even tried to call Dr. Grendel."

"So, you were angry with me that I was away."

"I was angry with my boyfriend."

"But you took it out on yourself."

"I always do that. You know that already."

"But why would you want to do that to yourself?"

"I don't want to talk about this anymore."

Here was my cue, according to Davanloo. This was avoidance—a resistance! If I just continued to confront the resistance, I would break through into the deeply unconscious murderous rage harbored by Brenda. I confronted.

"That's an avoidance."

"I said I don't want to talk about this anymore, doctor." The "doctor" was said with an ominous, bristly tone, a tone I had not heard since our second session. But back then, I had not been to the conference. Now I had. I pushed the technique, and found myself challenging the resistance, just like Davanloo.

"So at the end of today, you will walk out of the session and I will say, 'Well, I tried to help, but Brenda didn't want to get any help, she put up a wall.' Why would you want to do that?"

"I told you, I'm not going to talk about this anymore . . . I feel dizzy."

"Another avoidance."

In front of me, Brenda seemed to drift away. Her eyes began to glaze as she drifted into dissociation. She began to tell me not of the deeply unconscious murderous rage she harbored, but that she was starting to hear voices, to get paranoid. Was this another attempt to avoid talking about her rage?

Crap no!

She was really dissociating and becoming progressively psychotic.

I had tipped her into a psychosis!

I had to hospitalize her, where, for the next several days, she continued to regress, become self-mutilating, was restrained, medicated, and spawned more anger and resentment from the staff. Another *Borderline*.

* * *

I went to visit Brenda in the hospital. I had never done that before with any patient—and have never done so since. I may hospitalize a patient for safety, and will be in touch with the treatment team, but I will always wait until the person is out of the hospital, back in my office, and then process the events leading to their inpatient stay.

But this time, this once, I went to see Brenda.

Because I had made a mistake.

I had pushed her when she asked not to be pushed. In some real way, I had been abusive, confrontational, experimental.

And I wanted to apologize. I wanted her to know that I was sorry, I had made a mistake, and had never intended to harm her, let alone flip her into a psychotic process. I had tolerated with her for months her superficial scratching, even as our work had not been superficial. I was finally beginning to dip beneath her defenses, looking at what made her more or less suicidal, how cutting was a way for her to stay in control, and when that control was taken from her, she lashed out in fear and desperation, reminded brutally of the adult after adult who had raped her in the commune until she ran ran—ran for safety, for protection, for some sense of power and control.

And now she was back in a hospital, a locked inpatient ward where you had to ask permission to pee.

And with the label "*Borderline*"—the word alone a disrespect for how she had arrived at this most desperate engagement with her world.

Brenda and I had tolerated her provocations. Her suicidal tendencies. Because I had trusted her to live. Because I had treated her with dignity and respect, amazed at why she was not doing worse given the outrage of her life. I'd tolerated her anger, her rebuke, her early disdain, and slowly, slowly earned what little trust she could muster.

And then I tipped her into a psychotic break.

I was there in the hospital to apologize.

* * *

"I made you something."

Within a day after my visit to Brenda, she had come off suicide watch, said she was safe, and wanted to be discharged in time for her next outpatient appointment with "Dr. Shrand—he's my psychiatrist."

She sat across from me, drawing out of her handbag a plastic baggie brimming with some form of, something. It was not immediately recognizable, strips of something that resembled peelings of a citrus fruit covered with opaque crystalline grains resembling sugar.

"I made this for you. It's candied grapefruit rind. Try one."

I do not usually accept gifts from patients. I don't go and visit them in the hospital either. But I am also not in the habit of making them psychotic.

Brenda took a piece from the bag and extended her hand. I extended mine and took the gift she offered.

She took out a second piece, and together we shared a moment, letting the bittersweet taste of the grapefruit rind embedded in crystals of sugar engulf us.

For the rest of the session, we spoke about the bittersweet quality of relationships, how sometimes allowing oneself to be vulnerable, to risk rejection, to risk intimacy, to trust, to love, to hate, to feel a rich range of emotions for a person, sometimes all at the same moment, was captured in the gift of a candied grapefruit rind.

She never thanked me for visiting her in the hospital, at least not with words. But as the next few months went on, she began to tell me of what had happened in the convent, how she had again been abused and molested, how the people her mother had, yet again, entrusted to protect her had betrayed her, exploited her, degraded and reviled her. For her sins, for old sins, for being a temptress, for being.

When I had confronted her, she explained, it violated our unspoken agreement that I would trust her to know her limits, violated the "I can live with it if you can" rule, penetrated the fabric and familiarity of the relationship we had developed, startled her, enraged her, terrified her as her unconscious desire to lash back at me, at her mother, at violator after violator conflicted with her wish to trust me, her *wish* to trust me, her desire and need to have at least one safe place where she could be honest and respected and not thrown into a psych hospital, not for her own protection, but because of the intolerance of those who were meant to trust *her.*

Bittersweet are relationships, the most honest ones, full of conflicts that dissolve into deeper understanding and appreciation, deeper love and dignity and respect, moving, changing, laughing, warm and able to embrace differences, enjoy strengths, see weakness as doing the best one can.

Brenda spoke about the convent, about her return, about her image of herself as useless and worthless and full of rage, often impotent, drawn out by the thin sliver of blood drawn from a superficial scratch.

She was not hospitalized again over the next few months.

I had been slated to do four years of adult psychiatry residency, but in the middle of my third year, I realized I wanted to be a child psychiatrist as well. I applied for a fellowship and was accepted.

This was February, and I was due to start in July.

I had four months to terminate with my clinic patients.

The majority of them were used to going from one resident to another, accepting the early change with muted resignation.

So did Brenda.

There was no escalation of cutting, no increase in provocation. She and I spoke about her next psychiatrist, and I suggested she allow me to find her an Attending, a "permanent" psychiatrist with whom she could continue to work on her therapy, and not another resident.

The clinic director agreed and we secured for Brenda an excellent psychiatrist. Brenda and I continued to meet every week until the termination session. It passed without event, and she walked out of the door to be seen the next week by her new psychiatrist. I wrote in the chart, "Terminated well. Continues to work on relationship issues. Diagnosis more consistent with Post-Traumatic Stress Disorder, but with symptoms of self-mutilation and volatility that could be interpreted as borderline features. However, was able to engage in meaningful insight-oriented therapy. Could not tolerate much confrontation without decompensation. Overall improved."

She had terminated without event. I was actually a bit surprised.

Two days later I received a message from Brenda on my voice mail. After a polite salutation, she went to the core of her contact.

"Can I come in for one more session? I forgot to give you the gift I have for you."

Sweat. I felt sweat bead up again. A second gift? For an instant the movie *Fatal Attraction* swept a hurricane path through my limbic system. Two gifts? The termination was too calm. A gun? Was it more difficult than she thought to say goodbye? We had terminated, but if I told her that we could not meet again, would this apparent rejection undo the trust she had built in me, and the trust she had that I had found her a new and secure and trustworthy and really good new therapist?

Another gift?

I picked up the phone.

I dialed her number.

She answered.

She was glad I called back. Appreciative. She had a gift. All wrapped. She had bought it and wrapped it and meant to bring it, meant to give it to me on our last session but had forgotten, yes, perhaps because it was harder than she thought to say goodbye—and could she come in just one more time so she could give me this gift all wrapped?

And I found myself saying words, intuitively, becoming aware that Brenda had not been struggling just with trauma, but with existence, with being. If she was abused, then she must have deserved it. We'd spent months looking at this same grotesque distorted perception: that no one deserves to be abused, but many who are begin to see themselves as useless, worthless, powerless, incapable, inadequate.

During our treatment, Brenda had begun to see herself as none of these, and now was reaching out to me even though we had "terminated." If she came in for one more session, what was the message I was sending to her? And how would that impact the work we had done? The work *she* had done.

I found myself saying words.

"Remember the grapefruit rind?"

"It's a different gift, Dr. Shrand."

"But do you remember?"

"Of course I do."

"So do I."

"I get that, you just asked me."

"But this is important. I won't forget those grapefruit rinds."

"But can you see me?"

What a question! Rife with a much deeper meaning. With enormous restraint to not get incredibly shrinky, I went on.

"I want you to do something. I want you to keep your gift for me, wrapped up, somewhere safe. Don't tell me what it is. I will always wonder what it is, and when I do, I will think about you, Brenda. You will not be forgotten by me, but I can't meet again for another session."

"Well, I just wanted to say thank you. For visiting me in the hospital. For letting me cut without freaking out. For getting to know me. Bye, Dr. Strand."

"Shrand."

"Just kidding. Good luck in your fellowship. And don't forget me."

"Thanks for teaching me about you. And I really will wonder."

We said goodbye.

Two years later, I heard that Brenda had stayed hospital free since I had caused her decompensation.

I still wonder and have not forgotten.

CHAPTER 8
I-M PERSPECTIVE: DIAGNOSIS

Diagnosis is the art or act of identifying a disease from its signs and symptoms. I was trained in this art in medical school, residency, and for the rest of my journey as a physician. Early on in my career, I recognized that the person sitting across from me in therapy is much more than a diagnosis. A diagnosis is a convenient way of quickly communicating a set of symptoms from one person to another. In the best of circumstances, it gives one professional a snapshot of the difficulty faced by the patient or person in front of you. For the most part, these are helpful guidelines, offered in the *spirit* of help, and with an unspoken promise to do something *to* help.

But a diagnosis can also have a dark side. It implies pathology or sickness, an idea of being broken and inadequate. Without meaning to, a diagnosis is also a hidden judgment that labels the person who "carries" the diagnosis. People "carry" a diagnosis, in many cases as a burden or yoke of judgment. One of the potential consequences of carrying a diagnosis is being seen as sick. If you think someone else sees you as sick, perhaps even as inadequate, you are likely to activate your biological fight-flight-freeze response, the result of an Ic Domain that thinks "you see me as less valuable."

This is what terms like "disorder" perpetuate. This is what the idea of illness, sickness, pathology, and disease perpetuate, because human beings are indeed inherently empathic, able to appreciate the point of view, feelings, and thoughts of another person. Each of us is interested in what the other person thinks or feels about us. Theory of mind can be a powerful tool to remind someone of their value.

But human beings are also really good at making the other person feel like crap, worthless, with no value, just a person to be dismissed. When our Ic Domain thinks someone else sees us this way—as Brenda felt—several other things may occur.

First, we may begin to believe what other people think about us and apply that to our self-concept. If seen as inadequate, we may begin to *feel* inadequate. If seen as unlovable, we may begin to *feel* unlovable. If seen as a bad person, we may begin to *feel* like a bad person. This was Brenda's experience, which had a huge influence on whether or not she could trust anyone. Wouldn't they just want to do harm to and punish a "bad" person?

When this pattern of being seen as inadequate is relentless, we may then begin to arrest our own Ic Domain. We may begin to stop using our own theory of mind. Why should we care or be interested in what someone else is thinking or feeling, or thinking or feeling about us, when it is always malevolent? Why should we want to know what someone else is thinking? This is the risk of a diagnosis—it may be perceived as such a judgment. It lumps a person into the category of "disordered," and isolates them from their protective group.

How does the I-M address the challenge of a diagnosis? An I-M is a current maximum potential. It is not a disorder or problem or fault. Everyone is now and always at an I-M, even though it is always changing in response to the influences of the Four Domains. My concern is that, unwittingly, if not done carefully, the application of a diagnosis to a patient, no matter how noble and presumably helpful the intent, can have a dark side consequence. My concern is that a diagnosis, perhaps initially just a small change in the Ic Domain, can have a negative ripple effect throughout the entire system.

The definition of "diagnosis" carries a hidden prejudice that the person in front of you is not doing the best they could. They may have a cold, a heart condition, or a mental illness. Perhaps they are overweight or have acne. A diagnosis implies an illness. I think this is what happens when a diagnosis and a judgment meld, as they do so often in Borderline Personality "Disorder."

In psychiatry, the diagnosis of Borderline Personality Disorder (BPD) often elicits an image of yet another individual who has a lot of problems. For a long time, it has been seen as intractable and incurable. The fifth edition of the *Diagnostic and Statistical Manual of Mental Disorders*, published by the American Psychiatric Association, may diagnosis a person with Borderline Personality Disorder who demonstrates "a pervasive pattern of instability of interpersonal relationships, self-image, and affects." [10] They fear abandonment and can appear to cling to and reject another person almost simultaneously. They have chronic feelings of emptiness, emotional instability with irritability, sadness, and anxiety. They are frantic to avoid real or imagined abandonment. They can be impulsive and often self-harm by hurting themselves and have difficulty controlling intense anger. A person who is recurrently suicidal, can become paranoid, and dissociate from reality. A person who other people don't like or trust. "Watch out—she's a Borderline."

The word "disorder" perpetuates stigma

You will never hear me use the word "disorder." If we are going to diagnose at all, rather than use the word disorder and perpetuate stigma and disdain, I prefer to use the word "condition." A condition can be defined as the circumstances affecting the way in which people live or work, especially with regard to their safety or well-being. In other words, the response to the influence of the Four Domains. Attention Deficit Condition, Major Depressive Condition, Obsessive-Compulsive Condition. (Granted, the acronym for Substance Use Conditions truly *SUC*s, but "condition" is far less stigmatizing and alienating than "disorder.")

The category of personality conditions includes borderline, but also paranoid, schizoid, schizotypal, antisocial, histrionic, narcissistic, avoidant, dependent, and

---

[10] American Psychiatric Association, *Diagnostic and Statistical Manual of Mental Disorders (DSM-5)* (APA Publishing: Washington, DC, 2013).

obsessive-compulsive personality. Very often, it seems as if the person with the personality "disorder" is cavalier and oblivious about their impact on you. For example, there is a difference between a person who has Obsessive-Compulsive "Disorder" and Obsessive-Compulsive *Personality*. A person who has Obsessive-Compulsive "Disorder" (OCD) is terrified that something catastrophic will happen if they don't have everything neat and in order, or count the steps, or wash their hands. (See the next chapter: My Five O'clock Patient.) Their obsession leads to compulsive repetitive behaviors that rarely provide any relief or satisfaction. Their behavior bothers them more than those around them.

A person who has an Obsessive-Compulsive *Personality* has rigid adherence to rules and regulations and feels calmer when everything is in order and neatly predictable. This controlling need for order makes them unwilling to yield or give responsibilities to others. Their entire character is impacted as they seek extreme perfectionism, order, and neatness, their need for control often making life miserable for others. The behavior of a person with Obsessive-Compulsive *Personality* bothers everyone around them: they are perfectly content with their obsessive need for order. The person with Obsessive Compulsive "disorder" is terrorized by their own need for symmetry, or cleanliness, or order; the person with Obsessive Compulsive personality terrorizes those around them with their relentless quest for perfection.

In this way, I like to think of personality conditions instead as *interpersonal* conditions. In fact, this may be the case. While the etiology of personality disorders is likely to be found in the Home, Social, and perhaps Biological Domains, the manifestation of the condition rests in the Ic Domain, the current concept of oneself. How I see myself and how I think others see me.

The Ic Domain has to do with theory of mind—the ability to appreciate someone else's point of view. There is ample literature showing that people with BPC (Borderline Personality Condition) have difficulty being empathic and recognizing their impact on someone else's Ic Domain. From an I-M perspective, the ongoing assault on the self-image of a person when they are abused, raped, or violated shuts down interest in what other people think or feel about them, but also shuts down empathy. Brenda was violated as a child. In a world where she was meant to be protected by adults she was, instead, abused.

A young child does not say, "Why did you hurt me?" They say, "What did I do?" *I have an intact theory of mind. I know you are meant to care for me. I know that when you care for me you make me feel valuable, respected, and good. But when you punish me or hurt me, or even abuse me, it must mean that I have done something wrong.* "I must be bad."

This happened to Brenda. Growing up abused, she shut down her Ic Domain early on. She did not care what her influence was on others, because she had stopped using theory of mind. She did not want to know what other people thought about her because it was usually malevolent.

Unfortunately, this belief was perpetuated by the diagnosis of Borderline Personality *Disorder* (BPD). A clear prejudice was implicit in the resident's note: "Warning. She's a Borderline." Why should Brenda want to know what her treatment team was thinking if it, too, was malevolent? Brenda had been abused. In some ways, the diagnosis of BPD was a perpetuation of that abuse, an invalidation of who she was and why she was doing what she was doing. She was being judged by her diagnosis, and by a twist of irony, her diagnosis itself was now interfering with "treatment."

When performing as medical director of a psychiatric hospital, I was always dismayed when a patient who had self-harmed out of anger and despair, out of a deep and profound psychic pain, would be sent to us from the ER. All too often, their wounds were not carefully stitched and sutured, but stapled together, quickly, with a meta-message that said, "You cut yourself so why should I bother caring for you?" The patient, usually a young girl, was dehumanized, stapled, creating an image of a Frankenstein.

Not only would they have their sliver scars as a reminder of their torment, but now the pockmarked atlas of a dismissive doctor whose first charge is meant to be "Do No Harm." How we view our patients can be profoundly destructive if we perpetuate the mythology that a person with a psychiatric or addiction challenge is somehow morally decrepit.

Our need to be seen as valuable and feel respected creates another cruel twist in the treatment of BPD, and perhaps in the use of a diagnosis at all. Feeling devalued by diagnosis and treatment, a person shuts down the Ic Domain, not wanting to see what you are thinking and feeling about them because it is disrespectful. But the treater still has an intact Ic Domain, including the interest in what someone else is thinking and feeling about them. The treater begins to perceive that the treated does not care how the treater feels. This activates a defensive response in the treater—the same fight-flight-freeze response of a human who feels devalued, disrespected, and at risk of being kicked out of the protective group. I have seen this happen so many times when staff interacts with a person who has borderline personality. And this is why so many people see them as horrible, difficult people with which to engage.

Seeing them, instead, at an I-M changes everything, especially your interpretation of their behavior and apparent dismissal of your feelings. When you use the I-M Approach, their response to you is understood as being a result of their shutting down their Ic Domain as a defensive and self-protective measure. Appreciating them at an I-M instead of as a "diagnosis," you can help rekindle their own sense of value by using the Ic Domain, as happened with Brenda.

Brenda arrested her Ic Domain after being repeatedly abused. Wherever she turned to her Home or Social Domains, there was a person of malintent, ready to violate her and see her as worthless. No wonder she was so reluctant to initially engage in therapy, and how astonished she may have been that I saw her as valuable, and trustworthy. It wasn't until I confronted her that she perceived me as dangerous, and then went into the ultimate "flight" mode: dissociation. This, as well, was the best she could do at that moment. Her I-M was to remove herself from reality.

I was also at an I-M. Freshly returned from that conference, mine was to try this new confrontational therapy technique. I was not trying to be disrespectful, but that is how Brenda perceived my insistence. She asked me to stop, and I did not—instead interpreting her response as a resistance, and totally missing that I was scaring her and re-creating her greatest fear: that her feelings were not valid or even precise.

When I went to see her in the hospital, acknowledged I had made a mistake, and affirmed her sense of value, it began to rekindle her own self-esteem. Being seen as valuable by somebody else is the path to self-value. And self-value is the path to self-respect. The I-M is a path to that self-respect.

I am not suggesting we abandon the use of diagnosis. This would be silly and harmful, as we do need to communicate swiftly and efficiently with each other, as well as determine how to help. But I suggest that the diagnosis is still an I-M, not a deficiency or pathology: it guides as to which domain may need a change, remembering that even a small change can have a rippled and amplified effect throughout the entire system. Through an I-M lens, there *is* no pathology. There is an I-M—adaptation to the Four Domains.

SMALL CHANGES CAN HAVE BIG EFFECTS

Rather than diagnose yourself and activate a fear of being less valuable, be honest with yourself about your current maximum potential. We diagnose ourselves when we see ourselves as less-than. Overweight, not good enough to get a job or a meaningful relationship. Not handsome enough, pretty enough, strong enough, sophisticated enough, educated enough, rich enough. Not a good enough parent, child, sibling, employee, employer, student, teammate. We diagnose other people the same way, criticizing their choices or dismissing their opinions. We live in a culture where other people may define our success and are quick to point out our failures. And while each of these is an I-M, you can again-look at why you are so self-critical.

Instead of making a diagnosis to explain a cluster of symptoms, again-look at why you do what you do based on the influence of the Four Domains. Was there a casual remark by someone that penetrated your self-esteem through the Ic Domain, and shifted your Biological Domain to feel angry, anxious, or sad? Was there a perceived snub that left you feeling devalued? Why was it that the best that person could do, *their* I-M, was to influence yours to feel disrespected? You can use the I-M Approach right now, today, and move yourself closer to success: ultimately, a reminder of your value. Respect leads to value and value leads to trust. When you trust yourself, you can look at yourself more honestly, without the fear that you will find you are less valuable.

YOU CONTROL NO ONE BUT INFLUENCE EVERYONE

Using the I-M as the constant baseline allows us to remove the inherent, if unintended, prejudice that accompanies a diagnosis. When you truly see someone as doing the best they can, they know it. They feel respected, valued, and can begin to see you the same way. When we see each other at an I-M, neither you nor I will worry that we will be "lunch" for the other. When you see yourself at an I-M, you can wonder, instead of worry, and be reflective instead of reflexive. Then, instead of having two people who may use the dark side of the Ic Domain, there are two people beginning to trust each other, and perhaps even sharing in a lunch of grapefruit rinds.

CHAPTER 9
MY FIVE O'CLOCK PATIENT

Rob was an hour late for his first visit. We barely had time to talk and make another appointment, as my next patient was in the waiting room.

Rob was an hour late for his next appointment. Once again, we hastily made another time, his apologies profusely and ardently convincing me to give him one more try. We set a time, and I made sure to make him the last patient I would see on that day. Rob assured me he would be there promptly at 6:00 p.m.

By 6:30, I was giving up hope. By 6:45, or what would be the end of his regular session, I began to close the office, but decided to wait a few more minutes, check my messages, write a note, skim an article.

While going to the bookshelf, I glanced out the window to see Rob getting out of his car, begin to walk to the office door, look back at his sedan, inspect its position, move his arms apart, holding his hands in an extended position of exasperation, shrug his shoulders, walk over, unlock the door, get back in the car, then begin a two-minute sequence of reversing, moving forward, putting on the parking brake, and getting back out.

He scanned his car now, neatly parked, checked his wristwatch, and literally ran from the lot into my building.

I heard the elevator start its moaning descent from the third to the first floor. As it drew more distant, its sound was masked by the rapid and methodical pounding of feet on the stairwell. Rob was running up the two flights to my office. Suddenly, the steps stopped. I heard a curse, but not the thump of a body falling or tripping. Then I thought I heard Rob reverse his course, go bounding back down the stairs, and then back up again.

This time he made it to my office door, and rhythmically knocked a request to enter. Bent over and panting, he reached up a hand when I offered a greeting, waved it but did not shake, and, gasping, walked into the office. He sat heavily in the chair that was obviously where patients sat, and I sat across from him, waiting for him to have breath steady enough to talk.

"So, what's the story?" I asked him.

Words staccato with intermittent deep and shallow breaths, Rob began to tell me his chronicle.

Rob had Obsessive Compulsive "Disorder," or OCD. OCD is not the same as Obsessive Compulsive Personality "Disorder" (OCPD), where people derive pleasure from having their shoes all lined up perfectly, or their beds neat and crisp with military corners, or the interior of their car pristine, or any other number of preoccupations with being orderly. People with OCPD struggle with others for control, may have difficulty expressing warmth and emotional intimacy, and, like other personality disorders, seem to bother other people more with their rigidity than they are bothered themselves.

OCD is very, very different. This is not about consciously or unconsciously making other people suffer. This is about feeling overwhelmed with anxiety that something horrible will happen to yourself or someone else if you don't precisely follow some ritual, a ritual that makes perfect sense to you on one level, is crazy on another level, and to another person is obviously senseless.

Rob had OCD. He never intended to be disrespectful or try to control the session by coming late. He didn't like being late for every appointment—with me, being late to work, the hours it would take before he could go into a supermarket, missing dinner with his wife. Rob truly believed something catastrophic would happen if he didn't. If he didn't . . . something really, really bad. If . . . He just couldn't say what.

He paused in his history. He knew that what he was about to say really did sound crazy. Part of him was incredibly ashamed.

OCD is about secrets.

Secrets. Usually shameful and, as with any secret, usually not about the secret itself, but about "how will someone else view me differently if they know my secret." In OCD, a person begins with an obsessive thought like, "Something horrible will happen if I do something wrong or don't do something right." Like the children's phrase, "Step on a crack and break your mother's back." Some people with OCD will have to step unbelievably carefully as they walk down the pavement, truly fearing that if they step on a crack, or don't step evenly with their left and then right foot, or if they don't parse out a particular number or sequence of steps before they get to the end of the road, that a catastrophic event will occur.

And they have to start over.

Walk the path again, but this time get it right.

And if they don't, then they start over again, and again, and again until the anxiety that has built up is finally relieved by getting it right—the right sequence, the right rhythm, the right . . . the right . . . the right something.

Here he was, sitting in front of me finally, on the third try. OCD is peculiarly personal, embarrassing, and crippling in its extreme.

"So, tell me about your OCD."

"Symmetry," sighed Rob. "It's about symmetry."

Running up the steps, Rob had stumbled slightly, and his left foot came down to what he perceived to be to the right of the step and not directly in the middle. He could not overcome the dread and anxiety that built up, so he had to do the steps over.

"But that didn't take up too much extra time," I said. "Pretty good that you only had to repeat once."

"Steps I can get over pretty quick."

"There's more?"

"There's more."

"Go on."

"Parking." I remembered seeing him get out of the car, then back in, then back out just before he came barreling into the building. "I have to get the car exactly in the middle, between the lines. It can take me an hour or more to park."

Rob was convinced that if he did not park perfectly between the lines, something catastrophic would occur. He could not say exactly what, but his anxiety would build and build until he simply had no choice but to adjust and readjust the car. He would park, get out, examine, get back in, and repeat this ritual over and over. He was always late, even if he arrived on time.

Our session was over for that evening and we made another appointment. I told him to come back the next week at 5:00 p.m.

I booked another patient for five and put Rob in for six.

The next week, Rob showed up on time: six o'clock.

We worked on addressing the anxiety he experienced with his parking ritual. We went out to the car and he showed me, reluctantly at first because he had spent an hour parking the car just right, the ceremony that absorbed his time. We talked about the anxiety that built up, and the as yet inaccessible catastrophe that he was averting by parking and re-parking his car.

Over the next several months, Rob never missed his "five o'clock" appointment. He learned and applied the basics of Cognitive Behavioral Therapy (CBT). He began to truly recognize the legitimacy of rule number one: that *what you think affects what you feel.* That if you think about something that makes you sad, you feel sad. If you think about something that makes you happy, you feel happy. And if you think about something that makes you anxious, you feel anxious!

You can't change what you feel, but you can change what you think, which then will help change what you feel. In some ways, this has to do with evolution. Human beings were driven by emotions long before they developed the capacity for higher intellectual function. In other words, we were guided by the ancient limbic parts of our brain and gradually developed the neocortex, the new brain, especially the frontal and prefrontal cortices where "executive" functioning live.

This is the "rational" decision-making part that distinguishes us from other animals.

One way to think about thinking is that the frontal lobe is much more accessible than the deeper, more primitive limbic system. Cognitive (thinking) Behavioral (action) Therapy capitalizes on the power of thought over emotion, in this case, the power of rational thought over irrational limbic response.

Although the initial thought that created the sense of dread in Rob if he did not park his car between the lines was elusive, he was able to recognize the second rule on the path to controlling his anxiety: that anxiety is like a wave. It goes up and it always comes down. Always. The human brain simply is not designed to sustain intense anxiety for very long.

But, if what you think affects what you feel, and you start to feel anxious and think, "Oh my God, I'm anxious. This is horrible. It's just going to get worse and never go away," what do you think happens? Right! You get more anxious. Isn't that the coolest thing? Without realizing it, if you really buy into the concept that what you think affects what you feel, you are already in control of your anxiety. It's just that you are taking it in the "wrong" direction. What you are thinking— "my anxiety is never going to go away"—is making the anxiety worse.

In fact, if there were an Olympic event for the person who could make themselves the most anxious, I told Rob he would have won hands down. I use this technique a lot when working with a patient with anxiety. Humor can go a long way, but always being respectful.

I used the following image with Rob:

Olympic flags are fluttering in the floodlights of Olympic stadium. Swiftly ascending the stairs, coming back down after a quick curse, and then ascending them again with more caution and ritual, Rob finally stands at the top of the podium. He bends at the waist, offering his neck to the official as the crowd roars, "USA! USA!" Rob proudly pulls himself erect, the Olympic Gold dangling from his neck.

OCD starts with an obsessive thought, which creates anxiety. The anxiety leads to a compulsive behavior, in Rob's case having to park between the lines. When the behavior is complete, the anxiety decreases. However, the anxiety came back the next time Rob had to park. His brain was conditioned (does the name Pavlov ring a bell?), and Rob knew what he needed to do to relieve it: park exactly, symmetrically, perfectly between the lines. Whew! Until the next time.

What you think affects what you feel. Think about something happy, you feel happy; sad, you feel sad; anxious, you feel anxious. Your anxiety is under *your* control. Rob began to recognize that he was thinking thoughts that make it worse.

Anxiety is a normal part of being human. It is the "flight" branch of fight and flight. When faced with perceived danger, we quickly assess if we are strong enough to fight and win. If so, we may activate anger, approaching the danger with the intention to get the dangerous thing to change.

If we do not think we are strong enough to win, we run. The problem is that fear can be subtle and insidious, activating our flight response before we even know it. We may think thoughts so automatically and instantaneously we may not even be aware we thought them. All we experience is the anxiety telling us to get away. Rob had automatic thoughts.

What you think affects what you feel. Change your thoughts, you change anxiety.

I taught Rob a simple technique to manage his anxiety, what I call the Four Rs: Recognize, Rate, Remember, Reflect.

Recognize that you are anxious, and don't avoid it. The biggest mistake people make when they feel anxious is to try and avoid it. They distract themselves. That's exactly what anxiety is designed to do: flight. Unfortunately, when you do this, you teach your brain you are not strong enough to deal with anxiety, so you have to avoid it. If you don't think you are strong enough, what do you think happens to anxiety? It gets worse because *what you think affects what you feel*.

Apply the first R right now: Recognize the changes in your Biological Domain that happen when you start to become anxious. Does your heart beat faster, do you get a funny feeling in your stomach? Do you get the cold sweats, or do your muscles tense up? These are actually elegantly designed biological domain responses to flee from that predator. Blood is diverted to your muscles so you can run. To do this, your heart has to beat faster and travel faster to your arms and legs, so your blood pressure increases. But we don't just make more blood. That blood has to come from somewhere, so it is diverted from the gut because there is no point digesting lunch if you are about to *be* lunch. That's where that sick feeling comes from. And blood is diverted from the skin, cooling you down so you don't overheat in case you have to run far to get away, the cold sweats.

Recognize these feelings and think, "I know what this is. It's my anxiety!" Recognition is a thinking function, so you have already begun to shift your brain into the prefrontal cortex, the bastion of rational thought which you will use to manage your limbic anxiety.

Now, *Rate* your anxiety between 1 and 10. Notice I don't say zero. Human beings are never at a zero. We are always at a low-grade anxiety called vigilance. We are aware of our surroundings. It's about survival.

Rating is also a thinking function.

I asked Rob to rate his anxiety right then between 1 and 10.

"Twelve," he immediately said.

"Really? Ten is panic, the most anxious you have ever been. Are you really panicking right this second?"

Rob paused, took a deep breath. "I guess not."

"You guess? You don't know? Guessing is another avoidance. You are really good at that! So, what's your anxiety, really, between one and ten?"

Rob paused again, reflecting. Yes! He was shifting his brain from the limbic to the prefrontal cortex.

"OK, Dr. Shrand. Not a twelve. I know, I know. No higher than a ten. It's not a ten. But it really is a seven."

"But not a ten? Now do the third R: *Remember.* Anxiety is like a wave. It goes up but always comes down. Always. You just proved it! If you think your anxiety will never go away, what do you think happens?"

"It never goes away? Oh, it gets worse because what I think affects what I feel."

"Yup. Your anxiety is under your control, and always has been. You've just been thinking thoughts to make it worse. How cool is that?"

Rob reflected as I went on. "If you think anxiety is out of your control, you are going to be more anxious. But when you recognize it has always been in your control, what do you think happens? You get less anxious because what you think affects what you feel. This step now begins to merge your PFC and limbic system, the part that is responsible for memory. You have conditioned your brain that you have to do that action to relieve that panic, which stems itself from the limbic system. It's as if your limbic system has taken control of your PFC.

"Now you do the fourth R: *Reflect*. 'What was I thinking to begin with that made me feel anxious?'"

I explained to Rob that this is the hardest part of the Four Rs because it may be difficult to identify anxiety-provoking thoughts. Why? Because those thoughts are designed to make you avoid something, in this case the very thought that is making you anxious. I explained that, for every thought that increases anxiety, you can construct an opposite one to decrease anxiety every time!

"You just have to create them, and then practice them." This fourth R— Reflect—combines limbic memories with PFC rational thought, shifting the locus of brain control back to what you think.

It is crucial that you do the Four Rs in order to manage your anxiety and put your PFC in charge.

Rob paused and said, "But Dr. Shrand, I'm afraid of dying. You know I'm going to die. I know I'm going to die. What's the opposite thought to that?"

"Rob, as long as you're thinking about it, you're not dead."

"What?"

"Every time you think you're going to die it means you are alive."

"Wow! I never thought of it that way."

"Right!"

It took several sessions for Rob to recognize how much he was actually in control of his own anxiety. After all, if what you think affects what you feel, Rob was really in the driver's seat of his anxiety. However, the initial anxiety-provoking thought was still elusive. Even so, he became very skilled at recognizing his anxiety, rating it on his own personal anxiety scale between 1 and 10, then remembering that anxiety is like a wave, that it goes up but always comes down.

Rob learned that anxiety is never a zero. Human beings are biologically designed to experience anxiety. Indeed, if, several hundred thousand years ago, one of our hominid ancestors fell out of a tree and looked around, thinking, "This is nice. I'm out of the tree," but did not experience anxiety, it could have been lunch! Some other animal would have come along and eaten it.

But the ancestor who fell out of the tree and said, "Crap! I'm out of the tree," and got the hell back up there—well, that ancestor lived another day, had babies, and those babies inherited the "anxiety" gene-environment complex that told them to get back up in the tree if they fell out. In this case, anxiety is protective. For humans, the low-grade anxiety level 1 is called vigilance. Consciously or sub-consciously, we are aware of our surroundings, an ancient and primitive protective device against becoming lunch.

However, imagine that same ancestor is up in the tree, getting hungry. It spies a mango, easily within reach. No chance of falling out of the tree, so it reaches over and grabs it. Yum. Good mango. In fact, it eats all the mangos within reach. Until there aren't any left except on the branches that are just a little ways further up or across the tree. "Hmm," the ancestor thinks, "if I creep over to get that mango, I may fall out of the tree and become . . . lunch. I'll just wait here for another mango to grow."

So what do you think happens? Perhaps the ancestor can wait long enough, but more likely it grows weak, its muscles atrophy due to lack of motion, and it falls out of the tree, either dead or ready to become lunch.

In this example, anxiety is not protective but inhibiting, interfering, destructive, and disruptive.

OCD presents similar anxiety. Crippling, overwhelming, obstructive. For Rob, it ruled his life. The unknown thought that propelled his anxiety may not have been readily accessible but learning how to control his anxiety was well within his grasp. Like the mango in our ancestor example. He just needed to practice.

Rob kept his "five o'clock" appointments faithfully. I knew he was getting better when he started showing up and encroaching on my *real* five o'clock. As his need to park between the lines began to abate, he started telling me of the enormous impact it had on other areas of his life: his work, marriage, and relationships with friends. Eventually, I switched the five o'clock to six and kept Rob in the five slot. He continued to practice his new way of thinking: *recognizing* his anxiety, *rating* it, *remembering* that anxiety is like a wave, and then trying to *reflect* on the thought that had made him nervous to begin with. It was as if he had learned a whole new set of skills.

He never did figure out what had started the anxiety to begin with but did tell me once about a kindergarten teacher whom he had despised. He had been a very creative child, but the teacher had insisted he draw and color between the lines.

CHAPTER 10
I-M PERSPECTIVE: FREE WILL

Rob was tormented by his obsessive-compulsive behaviors. Moving his car backwards and forwards, straightening and re-straightening and *re*-straightening again held no pleasure for him. Just the opposite. It was painful, relentless, oppressive, and an I-M.

How could Rob be doing the best he can? His behaviors were crippling, interfering with his ability to function. How can one maintain the argument that even such debilitating functioning is an I-M? In support of my thesis, I turn to the biological cell.

A heart cell doesn't wake up one morning and say, "You know, today I think I'm only going to beat half as fast." But if the sinoatrial node—the "pacemaker" cells—of the heart's Home Domain has been damaged, or the Social Domain of the heart (the rest of the body) is full of cholesterol, or if the immune system, through the Ic Domain, sees the heart cell as a foreign invader, or if the heart cell's Biological Domain—with its DNA, protein machines that perform the functions of the cell, "digestive system" to take nutrients into the cell, a system to extract energy, to get rid of waste, and to communicate with other cells, etc.—has been altered, then that cell may indeed beat half as fast. Change the environment, change the response. That cell is still doing the best it can, based on the influence of the Four Domains.

Using cells and cell function as an argument to support the principle of an I-M led one of my colleagues, Avrom Weinberg to challenge me around the concept of free will:

[If everything is doing the best it can, I worry about your] remarks above as an explanation of human nature, Joe, because, as evolution proceeded over millions of years, increasing cellular complexity developed with the integration of cells into organs and organismic systems and resulted in the incredible emergence of consciousness, mind, and human free will. The therapy that you and I practice is predicated on the belief that there is both determinism and free will, but your cellular explanation above does not seem to acknowledge or make room for the possibility of mental free will and the capacity of human beings to use their minds to make choices to change thought and behavior.

My friend Avrom has long passed, but his wisdom remains. This thoughtful concern, that the I-M Approach takes *away* free will, is also an I-M! An adaptation to the paradigm shift of the I-M Approach. Adaptation is always about choice.

Saying that we are always at an I-M is not the same as saying we have no choice. The I-M is not *determined* by the domains but it is *influenced*. Determinism is the belief that everything, including every human act, is caused by something and that there is no real free will. The word "influence," however, is defined as somebody or something being able to affect a course of events or somebody's thinking or action.

Affecting a course still leaves choices to the individual or system as to how they are affected. This is the power of influence and leaves to free will the choices one makes in response to those influences. The Four Domains have influence, but in the I-M Approach, the response is still the best you could choose at that time *given* those influences.

The I-M is actually the opposite of determinism. Every choice you make is, well, yours to make. The I-M is actually all about free will, in the context that our choices are constantly and fluidly influenced by the domains. Influence does not commit one to a particular course or choice but affects—not causes or controls—the choices made by the individual or cell or system. I believe that, once that choice is made, it is the best one can do at that moment in time given the influences of the domains. However, we still take responsibility for each of these choices, and how each one has an influence on someone else's I-M, and the choices and actions that they will take. You control no one but influence everyone.

In a sense, obsessive-compulsive behaviors could be seen as negating Rob's free will. Compelled by overwhelming anxiety, Rob had no choice but to park and re-park his car. The I-M of the serotonin regulation in his brain resulted in an action beyond his control. Those human acts were caused by something, and Rob, therefore, had no free will. At the very least, his free will had been subjugated and profoundly influence by his Biological Domain, which was dominating the effects on the other three domains.

Rob's obsessive-compulsive behaviors had an impact on other people as well. He almost got in a fight in a supermarket parking lot. He most definitely was not seen as being at an I-M! Imagine you have gone shopping and are about to park in the parking lot. You see an empty space, but next to it is a guy who is parking, and re-parking. His constant motion makes it difficult for you to get your car in, for fear he may hit you as he realigns his vehicle. It seems meaningless to you, and he is now encroaching upon your time. You may start getting angry, seeing him as an idiot, beginning to judge. You wonder, *what is wrong with this dork? Just park! It's fine!*

Without seeing Rob at an I-M, his actions truly do take on a deterministic perspective: Rob parked, became anxious that symmetry was not achieved, and activated a learned response to decrease his anxiety. His brain was feeling the discomfort of anxiety, a feeling I am sure most readers have experienced. This brain phenomenon was translated to his body: his muscles would tense, his heart rate go up (influenced by a change in the sinoatrial node), his breathing would get rapid and shallow (impacting the amount of blood flow and oxygen exchange), he likely got dizzy—and all of these discomforts could be alleviated, at least temporarily, by doggedly parking and re-parking until he got it right.

And the next time he was faced with asymmetry, and his anxiety increased, his brain would go, "Hey! I know what to do to get rid of this discomfort. I'll park and park until I get it right and feel relief." Until the next time.

Would you say his free will was taken away because he *had* to make this repetitive attempt at getting his car symmetrical? Or, do we say that this is Rob's I-M, the best he could currently achieve given the influence of the Biological Domain and the way his serotonin system was responding?

Despite the shame within his Ic that resulted from Rob's repetitive and apparently meaningless behavior, it was still an I-M. Rob was able to attain a different I-M with cognitive behavioral therapy, making the Four Rs as automatic as his previous anxiety-provoking thoughts, and the hard work he put in to influencing his domains. As he learned more skills, as he recognized that his thought had an impact on his feelings, he began to adjust the way his brain worked. As his neurons fired off their action potentials, he began to adjust the way serotonin was released and regulated in his brain.[11] This led to an adjustment in the control he had over his mind-body interaction: he was able to delay having to act on his compulsion to move the car to relieve his anxiety. And by this small change in one domain, he influenced an enormous change throughout the system. He recognized that *he* was in control of his anxiety. He could make it go up, or make it go down, depending on what he thought. His brain had changed, moving to a different I-M.

SMALL CHANGES CAN HAVE BIG EFFECTS

Rob's story highlights how an I-M does not always conform to what we normally think of as "doing the best one can." To most people, doing the best one can means

---

[11] Cognitive behavioral therapy, a thinking and feeling therapy, has an effect on brain function without the use of medication. David E.J. Linden, "*How psychotherapy changes the brain—the contribution of functional neuroimaging,*" Mol Psychiatry 11, no. 6 (June 2006): 528-38.

this is their personal pinnacle of success—the best they can ever hope to achieve. Not seeing Rob as at an I-M has an impact on you as well. If you were that person getting angry at Rob in the parking lot as he continued on with his compulsion, you are going to think he doesn't care about your time, is selfish, and is disrespectful. You are going to get angry.

But when you see him at an I-M, simply doing the best he can at this moment in time, I suggest you will not get angry but wonder about the influences of the domains. This small change in perception can have an enormous effect.

YOU CONTROL NO ONE BUT INFLUENCE EVERYONE

For millions of years, we have survived by instinctively following our compulsion to survive and thrive, but often at the expense of someone else's. Our Biological Domains have been compelled to get our genes into the next generation. Even our free will has been influenced by that implacable imperative. The I-M Approach helps you to shift that paradigm from fear and intimidation to unleashing the power of respect as the value maker.

Understanding the influence of the Four Domains helps you make more informed choices, emancipating free will from the slavery of your primal instincts, and taking you closer to your current definition of success. Perhaps, in our parking lot example, you would even get out of the relative safety and anonymity of your car and see if you could help a person struggling with the need for perfection.

Getting out of the car is a choice—free will—influenced by the I-M and the power of respect. When we respect each other, it is easier to appreciate their domains and volunteer to help. When you help someone else get closer to their goal, you increase their value and your own. A valued person simply feels safer, less anxious, and more capable of unleashing their unlimited human potential. In this way, we can continue to shift our brains from our impulsive, irrational limbic system, and think "what will happen next if I do this now." That is the highest enactment of our free will: to enhance and preserve the free will of everyone, not just ourselves.

CHAPTER 11
MUCH APPRECIATED

Mr. B. believed that he had made billions of dollars creating an entertainment park in Saudi Arabia. And with the money, he had bought the hospital where he now resided in the inpatient psychiatric unit. He was very distressed that we had dismantled his stem cell research lab in the hospital cafeteria, and routinely reported to me how he could buy me an entire country if I would just unlock the doors and let his private chauffer pick him up and take him to his Cessna.

He was never violent or aggressive, although mildly irritated at our unbelievable stupidity. Medication was not for him, as there was nothing wrong, and he had invented it anyway for the other people who needed it. Besides, this was not really a hospital, but part of his new Hollywood project, with hidden cameras capturing his most banal moves for prosperity. It was to be part of a ride in the Saudi Arabia theme park.

Mr. B. participated in the groups, kindly and sagely giving advice to the other patients on how to invest their disability checks, sometimes in exchange for a "much appreciated" cigarette. "Much appreciated" was the catch phrase for Mr. B. He used it as a thanks for cigarettes. He used it to thank the attendants who opened the bathroom. He used it when the nurse would offer him medications, which he would always refuse. And when he wanted to end the session with me:

"Much appreciated." I never knew if he was thanking me for talking with him, or for leaving him alone.

His delusion was fully functional and intact. He tenderly tolerated my gentle suggestion he try a medication, even asking me if I thought he was crazy. I explained it was unlikely that he was a billionaire, to which he responded blithely for me to ask myself how I could explain the Hollywood-like actors and actresses he had hired to play the parts of patients, or how he had just received the praise of the sheik of Arabia who had sent him a telepathic message saying how much he had enjoyed the rides in the Saudi Arabia theme park built by Mr. B.

Every suggestion about starting back on his medication was met with a kind but firm dismissal. He did not need medicine. He was fine. "Perhaps you need medicine, Dr. Shrand!"

One day, I walked into Mr. B's room to find him beaming and excited, almost bursting with an enjoyment that I had not seen in him before. He had taken two feathers from the art therapy room, the kind one would find in a pillow—small, fluffy. One was dyed blue, the other yellow. The yellow feather was balancing on his head, and he limited the movement of his neck and the tilt of his cranium to keep it in place throughout our conversation. It had a curve to it, resting on his head in a slightly flattened yellow arc, swaying gently back and forth. Precarious, likely to fall off at any moment, but kept in place by the concerted effort of Mr. B.

The blue feather, a delicate piece of down, was carefully placed and stuck in the center of his forehead like a religious marking. It hung there, a small piece of fluff, the slight movements of his head or surrounding air enough to nudge the insubstantial blue filaments like the ripples of flagella. It was actually quite elegant in its simplicity. After our customary greetings, I found myself asking the obvious.

"So, what's with the feathers?"

"Ah, Dr. Shrand. I'm celebrating." He pointed to the blue feather.

"Celebrating?"

"Yes. Celebrating." He again pointed to the blue feather, stuck somehow onto his brow.

"Celebrating what?"

"I have cracked the code."

"The code?"

"The code."

"What code?"

Mr. B. leaned in towards me, carefully keeping his head tangential to the ground so the yellow feather stayed on top. His eyes did the main work, scanning around and past me to be sure no one else was spying. This was an important and secret breakthrough. "The Da Vinci Code," he whispered.

"The *Da Vinci* code."

"Yes." His body was calm and he had a facial expression seen only on those who have made a tremendous and satisfying discovery. He carefully nodded his head slightly, being sure to keep the feathers in place. "I have cracked the code. We are all connected genetically, through a secret code that only I know. But as soon as you let me out of here, I am going to my publisher and tell the world. We are all related. So I'm celebrating." He pointed to the blue feather on his forehead.

"And the yellow feather?"

"Oh, I just like the way it looks."

"Ah."

"Much appreciated, Dr. Shrand."

Eventually, I had to apply for a commitment, which is asking a judge to substitute his judgment for that of Mr. B. Albeit reluctantly, Mr. B. began to take his medication: lithium, a mood stabilizer and an antipsychotic. His mantle of omnipotence slowly dissolved.

* * *

However, unlike my patient Dan in "Decaf, OK?", there was no sadness. Mr. B. was indeed a successful man who had manifested, in his early twenties, Bipolar "Disorder"—what used to be called Manic-Depressive Illness. Over the last twenty-five years, Mr. B. had been hospitalized many times. The first was when he had just graduated from an Ivy League college in the top percent of his class. He was energetic, enthusiastic, hardworking, creative, brilliant. He was slated for graduate school in political science and had an ambition to become an ambassador to the Far East.

Before graduate school was to start, Mr. B. was sent to the Far East by his father—a high-powered businessman who was so proud of his only son—for a "well-earned vacation."

The idea of being seven hours ahead and in another time zone swirled through the buzzing brain of Mr. B. On the plane to Riyadh, he became absorbed with the idea that time was accelerating and how, when he landed in the Middle East at 6:00 a.m. on Saturday, it was still going to be Friday in Boston! He felt that he, too, was accelerating, and that his movements were so swift they had to represent special powers that only he possessed. Upon landing, he saw people bowing down in worship. Dismissing their Muslim heritage, Mr. B. wondered if they were worshiping him.

He had not slept on the connecting flight to Paris, or from Paris to Riyadh, but still felt energetic and invigorated. At first his lack of sleep was attributed to jet lag and having his internal clock disrupted. But as the days went on, he slept very little, had abundant energy, and described his thoughts going so fast he could hardly keep up. He began to develop an extravagant plan for integrating oil and solar power into a mega-industry. He wanted to make an appointment to see the minister of energy, so he presented himself to the American embassy for assistance.

Mr. B. was sent back to the US by escort and admitted to a private inpatient psychiatric hospital. His father met him at the airport, having been hastily contacted by the American embassy that his son was in the throes of a psychotic, manic state. When Mr. B saw his father, he was delighted, believing that the US secret service had escorted him back to avoid the Saudis incarcerating him on trumped-up charges of violating their Muslim laws, so that they could get the secrets to his oil and solar power equations. He was as astonished to be hospitalized then as he was now, continuing to attribute his confinement to conspiracies designed to thwart recognition of his far-reaching and world-changing intellect.

Now, almost thirty years later and too many hospitalizations to count, he and his family had gone to Disney World. By a strange set of circumstances, his lithium had been left behind in Boston. Disney was enchanting. Every color, every sound, every ride was an experience to be tasted. He began setting up itineraries for his family, dragging them from park to park, irritated if they fell off his time schedule, snapping at his children for not appreciating the wonders he was providing for them.

They knew what was happening, they had seen it too many times not to know. But they knew that their dad was out of reach, that if they challenged him, he might suddenly take off and perhaps even fly to another country. He was manic. He talked so no one could interrupt him, had abundant energy, did not need much sleep, and slowly began to believe that not only had he *created* Disney World, he owned it as well as a new theme park in Saudi Arabia.

Mr. B. slowly began to resolve his delusion once he returned home. As the medication started to kick in, he was able to reflect on the experience. He acknowledged that it was not a coincidence that his bottle of lithium was left at home. He had thought that this time, perhaps, he didn't need it. He just wanted to have fun with his wife and kids—and Disney, well, what could be better than that?

And so, he'd left his medicine in its place of honor and easy access in the bathroom cabinet, and the one in the kitchen cabinet, and the one his wife had left in the car in case he forgot to take it before going to work. He got on the plane and lied to her, "Sure, I took it right before we left. Yes, yes, I packed it in my bag. No—I won't need another dose until we get to the hotel."

Perhaps this time, he hoped, *I won't need it. Maybe this time I'll be OK.*

Mr. B. was being discharged home. His wife had come to pick him up, take the prescriptions, hear his promises that "this time would be different" and that he would take the medicine religiously. He admitted that he did like the feeling of going "up," that hypomanic state just before he got delusional, but he didn't need to feel it anymore. He was done. He shook my hand before he walked out the now opened but previously locked door.

"Much appreciated, Dr. Shrand."

* * *

"I'm God."

Mr. B. sat in front of me robed in a hospital johnny, unkempt and unshaven, his hair a bramble. It had been almost six months since he had been admitted. This time, he was pulled over by a police officer after he was seen careening off a steel barrier that served as a median for the state highway. Mr. B. had been driving over eighty miles an hour with his eyes closed.

He got up to pace the floor, then sat down and began fidgeting.

"What happened?" I asked. "Driving with your eyes closed at eighty? What were you thinking?"

Alternating between sitting, standing, and pacing, adorned in his hospital johnny, he simply replied, "I'm God."

"God?"

"I'm God."

I knew if I challenged this delusion, I would be incorporated into it somehow. Instead, I found myself saying, "God!? That's an enormous responsibility, isn't it?"

His voice teeming with a sense of overwhelming appreciation for my acknowledgement, Mr. B. looked at me and said, "It is! I have to go back on my lithium!"

"Let's do it," I said.

He paused. As if relieved of an enormous burden, he put out his hand to shake mine. "Much appreciated, Dr. Shrand."

146

CHAPTER 12
I-M PERSPECTIVE: KNOWLEDGE

Mr. B. was delusional. By definition, a delusion is a fixed, false belief, and Mr. B. was adhering to his adamantly. He was a powerful and wealthy entrepreneur. Not only was he unwilling to take medication, but he truly believed everything he told me. His manic delusion made him feel more valuable, an intoxicating potion of omnipotence.

How can this be an I-M? Does the I-M apply to a person if they are unable to recognize the domains, their influence, and what needs to change? How could the I-M Approach—which asks one to explore the effects of the domains on one's current maximum potential—apply to a person who does not know he is psychotic?

The I-M effect is not dependent on whether you understand the concept. Everyone is at an I-M, even if they cannot appreciate it. For example, a person with significant cognitive delay (not an intellectual *di*sability, but an intellectual unique *ability*) may not be able to fully understand the approach, but that is their current maximum potential. They are still influenced by the Four Domains, even if they cannot appreciate their influence. In fact, we are all influenced by the domains whether we realize it or not.

I have a limited idea about quantum physics, but that does not mean I am not influenced by its effect. I know how to drive a car but am clueless how to change the oil. Just because I don't know something does not mean it does not have an impact.

It is the same with the I-M. The I-M Approach is applicable to everyone, even if a person is not intellectually able to appreciate the concept. In the case of Mr. B., his lack of insight into his delusion did not negate the efficacy of the approach.

The I-M is a current maximum potential. Whether delusional that he was the owner of the hospital, or clearing his psychosis with medication, Mr. B. was at every moment at his I-M. Even though he *knew* that he needed to stay on his lithium, the allure of his Biological Domain feeling just a little bit manic was enough to seduce him into stopping his medicine. From a high-functioning family man to a person needing to have a judge order him to take medication, each was an I-M on his continuum. Whenever he stopped his lithium, this small change in his Biological Domain had a ripple effect on his and others' I-M.

The I-M does not say you will always move "forward." Nor does it say you may regress and move "backwards." It does not say you will "learn" from your mistakes, nor that if you are unable to appreciate the impact of the domains, they will not have an impact. Some people may never grasp the meaning of the I-M, but that in and of itself is still the best that person can do.

A system also has an I-M: When Mr. B. became too psychotic to function safely in the community, he was involuntarily hospitalized. And when, in the hospital, he refused to take medication because his insight into his psychosis was in fact *blocked* by his psychosis, I had to petition a judge to give authority to make Mr. B. take medication. Indeed, if he did not take the pills by mouth, the judge had given authority to force Mr. B. to take the medication against his will by injection.

The I-M asks one to see the other as at their best, a position that mandates we treat each other with respect. But this does not mean we condone, like, or *enable* the other person to do what they want. The I-M presents an opportunity to take responsibility for one's actions, understanding them in the context of the Four Domains. Mr. B.'s actions were understood and respected in the context of his mania. But, although respected as the best he could do at the time, this did not mean that he should not be held accountable, nor that he should not be asked to do something to move his I-M to a different maximum potential.

EXERCISE: Knowledge is power

When I run a group therapy, I write the acronym "WORK" on the blackboard:

Why

Observe

Responsibility

Know

First, each member of the group spends a few minutes saying *why* they are there, and then *observing* the behaviors that got them there. Responsibility is the first step in moving to a different I-M. If it is always someone else's fault, you are never in control. If you are not in control, your Biological Domain will activate fight-flight-freeze—or anger, anxiety, and depression. As soon as you take *responsibility*, it may not be easy, but it begins to rekindle your value and a feeling of not being powerless. You then use the I-M Approach to *know* why you do what you do. How are you meant to change something if you don't know why you are doing it?

You can use the same acronym to address any of the stressful situations you may experience. When you use the knowledge you discover, you have shifted your brain back to the prefrontal cortex, and you can make a plan, execute that plan, and anticipate what will happen next as you move to your next I-M.

While there is always room to have a yellow feather just because we like the way it looks, at some point, taking responsibility for our actions and understanding them in the context of the influences of the domains allows us to truly "crack the code" of why we do what we do. Knowledge is truly power. And the I-M is a road to knowledge.

SMALL CHANGES CAN HAVE BIG EFFECTS

Try using the WORK acronym today. Pick something you want to see differently and use the I-M Approach to explore the influences of the domains and gain knowledge about why you do what you do.

YOU CONTROL NO ONE BUT INFLUENCE EVERYONE

You can use the WORK acronym at the Home or in your Social Domain so everyone can explore who they are and why they do what they do. If you are an employer or supervisor, teach other people about the I-M, and let them know you see them as valuable. It is amazing how such knowledge builds loyalty, and with loyalty everyone feels safer to take responsibility for who they are and why they do what they do.

CHAPTER 13
YOU'RE TAKING IT WRONG

Henry was working in the yard, raking a flower bed, when the rustling of a low-lying bush just on the periphery of his vision caught his eye. He stopped raking and turned his head to look, the rest of his body held motionless. The rustling had stopped, but Henry stood his ground. The very lowest part of the bush rustled again, now with Henry looking right at it. Out slithered a garden snake, harmless to humans, but not to mice or voles or other habitants of Henry's back yard. He let the snake slither away.

Imagine Henry was living a few million years ago, rummaging through the forest, perhaps looking for food, shelter, or a potential mate. The Henrys who stopped what they were doing to pay attention to a rustling bush probably survived better than Henrys who were not distracted by it, and instead continued what they were doing. If the rustling in the bush were a predator, they were lunch. But the Henrys that noticed and paid attention could at least try to run away or fight.

Getting distracted is normal. We all get distracted. Sometimes, we get distracted by a potential threat. But others, we notice something that seems more interesting than what we are in the middle of doing. We get distracted from one thing by another that, at least for a moment, "caught our attention." If we apply the human quality of getting distracted as normal, then Attention Deficit

"Disorder" is neither a deficit nor a disorder at all. Rather, attention deficit is instead a concentrated form of attention, very focused on one thing but not for very long.

Cynthia's Tale

"This medicine's not working. I'm not taking it anymore."

Sitting across from me, next to her mother, was Cynthia—sixteen, diagnosed with Attention Deficit Disorder, primarily the "inattentive type." Like many girls with attention deficit (AD), she had done well in school until about the seventh grade, when her grades began to drop. She would sit quietly in class, spacing out, inattentive, but not bouncing off the walls or drawing attention to herself.

Her organization abilities were compromised, and she had a hard time remembering what books to bring to class, or even to bring books at all. Her locker was a jumble of disarray. Her homework binder an impenetrable jungle of math assignments enmeshed with partly finished English papers and long lists of French words and their definitions rambling in between.

She had been an A student all through grade school. In primary school, most classes are contained. Math, English, and the sciences are all taught in the same room. The books are there, handed out by the teacher. It is does not require as much self-sufficiency.

That changes in sixth grade.

Then, kids are asked to travel from one class to the other. To bring their books, pass in the hallway, know how much time they have to spend at their locker, and what to extract from that steely cavern. They have much more homework, and much greater social expectations and navigations. It is a wonder they survive at all. And if you have a difficult time paying attention . . .

Cynthia had a difficult time paying attention. But no one at school had noticed that first slight slip in sixth grade.

If it were only at school that these dilemmas occurred, you could say, "Well, it's not easy being in middle school." Lots of kids have a hard time transitioning, learning how to get organized.

But the difficulty had started at home long before. Cynthia would get distracted easily and would get herself in trouble because of it. "Don't forget to empty the dishwasher," would become, "Cynthia—how many times do I have to tell you to empty the dishwasher?" She would be walking from the living room to the kitchen to make her contribution to the household, but the dog would run by, or a pencil on the table beckoned her to drag its tip along a nearby piece of paper, or the ticking of the clock on the wall would draw her attention, and before she knew it she was lost in another world, playing, then getting distracted from that by something else, her life a jumble of incomplete projects.

She had every intention of emptying the dishwasher, but on the way, life would distract her. And she would get in trouble for it. "I'm doing it!" she would say, honestly, forthright. Then, "Oh look! What's that?" And the dishes languished until another admonishment.

Cynthia was not just distracted at school.

Even when she had playdates, her friends would become frustrated. In the middle of a boardgame, or on the swings, or in a fierce contest of hide-and-seek, Cynthia would drift off, not spitefully, leaving her friend crouched behind a tree, or letting a ball go through her legs, or spilling a drink on the board because she was looking at a very interesting movement happening outside the window. She was oblivious—not malicious.

She had attention deficit without hyperactivity, primarily inattentive.

The hyperactive kids are easy to spot, running with the frenetic energy of a dynamo, moving from place to place, touching the stuff in the store even as parents berate them not to touch, breaking things, including bones when they impulsively, dare-devilishly decide to ride their skateboard off the roof. Like Cynthia, oblivious. But not to everyone else. The hyperactive kid is well noticed.

The irony of attention deficit, inattentive type is that, very often, no one is paying attention to these very capable students. That's a whole different type of attention deficit! The inattentive ones can go a long, long time ignored, becoming more and more frustrated, misunderstood, smart enough to do their work but too distracted to get it done. When a kid doesn't get good grades, they can become discouraged. And if the discouragement persists, they may give up. And then there can be trouble. The job of a kid is to go to school and succeed as best they can. That's where their pride and confidence live, just like an adult doing a good job at work.

Cynthia began to see herself as inadequate and unable to do her homework. As her Ic changed to "less-than," she became discouraged and was beginning to drift away.

The I-M Approach does not say that your actions at a given time are the best they can ever be, but it does adhere to the belief that this is your *current* maximum potential. Cynthia was noticed by her home and school environments as a girl whose grades had gone from good to bad. Her I-M had changed in response to the dynamic equilibrium between the I-M and the domains. I never said the I-M you are experiencing is going to help you "win." Success and failure are just two of the myriad of current maximum potentials.

Too much attention to attention deficit?

There has been enormous controversy over the diagnosis, or over-diagnosis of AD. "How can over 5 percent of all children be stricken with a disorder of attention? Where were these kids when 'we' were growing up? No one was on meds then!" (Of course, there really weren't any meds!)

AD: Over-diagnosed? A myth? A normal part of childhood as the brain struggles for frontal lobe control over the deeper impulsivity of limbic system responses?

Nah.

AD is real, perhaps over-diagnosed by practitioners who are not trained child psychiatrists, but when it is there, it is really there and needs to be treated so that a child can have the best chance of doing well in school, at home, with friends, in sports, their religion, theater, music, rock climbing—in whatever they choose to participate.

When it is real, and when it is treated appropriately, a kid may come back into the office and say, "Dr. Shrand, I had the best day ever when I started that medicine. I could concentrate, focus, stay on track, didn't fidget, didn't get distracted even when Tommy farted and the teacher swung around glaring. Sure, I laughed like everyone else, but I was able to get right back to work, like everyone else. I would never have been able to do that before."

How easily distracted are you? When watching TV, does your mind drift off? What about when trying to get work completed? Are you even having a hard time getting through this book? If getting distracted is getting in your way of success, then perhaps, *perhaps* you have AD or attention deficit with hyperactivity. My advice is to make an appointment at a clinic just to check it out. You have nothing to lose and a lot to gain.

Here are some easy ways to increase your concentration:

- Do an easy crossword puzzle every day.
- Do an easy Sudoku every day.
- Make a list, not an enormous one that is overwhelming, but one with three things on it that you can get done that day. (Small changes have big effects.) Cross them off, then save and collect those pieces of paper. You will be amazed how much you actually get done!

"Really? Ritalin?"

Cynthia's parents struggled. The idea of putting their kid on medicines had never been an issue when it came to antibiotics or asthma, or various aches and pains treated with the occasional Tylenol or Motrin.

But Ritalin!? Whoa there, Nelly. This was going to mess with their kid's brain. They asked questions, good ones, informed, not blindly accepting the need for this kind of intervention. They had heard of kids who lost all joy, sat in the class stunned and sedated, just to make the teacher's life easier, to make the parents' lives quieter, while the kid—the kid, a living shell, a zombie—had their neuronal net, their emerging, developing mystery of a brain, flooded with noxious chemical. What were the long-term side effects? Would she become dependent? Wasn't it like doing speed? Why their kid? Her parents' I-M was also influenced by the troubles of their daughter. In my office, they struggled with what kind of parents would they be to resort to medication. Did it mean they were also inadequate to help their kid, making them less-than-adequate parents?

But she was not doing well at school, was starting to have morning stomach aches, (never on Saturday or Sunday), began to say she was stupid, had no friends, and just wanted to stay at home.

This was getting serious, and this was their kid. And they felt a little, just a *little*, just at the beginning of . . . powerless. Their job was to protect her, and here was an invisible and unrelenting force that this "shrink" was saying impinged on her ability to function, this "Attention Deficit 'Disorder.'"

And they struggled with the stigma. They worried for their kid, and for themselves, and started to notice how dad had a little of it as well, and Aunt Jane, and cousin Billy, who had actually gone on meds and did really well. And their history grew more detailed, unlike the initial story where no one else had anything mental ever in any generation as far back as Adam.

"Really? Ritalin?!"

They allowed Cynthia to be placed on Ritalin at the end of seventh grade. Just for a two-week trial. After all, she had not been on medication her whole life. Two weeks was a worthwhile comparison. But they wouldn't tell her teachers, or anyone.

Cynthia made a dramatic conversion. Her grades improved. One teacher approached her parents in the hallway after school at an event, making a point of seeking them out to tell them how impressed she had been with Cynthia the last week, how Cynthia had really turned it around and was finally reaching the potential her teacher always knew she had. That she was a smart kid who seemed so much more focused than even just last week. "Good job," she wanted to say. "Keep it up!"

Her parents were pleased. And Cynthia's self-esteem began to rise and rise. For a kid in school, a good grade can be better than Prozac. Kids who do well in school, for the most part, don't come and see someone like me. For them, they are good at their job and doing fine.

Cynthia continued to do well until tenth grade. Then her grades began to slip again. Down, down, down. She denied doing drugs or alcohol. Her parents were at a loss, as she had done so well on the Ritalin up until then. Maybe it had stopped working? They were sure she was still taking it because the pill bottle kept getting lower and needed to be refilled right on time.

Cynthia came into my office.

An angry adolescent.

She seemed sullen, dismissive, indignant. I started off with one of my usual lines. "Before we get started," I said in my coolest let-me-connect-with-you voice, "I couldn't help noticing skid marks on the carpet outside my office. Were you dragged here? Oh no . . ." I joked, "not another adolescent dragged to see Dr. Shrand."

Nothing. No smile, no words. Just a glare.

"How goes it?" I continued.

More nothing.

"Do you know why your mom has brought you here?"

Nada.

"Any guesses?"

More nada.

"I see," I continued. "Looks like you have a strategy today. 'I am just going to sit here and not say a word to Dr. Shrand and perhaps he will go away and stop asking me these stupid questions.'"

Not even a slight smirk.

Cynthia glared. If I had been any less resilient, I would have shriveled like a plum turning into a prune. Adolescents are meant to be all-powerful, supreme, invulnerable, invincible. There is a reason for that famous bumper sticker that says, "Hire a teenager. They know everything." Perhaps more than at any other age, having to take medication for any illness is seen as an insult and betrayal. Whether it be insulin for diabetes, inhalers for asthma, or Ritalin for attention deficit, medication grates against the feeling of being powerful and omnipotent. For an adolescent, medication imposes an undeserved but unrelenting doubt on one's ability and readiness to fight big battles, to conquer dreams unbounded, to explore, unfettered, a world waiting for you and only you.

Cynthia was no exception. It didn't matter that her grades had ascended to the honor roll level, without any side effects from the medication—no drowsiness, appetite impairment, or difficulty sleeping. Despite its proven benefit in her grades and in her relationship with her parents, she resented this Ritalin that she had to take. She resented this diagnosis of ADD that clung to her, an abscess uninvited, unwanted, and unwelcome, an annoying brake on her growing omnipotence.

Had the medicine stopped working? Had she outgrown the dose? Was she selling it or trading it for some other goodie? Was she hoping to reveal to her parents and to that stupid Dr. Shrand that she had been pretending to take it all along, and her successes were the result of simple hard work and sweated brow, not methylphenidate and the stimulation of dopamine secretion in her brain? [12] That it was her work and her work alone that had improved her grades? Not a medicine but *her*—her alone all along.

The glare from Cynthia became a supernova peeling off the paint, igniting the furniture, incinerating my myriad of diplomas and framed certificates, a soundless explosion that shouted, "You have one minute before I walk out of here and blithely reduce your entire office building to ashes."

I better get right to it, I decided.

"So, Cynthia. I have to ask you something. If you answer only one thing today, this is the one: Your mom tells me your grades are going down and she wonders

---

[12] Dopamine is another neurotransmitter intimately involved in brain function. In this case attention, but also implicated in depression, psychosis, pleasure, reward, and addictions. It is made in many parts of the brain, including the substantia nigra of the basal ganglia. When cells that make dopamine in this part of the brain die, the result can be Parkinson's Disease.

that perhaps the medicine may not be working any more. So, I gotta ask—are you taking the Ritalin?"

Cynthia wasted no time. Her retort was as tart and crisp as an autumn apple. "Sure, I'm taking it," she growled. "I'm shoving it up my ass!"

While her mother cringed in embarrassment, I seized my opportunity. Mustering all my skill as a board-certified child-psychiatrist, I said with astonishment and conviction:

"Well, no wonder it's not working. You're meant to take it by mouth. If you shove it up your ass, of course it won't work. It just won't do you any good at all."

Unable to control herself, Cynthia cracked up. She went back on her Ritalin and did fine.

CHAPTER 14
I-M PERSPECTIVE: FAILURE

We all get distracted on occasion. We may lock our keys in the car or forget why we went into the study. We all get impulsive, perhaps spending money we really shouldn't or saying something we wish we could take back. Attention deficit is the far end of that spectrum—so why see it as a "disorder"? It is an I-M.

If someone is always at an I-M, why bother giving them medication? Because a small change in the Biological Domain can have a big effect.

Cynthia had refused to take the medication that was influencing her I-M. With or without it, she was still doing the best she could *at that time*. Without the addition of Ritalin to her Biological Domain, she struggled at home and at school. Cynthia's Ic began to "see" herself as inadequate and unable to do her homework. As her Ic changed to less-than, she became discouraged and began to drift away.

Her parents' I-M was also influenced by the troubles of their daughter. In my office, they struggled with what kind of parents they would be to resort to medication. Did it mean they were also inadequate to help their kid, making them less-than-adequate parents?

The I-M Approach does not say that your actions at any time are the *best* they can ever be, but that *this* is your current maximum potential. Cynthia was noticed by her home and school environments as a girl whose grades had gone from good to bad. Her I-M had changed in response to the dynamic equilibrium between it and the domains.

Human beings seem to equate "doing ones best" with success. Anything less than success means you are not doing your best. When we see someone as inferior, not living up to their potential, making stupid choices and taking stupid chances, we are imposing a set of morals, values, and beliefs upon our perception. The I-M Approach challenges this idea. I never said the I-M you are experiencing is going to help you "win." Success and failure are just two of the myriads of current maximum potentials.

What happens when you judge someone as a failure?

When you view someone else as a "success" or "failure," and not simply at an I-M, what happens? What happens when not only do you not like or condone an action, but see the person as stupid, or a failure, or incompetent, or dangerous? How does the person you are judging begin to feel? How does a person integrate their awareness that you see them as a failure within their I-M? What happens to you when you are seen as a failure? When your boss is unhappy with your work and criticizes you? When your significant other berates you? When your child doesn't listen, or you get a call from school? When your parent thinks you are never going to be successful? When your teacher thinks you are not trying your hardest?[13] When you see yourself as being a failure?

You do not feel good.

You do not feel successful.

Sometimes you believe you cannot change.

That's where you use the I-M. Even seeing yourself as a failure is the best you can do at that moment—a limbic, emotional, irrational response. When you use your PFC to recognize how you are influencing your Ic by seeing yourself as a

---

[13] I know one teacher who had a sign on his wall that said: "Good is not good enough." His motivation was to inspire, but the children felt they could never match up to his expectations. After learning about the I-M Approach, he changed the sign to: "Respect = Respect."

failure, you can step back and respect why that is happening. You are not a failure, just at an I-M you may not like.

The basic drive for feeling valued is active in every interaction between people. We wonder what people are thinking or feeling about us, and we react. When I begin to recognize that you see me as a failure, I may choose to disengage: why would I want to know what you are thinking about me if it is so "bad?" Why would I want to attach? Why would I want to trust? That happened with Jan, with Dan, and with Brenda before I met them, and it changed once they realized I would only treat them with respect.

And this was happening when Cynthia entered my office. Perhaps she was afraid that I would judge her a failure. Perhaps she felt angry, a clue that she felt disrespected by others or angry at herself. Teenagers are meant to feel omnipotent, but Cynthia was beginning to feel broken and inadequate. By treating her with respect, she was eventually able to say her few but powerful words. But I did not let her activate my mirror neurons and become offended. Instead, I saw her at an I-M. By my using humor instead of taking the bait, she was able to appreciate that the only agenda I had was *her* agenda, whatever that may be. I am a psychiatrist, not a judge.

But you don't need to be a psychiatrist in order *not* to be a judge of others. Seeing people at their I-M helps you do just that; when you really see someone at an I-M, they are more likely to treat *you* with respect and see you at an I-M as well. We all want the same thing: simply to be valued by somebody else. Whenever you remind someone of their value, you increase your own value, enhance your relationship, and can feel safer in the protective group you are creating.

Cynthia stopped her medication because taking it meant something negative to her. I have worked with a lot of people—children, teens, and adults—for whom the act of taking a medication implies they are not strong enough, smart enough, disciplined enough to "get over it," whatever "it" may be.

I have developed a pattern to address this sense of being broken. I did not have to use it with Cynthia but would have if needed. I start off asking, "If you had to climb a mountain, would you do it in your bare feet? And what would happen?"

Usually, the patient will accept that trying to climb a mountain in bare feet will lead to bloody feet and a poor chance of actually getting up the mountain.

I then continue. "To climb a mountain, you need the right equipment, and I don't care how much equipment you need. Family, friends, religion, medicine, music, therapy, sports, art, whatever equipment you need to climb your mountain. Medicine is just a piece of equipment. It is technology. *It does not define you* but is merely there to help you climb your mountain." This view of medicine, as a piece of equipment, helps to de-pathologize the patient, as well as de-mythologize medication as an indicator of disease.

A lot of people don't want to take medicine because they worry that their Ic will be seen as less-than, which reduces their value. But when a person takes a medication, all they are doing is making a small change in the Biological Domain: change the environment of those brain cells, change the *response* of those brain cells. The medication does not define the person. Taking the medicine has shifted their I-M. Small changes can have big effects.

Cynthia was reluctant to take medication because she thought it meant that she was broken. Even this is still an I-M. But during the office visit, with my acknowledging her defensiveness without judgment, and using humor when she may have expected a less respectful response, she was able to go back on the medication and do well.

Cynthia was not a failure. She was at an I-M. As she recognized that she was really doing the best she could, she chose to make changes in her domains and went back on medication. This small choice had an amplified and ripple effect throughout the system. The medication influenced her Biological Domain. Taking the medication could not have happened unless her Ic domain had shifted. As her grades began to improve and she became less disruptive to other people's I-M, her Home and Social Domains were influenced, including those of her parents and teachers. As Cynthia began to see that her ADD was not her fault but her *responsibility*, she was able to again-look at the influence of the Four Domains, rekindle her sense of value, forgive herself, respect herself, make a small change, and move to a different I-M.

Adult Attention Deficit with Hyperactivity

I once treated a Hispanic woman in her late twenties, who I will call "Veronica." She came to me angry and frustrated by her inability to finish things she started. She had not done well in high school, so had not even bothered to apply for college. Her boss at the hair salon often gave the best customers to other hairstylists, as Veronica took too long and was often distracted. Veronica's son, an active seven-year-old, was overwhelming to care for. Veronica could not organize herself to help him with his homework, and at school he was beginning to be seen as a difficult child.

Veronica was depressed that her life was so out of control. She cried the first time we met, feeling useless and inadequate in every domain of her life.

Inattentive, distractible, unable to finish a project, Veronica presented with many symptoms of an undiagnosed and untreated attention deficit.

I wrote her a prescription for a low dose of Adderall and instructed her to come back in a month.

When she returned to the office, she was a different woman. While the dose was not high enough to last the whole day, she was already more productive at work, was able to see more clients and make more money, and her boss had praised her for the accomplishments.

I raised her dose and directed her to take a second dose at 1:00 p.m. Most AD medications only last a few hours, so a second dose is often necessary.

The next month, Veronica was ebullient. At home, she was able to do homework with her son and had received a report from his teacher that he was doing far better, appeared happier, and was following direction and getting along better with peers. I had to ask Veronica if she had given any of her medication to her child, as he was so improved as well. Of course she hadn't. She understood why I'd asked, but said she was simply more organized at home, and even more so with that second dose of Adderall. Then she said wistfully, "I wish I had taken this in school. I always felt so stupid. There was no way I was going to go to college. But now I know I'm not stupid, just scattered. Perhaps I will go back and take some classes."

As the months went on, Veronica blossomed more and more. Her confidence increased, her productivity increased, her money increased. One day, she came in with pictures of her son's birthday celebration. She had meticulously decorated the living room, wrapped presents, baked a cake, made goodie bags, and thrown the best birthday party her son ever had. It was really a party for both of them—as Veronica had regained her self-esteem.

Cynthia had made an impulsive choice to stop taking Ritalin. It was not that she was distracted and forgot to take her medication. She thought taking Ritalin meant she was broken, so she rebelled against that particular Ic by going limbic. Her declining grades just made her angrier, resentful that she had a "disorder." No way was she going to validate that by taking Ritalin. Another impulsive and limbic response.

Then she began to shift from her emotional limbic I-M to her emerging and more rational PFC I-M—and began to think things through. She could remain at an I-M with or without Ritalin. It was her choice. She was in control. The question really was: which I-M did she prefer? The one getting good grades, or the one not getting good grades? She got to choose.

Learning from our mistakes makes our failures precious gifts of knowledge. My father was a pediatrician and acknowledged he had made every mistake there was to make. But only once. Each mistake bolstered his knowledge, and each failure became the potential for a next success. We can all approach the world this way. There is no such thing as failure, only an I-M that you don't have to like but can respect to understand the influences of the domains that led to your choice.

SMALL CHANGES CAN HAVE BIG EFFECTS

If you have been given a diagnosis, you can use the I-M Approach to reframe how you understand that label. You are not a disorder or a failure. When you feel like a failure, use the I-M to adjust your definition of success. That small change can have a big effect.

If you feel like a failure, it means you still care how other people see you. There is nothing wrong with caring. Are you sad and mad because you didn't get a good grade, didn't perform as well at work, feel guilty about a relationship? Those feelings mean you care.

You care what other people think because you care about yourself. That's also a good thing. Rather than beat yourself up about being less-than and activating your limbic fight-flight-freeze response, again-look at why you do what you do based on the Four Domains. Use your prefrontal cortex to wonder instead of worry, to be reflective instead of reflexive. Make a small change in any of the domains, using your PFC to anticipate what will happen next. Keep it frontal, don't go limbic.

When you recognize you do care about yourself, you are one step closer to a new level of success. As you shift your I-M from seeing yourself as a failure, your Biological Domain will change, your cortisol and stress hormones will decrease, and you will begin creating your next I-M. You have not failed but found another way to succeed.

YOU CONTROL NO ONE BUT INFLUENCE EVERYONE

See other people's success, even if they can't see it themselves. Remind someone of their value and explore what they see as failures. Every failure is a step towards a new level of success. You can remind someone of that by modelling it yourself.

CHAPTER 15
ROSES

"Of *course* I love my mom. Why do you think I want to go home?"

Abel was eleven, and a patient in the locked inpatient psychiatric ward for children.

For the first eight of his eleven years, he and his mom and dad lived as an average family in an average town, his parents with an average marriage and an average income. The family had an average dog, a really nice lawn, and his dad's prize rose bushes that all three helped to take care of—the deep red grandeur of the blossoms invigorating the yard and the vases throughout the house. Abel spoke of that time with little affect, matter-of-factly, and continued with the same nonchalance.

"And then dad died."

Within the space of a heartbeat that never was, Abel's average life was no-more average. He never knew that the insurance money was not enough to keep them in their house, he just knew he moved away from his average town and his average school, and that his mom didn't smile much, and that he'd lost his dad and his street and his house and his friends and his school—which he told me twice because he really liked it.

He never knew that his mother, every night, held a wedding picture to her chest as she told him about her day—just that she would read to him until he fell asleep, and sometimes they would talk about Dad and sometimes not, and sometimes he didn't want to and would feel guilty.

He never knew that her job barely paid the rent, and she did not have enough money for a down payment after selling the house at a loss, but he knew that the light in the parking lot outside their apartment flickered too much and the upstairs neighbor made a strange noise, and the downstairs neighbor smoked in the hallway even though he wasn't supposed to, and that it was so much better when Mom was home.

He only knew that he was in an apartment and in a new school trying to make new friends, and that his mom would say goodbye in the morning, and he waited to say hello when she came home. He only knew they had brought with them three of the smaller rose bushes, which the landlord had agreed to plant outside their apartment, abruptly placed between the still-too-small pale blue and purple hydrangeas, the deep red blood of the roses a stark statement of his lost demesne.

Once a week, he and his mom would go and cut a rose, place it in a clear cut-glass vase, and watch as its petals slowly lost their vitality, each day a little drier than the day before, a slow an inexorable wilting demise.

And then she started getting sick.

Abel told me the story as we sat in the large, brazenly decorated day room. On the walls were paper cutouts, bright and crayoned with smears way outside the lines—pictures drawn by patients as they channeled their emotions into "art." Some of the lines were light and airy, faded red, green, blue, and orange, unsure if they were worthy to exist, wisps of crayon timidly placed by an uncertain hand, trying to disappear. Other lines were thick with rage and impulse, dragged darkly across the paper, a statement of defiance and alarm, a shout that they are here and not to be ignored.

Abel's drawing was neat and even, the pressure just right for the page, the colors unsurprising, the house placed neatly near the middle of the page with a perfect lawn and an average fence with rose bush blurs of brown and green and dots of reds in front, and an average sun with its average rays long and deep yellow, piercing the top of the roof.

"That's my house before we moved." He paused in his story as we admired together the safe and simple drawing, well-contained and at peace. "My mom was never sick at the house, just the apartment."

At first it was a mild flu. Achiness, nausea, chills, sweating. The first time lasted a day or two, not bad enough to keep her home from work. In the morning, she felt more tired than usual, but made Abel his breakfast and put him on the bus to school. Home that evening, feeling sick to her stomach, a little feverish although the thermometer did not reveal any fever, Abel told me proudly how he brought her hot orange juice sweetened with honey as she lay on the couch, gently tending to his mom who gave him a kiss with, "How lucky I am to have you take care of your old, tired mother."

"I told her she wasn't old, just sick and tired and we both laughed . . . So, when can I go home?"

"That's going to be up to your team," I hedged, not wanting to lie to Abel but also honestly not knowing when he was going to go home. I was the covering attending psychiatrist for him, as his regular psychiatrist was on vacation for that week. There is an expectation when you are away that your patients will still be able to contact a physician, and so arrangements are made with friends and colleagues to "cover" each other, in essence being available to answer the questions of people whose lives you do not know, and whose psychiatric dilemma may range from a prescription refill to a life-threatening crisis.

In a hospital setting, there is a bit more comfort when covering. The patients are usually known to the nursing staff and social worker, the files and records are at a fingertip, and the patient is being monitored twenty-four hours a day, seven days a week. Often, the task of the covering psychiatrist is to be sure the treatment plan is continuing to progress, minimally changing the direction of care if at all.

Abel had been in the hospital for two weeks the first time I met him. At that point, the plan was for him to go back home, but he had started missing school when his mom got sick, and he fell far behind. When he returned to class, he became increasingly depressed, withdrawn, avoiding other children. His mom had more difficulty getting him on the bus, and she was often torn with having to risk losing her job and tending to the needs of her child. At one point, she tried giving him a picture of herself to take to school in an envelope with a few dried rose petals. The novelty got him to school, but only for a day, and she found herself more and more desperate.

The school guidance counselor called her at home. School avoidance was deemed a psychiatric emergency. She needed to get him in. He would yell and cry with a sudden anxiety that had been dormant for the months since the death of his father. Her friends told her to expect this. Abel had taken the death far too easily, it was not normal, the feelings had to be somewhere.

So perhaps her illness precipitated his, not an illness but a connected fear that he would lose her, as well.

Abel was hospitalized for his own safety. It was about a year after his dad had died. An "anniversary" admission, as neat an explanation for the rapid emergence of his symptoms, his anxiety and depression.

The plan was for him to stay long enough to get started on antidepressants, monitored for safety, begin the grieving process, then go home.

Acute inpatient psychiatry. Patients and their families expect something else. They expect a patient to stay long enough to get better. But that's not what acute inpatient psychiatry is all about.

Imagine you break your leg. You go to an emergency room, they X-ray your leg, figure out where the break is, put you in a cast, perhaps keep you overnight, then send you home with a broken leg in a cast.

That's what acute inpatient psychiatry is all about.

We assess the problem, figure out where the break is, start treatment, and put enough supports in place so that when you go home you have more tools with which to stay out of a hospital. The healing takes place outside the hospital. We just send you home in a "cast."

Abel was going to go back home, with a medicine that was beginning to work, enhanced contact with and in the school, a play therapist to deal with the loss of his dad, and children's books on grief and the loss of a loved one. His mom was also going to get a counselor so that she could talk about what it was like to be a single mom and the far-reaching range of emotions she felt towards the loss of her husband.

At the end of that week, I said goodbye to Abel and did not expect to see him again.

Six months later, I was again covering the pediatric psychiatry unit. There was Abel, coloring at the dayroom table. The same well-balanced scene of his old house, the sunrays firmly shining down until they touched the roof, the fence with the swirls of rosebush speckled in front, the only sign of chaos in the otherwise ordered drawing.

"What happened to you?" I asked him with a tone that implied curiosity and respect, honed by technique to avoid any hint of castigation or blame.

"I came back. My mom got sick again."

This time it was more serious. She'd begun to get dizzy and have tingling in her toes and feet. At one time, she seemed to spontaneously break into bruises. Her gums bled a little after she even gently brushed her teeth. The nausea would at times become vomiting. She had to stay home from work but was proud that Abel went bravely off to school each day, onto the bus, not even calling from the nurse's office to tell her he was sick with an ache or a pain or just not feeling well and wanting to go home.

Instead, he would meet his mom at home when he got back from school, quietly opening the door so he did not wake her sleeping on the couch or in her bed, wherever she could rest, since she was so, so tired. He would make her hot orange juice sweetened with honey and warm up some instant chicken soup.

And each week, he would cut a rose and place it in the clear cut-glass vase. Once, he left a picture he had drawn of him and his mom and dad outside their house, placing it amidst a scattered blanket of dried rose petals.

But she did not get better quickly this time. The doctors thought it was multiple sclerosis, others thought it was the stress of losing her husband and raising a child alone, others thought she was depressed herself and her symptoms the conversion of her conflicts into the array of concerns she expressed. Her muscles would cramp or begin to writhe and twitch, and she was clumsy, at times slurring her speech. Her own mother worried that her daughter had developed a drinking problem after the school called her to say that she had come to a school meeting appearing confused and uncoordinated.

Abel told me how once he had come home and his mom had wet herself and the couch. Another time, he had to call 911 because she started having trouble breathing. His grandmother had to stay over, but his mom came home from the hospital the next day.

And everyone started worrying about her. And who would take care of him if she died? There would be people over at first, making a meal, washing a dish, keeping the home clean. From the old neighborhood, telling average stories of the average town and how different it was without the three of them.

But the distance was too far, and all he knew was that they didn't come to visit as much, which was OK with him because he could do just as much as they could, and didn't he know her better anyway? But even so, his grandmother started coming over more often, but he didn't like that because he didn't get the time alone that he loved with his mom.

And then she began to get better. Her strength came back. Her energy returned. She stopped slurring her speech. Her muscles relaxed. Everyone breathed a sigh of relief even as the doctors puzzled and scratched their heads about her recovery.

Someone even wondered if Abel had been giving his mom his antidepressants because she just seemed so much happier. But his mom said no, because she gave them to him every morning as part of their ritual before school, and the bottle was being refilled right on time. Besides, she didn't need an antidepressant anymore now that she didn't feel sick.

"She got a boyfriend."

"She did?"

"Yeah, the landlord, the guy who takes care of the roses."

"How was that for you?" I asked.

"I didn't care. But he's a jerk."

"And you don't care?"

Abel colored in the last of his rosebushes, with perhaps a bit more energy than before, the crayon pushing down onto the paper with an almost imperceptible increase in force.

"Not really. Besides, we may move. Mom thinks there's something she may be allergic to in the apartment. She got sick again. Almost as bad as before. So I came back here."

"Because your mom got sick? Where was your grandma?"

"She was even sicker. I stopped going to school again so I could take care of my mom after Grandma had to stop because she was getting sick too."

"So, what's the plan?"

"When can I go home? I miss my mom."

I did not see Abel again for a year. He had stayed out of the hospital and was not on the unit the few other times I covered over the next twelve months. He was now an "old" twelve—a few months shy of his thirteenth birthday. He had grown, the faint traces of childhood clinging stubbornly to the budding frame of an adolescent. He was taller, wider, but still the self-contained child he had seemed almost eighteen months before.

"Geez, it's been a while."

"Hi Dr. Shrand."

"What's going on?"

"Didn't you talk with the nurses?"

"Not yet? What's up?"

Abel looked at his lap. He did not reply until a pause too long for spontaneity. He was thinking about his answer. Without looking at me he said, "When can I go home?"

Now I paused. His eyes averted. Abel seemed diminished from before, his gangly body becoming too large for the child-sized chair at the coloring table. He was drawing a rose, it covered the page, a swirl of petals and a harsh, stark stalk, well-endowed with thorns.

The tone of voice, the inflection, the hushed request seemed too full. Something had happened, and he knew he may not have home as an option.

"I don't know. It's up to your team. You know that."

"I don't think they're going to let me."

"How come?"

"I just know."

Abel didn't want to talk anymore. I left him as he carefully, neatly, calmly continued to color his rose, meticulously outlining each thorn even as the petals blended together on top of one another, a deep rich red.

The nurses and social worker filled me in.

Abel had gone home to live with his mom in the apartment. She had recovered enough to care for him, but her own mother had become too ill and incapacitated. She could barely walk. Abel also had symptoms on occasion, complaining of diarrhea, perhaps an extra ache or two. He was able to go to school, but the phone calls home from the school nurse increased until he had to spend a week at home. His pediatrician thought it may have been viral, but then began to wonder if there was something in the apartment to which they were being exposed. His mom thought it may have been her son's reaction to the deepening relationship with the landlord.

She stopped seeing the landlord, Abel crying when she and the "he's-not-daddy" man would try to go out for an evening. Abel tensing when he saw the man tending the hedges and the roses, rageful and furious when the man brought his mother one of *his* roses, *their* roses—Daddy's roses.

So she stopped seeing him.

And the tantrums disappeared.

And the symptoms disappeared.

And then everyone got better. Slowly, but better. For months, Abel and his mom were symptom free. No stomach aches, no fevers, no tiredness. Content.

Abel returned to his calm and placid self. Just enough friends at school, average grades, an average mood, no excitement or distress. He even made up with the landlord, and this gesture encouraged his mom to renew the relationship.

Abel did not protest.

His mom would go out, and Abel softly smiled and simply asked them to hurry back.

His mom would come home late from work, and Abel would not suspect she had been first to see her boyfriend.

On weekends, the three would go to a park or a movie or a restaurant, as the man tried to become his friend.

And then the man got very, very sick.

Very sick.

He started bleeding from his gums, he had a seizure, he was rushed to a hospital where Abel's mom was told she was not next of kin, and they couldn't tell her anything because they did not have a signed release. She went home scared and distressed, and Abel made her some hot orange juice sweetened with honey and cut her a fresh rose for the vase.

She vomited that night.

Her muscles ached over the next week.

Abel would come home and take care of her, comforting, soothing, telling her everything would be fine, that he was there to take care of her. He was almost thirteen and he would take care of her because she was his mom and he loved her.

I heard the rest of the story from the nurse, bewildered, and went back to talk with Abel.

"I got most of the story from the nurses, but what's going on. What happened?"

"When?"

"Right before you came back in. Take me through the day. You woke up . . ."

To my astonishment, Abel began to tell me the story. Perhaps it was the familiarity, perhaps it was the "taxi-driver phenomenon" where a person tells a stranger the deep dark secrets of their life knowing they will never see each other again. Perhaps it was catharsis, his cavernous and forlorn need to purge himself of guilt, although he still spoke with the same effortless incongruity of emotion which had characterized our each and every interaction.

"I went to school as usual. Mom was at home, sick again. I didn't call her or go to the nurses because I knew she was going to get better soon, that she wasn't as sick as she had been before."

"How did you know that?"

Abel ignored a direct answer and continued with his narrative.

"I just knew."

"And then what happened?"

"I got home from school. There was a police car outside the apartment. I thought Mom had gotten worse, so I ran in to see her. She was sitting at the kitchen table. It looked like she was just staring at the rose, but she looked up at me when I came in. She started shaking her head from side to side, talking with the policeman but looking back at me saying, "It can't be. It can't.""

"What 'couldn't be'?"

"Abel?" the policeman said. As Abel told me his story, I felt that I was there in the kitchen with them all, his mother sitting, her nightgown covering a slighter body than the week before because of the nausea and lack of appetite, a bathrobe loosely knotted by her waist. Two blue-outfitted policemen, their batons and guns guarded and attached to their belts. And another man, in a loose-fitting suit, who identified himself as a detective.

"Abel?" the detective took over. "I'm Detective Shane and I'd like to ask you some questions. Your mom can stay right here with you, OK?"

In the locked confines of the child psychiatry unit, the crayons put aside, the rose complete, Abel told me about the interview with the detective. At first, he denied everything, his mother's voice adding to his resolve but her body betraying with an attitude of doubt, a fierce attack on her certainty of her son, *her* son.

"So why did you do it?" I asked, not really expecting him to answer. He was only twelve.

His words remain preserved in my memory all these years later. The cast of light on his face, the hush and paralysis in the room, the tranquil measurement of his voice.

"I like taking care of her. She's my mom. I love her."

Abel had been poisoning his mom for almost two years. Just a little, not too much, just enough to get her a little sick but not enough to kill her. Usually it was the liquid Malathion they used to keep away the bugs from the rose bush. Orange juice. Tea with honey. Just a little—a little drop or two, that's all. Once or twice a fleck of d-CON from the apartment basement where the landlord put it so safely and out of reach. Unless you really wanted to get it.

"I wanted to be the one to care for her. Dad would have wanted me to. It was my job now." So when his grandmother came over, she got sick too.

And then the landlord. She started to like him too much.

Abel said he never got angry, never impulsively put the d-CON into the open can of soda the man would drink as he tended the apartment complex. He had started with just a little, like before, just enough to hear his mom ask, "How did you get that bruise?" And then a bit more, and then when they got back together, he wanted to just be done with it in case they got too serious.

Abel never knew that the man recovered and gave his mom permission to visit him in the hospital. He never knew that the doctors had quickly figured out the cause of the bleeding. He never knew that his mom had wondered if the two of them had been exposed to the same toxins, perhaps while she watched him work. He never knew that when his mom got sick, she called the man—who called his doctor, who called her doctor, who ran some tests and was astonished.

All he knew was that he had been able to take care of his mom when she was sick, and that he was talking to a detective.

A few months later I was back on the pediatric unit. The attending psychiatrist was home with the flu. Abel had been transferred to a longer-term hospital. He had not gone home, but that was all that I knew.

CHAPTER 16
I-M PERSPECTIVE: CRIME

I placed this following perspective on crime right after the perspective on failure, as the two often merge in our society: In every crime, one party's value increases by diminishing the value of another. A person who commits a crime is considered a failure in their life, resorting to methods unacceptable in a society. It seems inconceivable that a person who goes against the morally acceptable standards of a community is at an I-M.

My colleague Avrom Weinberg offered the following insight after reviewing the first draft of this book:

Some particular issues that readers will want to see addressed with your I-M theory are: how a student who chooses to not do his homework because he feels that nobody can make him do something he doesn't want to do is achieving his maximum potential at that time, how a person who completes suicide is at their maximum potential at the moment of that action, how a person who murders another person is at his maximum potential at that moment, how a person who gets in a car and drives drunk is at his maximum potential at that moment, how a person who chooses to not do things because of a fear of failure is at his maximum potential at that moment, etc.

This is a critical observation. It *is* hard to see a person at an I-M when they may be taking away from another person. Everything in our survival brain tells us that the offender needs to be punished and held accountable, but that can impede a deeper understanding of the person who we judge, as they will not want to engage with us and thereby confirm that they have less value because they diminished the value of someone else.

The student who chooses not to do their homework may not be able to foresee the consequences of such a choice. But they are there. I have often said to a student refusing to do their schoolwork that the grade they are now in could end up being the best *two* years of their life. I am not forcing them to do their work, just asking them to reflect on what is probably going to happen if they don't.

The I-M never said you were going to win and be successful, it just said you were always going to try to adapt. Sadly, for some people, completing a suicide is their final solution. For many, they have looked into the future, but all they see is more here and now, determining that they will never have value.

There are some people who may never have empathy and will only and always see other people as objects to exploit. I am not endorsing this type of influence, but rather than judge them, I am interested in *why* this is the best that person may be able to do. The approach says that even though it is your I-M at that moment, you do not get a free ride. You will be held responsible because every action has a natural consequence.

Drugs and alcohol interfere with judgement, as the Biological Domain of several brain areas are influenced. Change the environment, change the response. Sometimes that can create an influence on other people that can damage or even kill. It is still an I-M, and again the person is held responsible.

Some people are so scared of losing their value that they go into the freeze mode, what my friend describes as fear of failure. The I-M Approach can help them use the Four Rs that Rob used and identify the sources of their fear.

Abel poisoned his mother, his grandmother, and the landlord in response to a massive change in his Home and Social Domains. By society's standards or really anyone's, what he did was wrong, but it was still a choice based on the influence of the domains. And it was an I-M that the Social Domain deemed as unacceptable, and Abel was placed in a locked inpatient psychiatric unit.

There are rules in a society. Most of them revolve around treating each other with dignity and respect, preserving the value of the individual or the institution. As such, behaviors such as stealing, lying, killing, hurting, cheating, and other behaviors that violate the integrity of others and reduce their value are not tolerated.

Our Ic Domain can activate our own reflexive response to treat the offender in the same way they treated their target. We mirror their behavior and squelch compassion and empathy. Why should we care what was happening in their Four Domains if the best they can do is to hurt someone else? Let's hurt them back. They deserve no less. Do unto others.

Outside of the courtroom, we can be angry and want that person to change. Quick to blame and judge the other as less-than and broken, criminal, a bad person. It is another label, another stigma. Blame is shaming, devaluing, a direct impact on the Ic. More often than not, when we blame someone we elicit anger, withdrawal, and resistance, which creates a barrier between you and the very person you are trying to reach. The other person, afraid of being devalued themselves, becomes defensive, leading them away from what we wish they would do instead: Apologize. Make restitution. Restore the value of the devalued. You control no one but influence everyone.

There is another choice.

The I-M Approach does not endorse antisocial behaviors. It is not an excuse for doing bad things and then hiding behind the phrase, "Well, it's still an I-M and therefore there are no consequences." Absolutely not! The I-M is not about enabling "bad" behavior—but trying to understand *why* this is the best that person can do.

The I-M Approach holds a person responsible for their actions. If it is always someone else's fault you are never in control. And if you are never in control, you will always be angry, or anxious, or sad. That's why blame and shame never work:

they decrease a person's value and activate their fight-flight-freeze response. When we ask someone to take responsibility for their I-M, we explain that taking responsibility may not be easy, but it the first step in regaining control. Control helps to decrease our fight-flight-freeze response. And when less limbic, we can think things through and recognize that we can feel in control without exploiting and violating the personal and emotional rights and dignity of others. We can have a different influence.

Responsibility is different than blame. Responsibility is empowering, over time restoring the Ic as a person regaining trust. The I-M Approach paves a nonjudgmental path so a person can take responsibility for their actions, and then look to see what needs to change in the domains so they can move to a different I-M. By viewing each other as doing the best we can at this moment in time, the I-M Approach removes the overlay of morality and allows us to interact in a way that, I believe, is more meaningful and productive. It encourages us to take more and more responsibility for our actions influenced by the Four Domains.

The I-M Approach does not hold out as a judge, but simply sees a person as doing the best they can, given the influence of the Four Domains. When you apply the I-M, you again-look at why a person does what they do. You don't have to like or condone their action. The person will be held responsible. But seeing them at an I-M creates an environment with the greatest chance to move to a different I-M, by safely exploring the influence of their domains on their choices.

This is a critical insight, because it allows each of us to have greater control over our lives: by understanding the influences broken down into exploration of the Four Domains, we can gather knowledge, and knowledge is power. While behaviors and actions that go against the expectations of a society may not necessarily be one's *fault*, they are one's responsibility.

EXERCISE: We have all committed "crimes," big or small

This will be a much easier exercise when you apply the I-M Approach. Instead of judging yourself, use the Four Domains to find out why you made that choice. Write a list of things you have regretted doing and see which ones have taken away from someone else's value. When you take responsibility and restore that value, even with an acknowledgement, you have shifted to another I-M.

The I-M and the courtroom

Society needs rules and guidelines: a society itself has an I-M. When a person breaks a rule, we have a set of laws, law enforcers, lawyers, judges, and juries whose job is to respond and issue an appropriate consequence. A system has to respond to such behaviors to maintain its own I-M.

A system will judge when a crime has been committed: when the influence of one person has diminished another person's I-M. It is the role of the court to measure the I-M of a person and determine the consequence. It is safer for the Social Domain at large for some people to be imprisoned and to remain separated from the rest of the community.

When a system applies the I-M Approach, it can lead to a very different outcome. Yes, small changes can have big effects and you control no one but influence everyone. Yes, a person is held responsible for their actions because what we do has an influence on someone else's I-M. But when we explore the *individual's* I-M, and their response to their Four Domains, we can design a more appropriate and lasting intervention far beyond the simple removal of them from society.

What happens in jail, in a "house of correction?" We can apply the WORK acronym to a prison population, exploring why they are there, observing the behaviors that got them there, getting them to take responsibility, and then using the I-M Approach to explore why they did what they did and what small changes they can make when back in society, so they are at a different I-M, motivated to help rather than hurt. The I-M Approach can illuminate the influences that led to the offense, explore what needs to be "corrected," and serve as a roadmap to actualize the change in the offender and move them to a different I-M.

I had an opportunity to interview some men who had been released from jail, listening to the lack of preparation they received to reintegrate into their community. And how they continued to regret what they had done but felt unsupported and stigmatized as "just an ex-con." It is understandable how they gave away their trust, but does that mean that we, as a society, can never trust them again? The men I spoke with got involved with a group that encouraged them to write poetry about their experiences. Those poems were published in a book. When others read the poems of these men, it reminded them of their value. Had the men who had been released from jail "failed," or moved to another I-M?

A system has a remarkable opportunity to use the I-M Approach to look-again at who that person is and why they do what they do. Imagine recognizing the influences on a behavior, treating that person with respect, rekindling their sense of value, and having them *trust* the suggested small change that can take them to another I-M. Imagine continuing to work with that person once they are back in their Home and Social Domains, after their incarceration in the Social Domain of jail.

The I-M Approach moves away from morality and judgment. While you could argue that seeing someone at an I-M *is* a judgment, I would disagree, in that it simply says that, given the influence of the domains, this is the best they can do. There is no gradation. The I-M just is. But if you don't like it, you can change it.

Crime on a societal level

The United States is a Home Domain to millions of people. Its Social Domain is the interaction with the rest of the global community. The United States has an Ic Domain—the way it sees itself and the way other nations see it, which may be very different now than when George Washington was president. And the U.S. has a Biological Domain, comprised of all its resources and people, each of which has an I-M.

A system is also influenced by the Four Domains, and small changes can have big effects. Crimes are responded to by a system with varying degrees of "consequences," as everything you do has a natural consequence. The I-M does not excuse a behavior, but tries to explain it within a context: how has this person been influenced by their domains?

War, the exploitation of other people, destruction of the environment—these can all be seen through an I-M lens. Using the I-M Approach, these insults and crimes to humanity and our world can be understood, explored, and, one hopes, ultimately shifted to another I-M. Historians have known about this for a long time, trying to place events into the context of the political landscape of the time. A historian looks at how a country interacts with other countries, how the country perceives itself, how it thinks it is seen by others, and how its people react to the world around them—each with their own individual I-M. Historians wonder if wars or civil rights movements are a result of an individual or a nation's economic hardship, or a perceived insult to their national or personal honor, the threat of invasion, the competition for a limited resource, being excluded, or not being allowed to vote. Each of these are the result of having diminished value or not being valued at all.

The I-M helps to organize and explore how some people have become leaders of others capitalizing on the wishes, desires, vulnerabilities, anger, fear, and other emotions to rally their communities or country around a common cause. Even the outrage of a Hitler can thus be appreciated as an I-M. One does not have to like it or condone it but understand and again-look in the context of the influences of the Four Domains. There is enticement in increasing your value at the expense of someone else. It is about being part of a tribe that is more "successful" than another tribe—an example of our ancient need to survive. The only future that then matters is being superior to others, and with greater access to a perceived resource. It is compelling, but limbic.

Crime on an individual level

A patient recently told me that he likes to rob people. They are strangers to him, and he feels no emotional attachment. He speaks cavalierly about how many people he has robbed, mugged, punched, and taken their money. Even this is an I-M. As he explored the approach, he began to look at how the Home Domain of his early childhood, growing up with an alcoholic father and an abandoning mother, led him to drift from school to a Social Domain where being accepted meant being dangerous and feared. He looked at how he began to see himself, and how others began to see him: a delinquent, not to be trusted, discarded. His brain filled with rage and he began to rob people, not seeing them as individuals but as vehicles for wallets, jewelry, possessions, in a desperate attempt to increase his own value while diminishing the value of others.

His actions are not acceptable, or condoned, but have to be respected as the best he could do given his situation. He will have consequences—likely going to jail—but the opportunity to understand the context of his actions using the I-M Approach as an organizing principle has already helped him recognize how his behavior impacted the I-M of those he robbed, how it perpetuated his self-image as a bad kid because others saw him as bad, and how this view by others influenced his continued withdrawal from connection. After all, why should he connect to anyone if they always see him as bad?

But when he began to see how he contributed to his own view of himself, how he was really more in control of it than he imagined, how he could not control anyone but could absolutely *influence* them, he began to make a small change. He recognized how the domains interact. How a small change in any one domain can have a ripple effect throughout the entire system. As he began to explore how his behaviors were influenced by *his own choices*, he began to recognize that he could change the way other people saw him by not robbing anyone. Perhaps even more powerful, he began to recognize he had not *lost* that trust by robbing others; he had *given* it away. He had given away the trust, and he could take it back.

He could regain trust, and as he regained trust, he could regain his own lost sense of value. It was this feeling of being dismissed, and of not being valuable, that had been influencing his antisocial actions. Rather than blaming his parents for drinking or abandoning or neglecting, he began to see that they too have an I-M, and that what they did as parents was still the best that they could do.

He did not have to like it. He did not have to condone it. But he had to respect it. And as he and his parents began to talk about this new insight, using the I-M Approach as a guide for exploration, they began to accept responsibility for their actions and the influence on each other. They began to forgive themselves, to forgive each other, and to make small changes with a ripple effect throughout the system.

I never knew whether Abel reached this epiphany. He was transferred to another facility, perhaps committed for a long, long time. By many, he was considered to have antisocial personality "disorder," which is an inability to have empathy. But I don't think this was the case at all. He felt proud that he could care for his mother, protect her in a way he could not protect his father. And when he felt that the landlord was going to usurp his position as his mother's caregiver, he did what he thought he needed to do: remove him from the equation. Abel very much wanted to be the one seen as able to ease his mother's pain. It was just that he created her pain for him to heal. He was, perhaps, the thorn upon the rose. But even that is an I-M.

SMALL CHANGES CAN HAVE BIG EFFECTS

Do you see Abel differently now than when you first realized he had been poisoning his mother? That small change is actually huge—looking again—respecting why Abel did what he did. When you recognize that we are all really good at judging ourselves and each other, but you can now use the I-M Approach not to judge but to wonder, it will change your world and the world of others.

YOU CONTROL NO ONE BUT INFLUENCE EVERYONE

That small change results in you becoming a different influence. No one wants to be judged. Everyone wants to be understood, even if they have done something wrong. And when someone does not agree that they *have* done something wrong, that presents an opportunity to engage, rather than become entrenched in disagreement; turning our backs on each other, rather than having each other's back, because we disagree. Which kind of influence do you want to be?

CHAPTER 17
ONE LESS HAT

Chip had been terrorizing his mother and other children at his preschool. In fact, he was so aggressive that his mother showed me the bruises he had left on her arms and legs from kicking and hitting her. Looking at him, one would never guess he had this approach to the world. He was a five-year-old boy, slightly small for his age, blonde hair, blue eyes, who initially sat on his mother's lap, reluctant to leave what was the apparent comfort of her closeness.

Slowly, he began to move away from her and explore the office, picking up various toys, looking at me and his mother for permission to open the large toy chest before he did. As his mother began to tell me the story of their lives, Chip carefully and methodically took out all the hats and costumes he found in the chest.

Chip was the product of a marriage that had quickly become abusive. His mother was still traumatized by the domestic violence that had been thrust upon her by her now ex-husband. Chip had seen and heard her being beaten, having her jaw broken, and himself was briefly kidnapped by his father at gunpoint. His mother was now terrified that the father, who was living in a different state, was going to go through the legal system to secure guardianship of her son. Indeed, she was so worried that he would appear and abduct her son that she got a job at the same daycare center where Chip was enrolled, working in a classroom just down the hall.

His mother described Chip as fluctuating between clinging to her when she tried to drop him off at his classroom and shunning her upon return to pick him up.

When she dropped him off, she would reassure him that she was "just down the hall," but this only seemed to exacerbate his crying and clinging. When she finally was able to extricate herself from his grasp, he would haul back and punch her in the arm, kick her in the legs, then reluctantly allow the classroom teacher to bring him into the room. The other children would witness this violence towards his mother, and usually were reluctant themselves to engage in play with Chip. As such, he often found himself on the outskirts of the games, despite the teacher trying to have the other children include him. When they did try to involve Chip, he would become aggressive towards the other children, have difficulty playing, and was possessive of toys and quick to try to monopolize the teacher's attention if another child was in need.

When his mother would come to pick him up, he would ignore her and not listen to her request that they leave. Another struggle would ensue, with Chip becoming increasingly oppositional until he again would kick and punch her, then finally allow her to hug him, take his hand, and lead him out the building. She described an enormous shame and embarrassment at his behavior, and the sense that she was inadequate at "controlling" him. She wondered what the other people at work thought of her but was astonished when the preschool director told her that she needed to get "professional help" for her son.

Chip was sorting through the chest of costumes as he listened to his mother telling the story. He carefully and methodically looked at the different hats, examining each one for its merit. He was not impulsive and did not toss around the different things he found. In fact, his inquisitiveness was not at all consistent with the impulsive and aggressive boy his mother described, as he would on occasion take a piece of costume to his mother for her approval and inspection. He presented these things to her quietly. His mother would gently but superficially acknowledge the garment, but then dismiss him as she went on, determined to tell the story.

Chip chose his costume. With a somber excitement he slowly and carefully put on a gray plastic helmet, a gray plastic breast piece, and two gray plastic wrist protectors until he was fully adorned in the armor of a Roman gladiator. There was a gray plastic shield that he found, and then he asked for a sword.

His mother shuddered, and quickly voiced her objection of his wish for "a weapon."

I intervened. "I don't have a sword, but we can make them out of paper," I offered. For the first time, Chip came over to me.

"How do you do that?" he asked. We began to roll up pieces of paper, then use sticky-tape to keep them from rolling apart until we had each made a sword. Chip immediately began to wave his around, posturing in a gladiators pose, gesturing with the sword, protecting himself with the shield.

His mother cringed. "Do you really think he should be doing that? I mean, it's a weapon."

"Let's see what happens." I tried to assure her that Chip was playing with a paper sword and handed her mine. At first, she pushed it away, but Chip picked it up and handed it to her. She sat with the sword held limply in her hand, while Chip began to brandish his with some enthusiasm, waving it around, but not too close to his mom. The session came to a close with Chip carefully removing his armor and putting it back into the chest. His mother took the paper swords, crumpled them, and threw them in the garbage.

For the next several weeks, Chip and his mother came to the office. She was reluctant to leave him alone but tolerated the making of the swords. One, two, and now a third one for me. Chip would excitedly roll them up, tape them, all after extracting and donning his armor. On the fifth week, his mother finally felt comfortable enough to leave Chip and I alone for the majority of the session. A pattern had evolved, in which she would report his complete lack of progress over the previous week, his aggressive behaviors, her bruises, his reluctance to separate, and his anger at reconciliation. I learned that he would not sleep in his room by himself, despite a long and complex ritual of reading, rubbing his back, and singing. He would fall asleep for a few minutes, then wake up abruptly, distressed and screaming for her, and rush into her bed. She was exhausted and concerned that he was turning into as "abusive a man as my husband."

Identification with the aggressor, I thought. This little boy had seen his father hurt his mother, had been kidnapped by the large and scary man, and probably felt powerless. So now he wanted to share the power. To feel strong, in control, dangerous.

But it left his mom feeling scared and intimidated.

Chip had a dilemma. Even as he became more aggressive and threatening to his mom, I suspected part of him desperately wanted his mom to be stronger than him, to protect him from his dad, and even from his own desperate rage. But the more he tried to mobilize his mom, the more he drove her back into her stance as a victim, also powerless to move, to change, to protect.

Human beings are nothing if not ancient survival machines. Through evolution, we have developed techniques to avoid being prey to another more dangerous, hungry, and perhaps more desperate competitor. As one of thousands of species, we developed a brain that engaged in the "fight-flight" response. Our brains, activated by the threat of personal extinction, being lunch for something else, or being destroyed as a potential competitor of a limited resource, we go into a limbic-driven mode: either we mobilize and fight, or we get the hell out of there to live another day.

But there is also a third response.

Freeze. Paralysis.

When an organism cannot fight, and cannot flee, it will just stop, freeze, try not to draw any attention to itself at all. Try to make itself as small and innocuous as possible, try to ride out the danger, try to disappear.

It submits.

I worried that Chip's mom had taken this role, frozen by her own sense of inadequacy but terrified of her son's violent reminder of her ex-husband. And that Chip, his innocence stripped by witnessing domestic violence, was trying to desperately get his mom to become strong, capable, and move from the defensive to the protective position.

At first, she justified not leaving the session based on her experience with trying to leave him at the preschool to go down the hall and tend to the other children. "He can even see me there, but he still makes a fuss. Look at *this* bruise."

On the day that she left us alone, Chip was already in his armor, having made and handed me my sword, and with both fists full of the other two. As he handed his mother her sword, she stood up and stated she would wait outside. To both our astonishment, he made no protest at all but crumpled up her sword and put it in the garbage, watching as she left the room.

He turned to me and began to wave his sword in front of me.

"What should I do now?" I asked.

"You can use your sword too." He began to strike at my sword with his. We began to play. As his sword struck mine, I tentatively swung back. The force was too great, and his paper sword bent with the contact. He stopped, fixed it by adding some extra tape, and started to wave it at me again, egging me back into the game. Again, our swords made contact, and again, his collapsed.

Chip stopped. "I need to make a new sword," he announced. He took a piece of paper from my desk and began the folding process. He then instructed me, "Dr. Shrand, pick a hat."

"A hat?"

"From the chest."

"Which one should I pick?"

"Any hat." I picked a farmer's cap. "Now put it on, Dr. Shrand." I put it on.

"Like this?" I was sitting in my office chair, with Chip building his sword as he looked with a careful gaze of approval.

"Good."

"Good hat?" I asked.

"Good hat. Now put on another one." I went to take off the cap, but Chip stopped me with his words. "Oh no—keep that one on."

"You want me to keep this hat on?"

"Yes, and put on another one." I found myself putting a baseball hat on top of the farmer's cap.

"Like this?"

"Good. Now another one." Over the next several minutes, I was told by Chip to put one hat on after another. A cowboy hat. An astronaut's helmet. Another and another. Finally, I put on a large, multi-colored floppy top hat, like the one worn by the Cat in the Hat in Dr. Seuss' world. I had to let go of my sword and use both hands to keep the hats on my head. The hats towered above me, over a yard's worth of hats precariously balanced on my head.

"Now don't you let any of those hats drop, Dr. Shrand," instructed Chip. "Don't you let one drop."

I sat with my hands above my head, my arms completely outstretched and vertical, desperately holding on to the multitude of hats, balancing them, moving and adjusting my head and neck to keep them on, while Chip watched with triumph. He had completed his sword. His armor was in place with his helmet, shield, and wristbands. And he began to wave his sword up to my face. He never actually touched me, but was menacing, delighted with his new game.

My arms became heavy, but every time I would make a gesture of dropping them, Chip would flourish his sword with more ardor, and command me not to let one hat drop. "You better not let one of those hats drop, Dr. Shrand."

"What would happen if I did?" I asked with a practiced, feigned timidity and worry.

"Just don't let one of them drop."

For the next eight weeks, Chip would repeat this game. For the next eight weeks, his violence at school and towards his mother was unabated. I began to wonder about my abilities as a psychiatrist. What was going on here? How on earth was this helping? Perhaps his mother was right, and I was perpetuating this boy's violence and aggression by allowing him to play with paper swords.

I found myself sitting in my chair, my arms tired, the hats piled on top, Chip waving his paper sword, his mother sitting—perhaps frustrated but perhaps triumphant—outside, bruised but vindicated.

I was useless. I was powerless.

And then it hit me. I was *powerless*. I got it.

Chip, in his full armored regalia, was merrily and menacingly threatening me with his little paper sword, and I could do nothing.

"Don't let those hats drop, Dr. Shrand. You better not let one of them drop."

The words came out of me with a deep sincerity and worry, my arms above my head, the paper sword close to my face. "Wow, there is nothing I can do. I feel totally weak. You could do anything to me, and I wouldn't be able to do a thing."

"Yeah. How does that feel, Dr. Shrand?"

"It feels awful. I can't do anything."

Chip paused. He looked at me, locked his eyes onto my eyes, and squinted, just a little. His voice was stern but steady. "Then you can take off one hat."

Powerless. The most difficult emotion for a human being to tolerate. Chip may have been identifying with the aggressor, but it was to defend against the overwhelming biological fear that he was too little, too weak, too vulnerable. He was powerless to make any changes in his world, powerless to protect his mom, powerless to fight or flee.

And through his play, he helped me understand who he was, how he viewed himself, how he thought others saw him, and how he wanted to be seen. He wanted to be seen as a dangerous boy who you better not mess with . . . like his dad!

Over the next few weeks, Chip allowed me to take off one hat, then another, and another. His mother reported that he was still hitting her but was able to play nicer with the other children at the preschool. She began to wonder if it was actually more difficult for him having her there and having to "share" her with the other children, in sight but out of reach. He still had difficulty separating from her, and reconnecting, and was still punching and kicking. But the tantrums did not last as long and did not seem as intense. He began to talk a little about his dad, and even told her he had a nightmare that Dad had come back and kidnapped him and had hit her. In his dream, he had killed him, but then got sent to jail forever.

Each week, I had to put on one less hat, until one day Chip chose to create a different game altogether. He would still put on his armor, but he did not make any more swords. He began to play with the toy plastic dinosaurs. He chose three. One was a large Tyrannosaurus rex, the other a Brontosaurus, and the third a Stegosaurus with a large spiky tail. The game was invariably the same. Adorned in his armor, he would arrange the three dinosaurs with the Stegosaurus always in the middle. The two larger creatures were the mommy and daddy, and the Stegosaurus was the baby. The first part of the game was comprised of the family-of-three doing something nice together. They could be at home, they could be out, but they got along.

Then a conflict arose. It was usually over something minor. Chip played all three parts, fluidly interchanging his voice from a low-pitched daddy to a high-pitched mommy to his own voices as the Stegosaurus. An argument would start. The T. rex would begin to attack the Brontosaurus. "Look at those teeth!" Chip would comment—as Chip and not any of the characters.

"They sure look dangerous," I would say.

"Yeah, they are," Chip would answer. "That mom has nothing."

"Help me, help me!" Chip would say using the mom voice. "Won't anyone help me?"

"I'll help you," Chip would say using his voice now as the Stegosaurus. And then an interesting thing would happen, again and again. Coming between the daddy and mommy would be the baby. It would struggle to incorporate itself between the two larger dinosaurs, swinging itself between the daddy and mommy. But as it turned to face the father in an attempt to protect the mother, its large, spiked tail would strike and knock the mother down.

Again and again, this game was recreated by Chip. Again and again, the Stegosaurus would try to protect the mother only to knock her down. Again and again, the father would storm away in triumph and the baby would go and gingerly, carefully, put the mother back on her feet.

No more hats. No more swords. Just the three dinosaurs trapped in their invariable pattern of play. And one day I said to Chip, "Boy, it sure seems like that baby wants to help his mom, but he keeps hitting her with his tail."

"Yeah. That's gotta stop, Dr. Shrand."

"So what can that baby do?"

Chip took the three dinosaurs. He put the Stegosaurus between the two grownups. "Get out of here!" he yelled in his Chip voice. "Go on, get out of here!" There was a pause. The Stegosaurus held his ground, facing the T. rex, his back to the Brontosaurus but his tail not touching her. "Go on!" Slowly, Chip turned the T. rex around with his left hand, while holding the Stegosaurus with his right. Little by little, unhurriedly but determinedly, he moved the T. rex away from the triad until his arm was fully outstretched. He let it drop and the T. rex, without the support and balance of Chip's hand, collapsed onto its side. He turned the Stegosaurus carefully towards its mother, being sure that the tail did not touch her, then exchanged hands so he could steady both the two remaining dinosaurs. "Let's go home, Mom." And the Stegosaurus and Brontosaurus were walked away by his hands.

The next week, his mother reported she had not been hit once by Chip. He began to sleep in his own bed but would still crawl in with her in the early morning for a snuggle. She decided to work at a different nursery school, and Chip began to separate easily from her, and run to her when she came to pick him up.

One day, Chip came into the office, but he didn't put on the armor. He told me how scary it had been to be taken by his dad, how the police came, and how his dad was taken away in a squad car. He cried telling the story. He asked if we could get his mom from the waiting room, which we did together. He told her, and me, that he was ready to go, even though there was more time in the session. He turned to me, reached out his hand—then changed his mind, looked up at his mom for permission, and gave me a hug.

One less hat.

I heard from his mom several months later that he was about to enter kindergarten, and that they had moved to a different state so his father couldn't find them. He was doing great. And she didn't have any bruises.

CHAPTER 18
I-M PERSPECTIVE: AGGRESSION

Chip was aggressive to his mother, and to children, and teachers at school. He was seen by others as an aggressive child, from whom other children would and should keep their distance. Chip knew he was viewed this way. Chip had an intact Ic, able to appreciate what other people were thinking and feeling, and what they were thinking and feeling about him. Being seen as aggressive did nothing to abate his anger and violence. Indeed, it may have made it worse.

Aggression is a natural response to feeling threatened: one option of the flight-fight mechanism. Aggression is the enactment of anger.[14] Disrespect, or the *perception* of being disrespected, is the strongest predictor of anger, aggression, and shame. Seeing yourself as being disrespected triggers a sense of danger, and the limbic system responds. If respect leads to value and value leads to trust, disrespect leads to feeling devalued, and feeling devalued leads to mistrust.

How other people respond to aggression may unwittingly exacerbate the fear of danger. For example, aggression can breed aggression if you see yourself as being threatened. We fight back or try to isolate the aggressor from the community. In this latter scenario, as human beings rely on each other for the protection of a group, being isolated may increase anxiety and the sense of danger

---

[14] I explore anger in depth in Outsmarting Anger: 7 Strategies for Defusing our most Dangerous Emotion.

on part of the "offender." This in turn may result in the person becoming more aggressive, a response to their perception of increased vulnerability. Without understanding the domains and their influence, without applying the I-M Approach, a person who is aggressive is rarely seen as doing the best they can. Instead, they are seen as not complying with social expectations, and therefore "bad."

Chip was progressively seen as a bad boy who was being bad to other people and his mother. He was given more "timeouts," and was being systematically ostracized by his peers who were afraid to play with him. The approach of timeouts, it was hoped, would break him of his habit of his aggression towards others. The unintended consequence of this strategy, however, was an increasing isolation which exacerbated his sense of vulnerability. Seen as a boy not to be played with did not enhance his sense of value and self-esteem.

But Chip could not stop. He had been influenced by his Home Domain, where he witnessed and was subject to domestic violence. And this was now influencing the choices he made in his Social Domain. As these choices were enacted, it influenced the way he was seen by others, and the way he began to see himself. And his brain and body, likely flooded with emotions and neurotransmitter activity, responded with a punch here, or a growl there.

He was caught in a self-perpetuating loop: part of him was desperate to be included in a group for both protection and validation, but he was conflicted with the risk of being vulnerable to both rejection and de-valuation. As his Ic turned more and more to the dark side, and as he recognized that he was perceived as "bad" and a person not to be trusted or played with, he began to arrest his ability to engage in theory of mind, just as Brenda did. It was too painful to be seen as the kid you couldn't play with, and his external aggression increased.

How can being aggressive and violent be an I-M? How is one meant to respect someone who is being violent, violating the integrity of another person? As in the I-M perspective "Crime," adhering to the I-M Approach does not mean one condones or approves of a particular behavior, but one has to understand and respect it in the context of the Four Domains. For Chip, his aggression and violence were a function of his feeling inadequate and vulnerable. I never knew the story of his dad and the life he led that resulted in domestic violence being the best he could do at that moment. But even that behavior—even Chip's dad—was still at an I-M.

Anger is part of our human character. The *feeling* of anger has never hurt or killed anyone. It is what we *do* with that anger that can hurt or kill: when the feeling of anger becomes an action of aggression or violence. If one accepts the premise that the strongest predictor of anger is feeling disrespected, then the I-M offers an approach that can decrease the incidence of anger and subsequent aggression and violence by not activating that limbic response. The I-M is an approach of respect. When is the last time you got angry at someone treating you with respect? This is another power of respect: it can lead to a decrease in violence and aggression.

This does not just apply to an individual: A system has an I-M. As in my commentary in "Roses," a system will respond when individual aggression impedes on the rights and integrity of others. Jail for some, psychiatric hospitals for others, and so on. Violence is not to be tolerated, whether an I-M or not. But aggression, the external manifestation of the internal emotional experience of anger, needs to be understood in the context of the Four Domains. The system, at school and at home, could not tolerate Chip's aggression. The small change in response: Chip was brought to me for therapy.

Even though Chip was aggressive, he was anxious about leaving his mother, and his mother was anxious about leaving Chip. Her own reasons are not part of this discussion, but they could certainly be seen in the context of a mother both afraid her son would be kidnapped again, and ashamed and embarrassed that she was somehow to blame for his intransigence. She did indeed see him as a dangerous boy, but she did not want to leave him. How this recreated her relationship as an abused spouse was for her and *her* therapist to address. In Chip's therapy with me, the focus was how Chip thought others saw him, and why he chose to do what he was doing.

In Chip's case, he was accurate in his perception of being disrespected by his father, and being feared and not respected by his peers, teachers, and his mother. However, all of them had a distorted view of why Chip was being aggressive. They were beginning to believe that Chip was indeed a "bad" kid, like his dad, and that his aggression had no meaning or purpose. He was brought to therapy to stop the aggression, not to necessarily understand it in the context of the Four Domains.

When seen through the lens of the I-M, that the best this little boy could do was to thrash out at his mother and the world, it changed the understanding of why Chip was doing what he was doing. With Chip, it then became possible that his aggression was, in a distorted way, defensive and protective; he would not let anyone hurt him the way he saw his father hurt his mother.

Chip was treated with disrespect at home by exposure to domestic violence. This profound violation of his rights, terrifying enough to adults, pushed this child into a very different I-M. He transformed his Ic from being small, inadequate, defenseless, and powerless to where he was the one to be feared. Terrorizing his mother, teachers, and other children was the best that Chip could do: he was at an I-M.

He was at a different I-M in the therapy sessions. As Chip held me hostage, vulnerable with one hat atop another and another, he made a choice *not* to be the aggressor. Perhaps it was because I did not threaten him, with my hands high above my head. Perhaps it was because he felt safe and in control, and I respected his wish to keep those hats balanced. Perhaps with the influence of this small change in his Social Domain, he could then make the choice his father did not. How did he want me to see him? How did he see himself? What was it like to be seen as an aggressor by his mother, when it was all he knew and when it was yet the best he could do?

Chip began to have a shift in his Ic when I told him I felt helpless. At that moment, he was powerful, and when he told me to take off a hat, he became beneficent. From there, he began to change his relationships at school, and was not a bully. He began to treat his mother with more kindness, and both of these changes had an impact on the I-M of those around him. His anger began to calm, impacting his limbic system and the multitude of brain connections that now responded differently to his external world.

And in response, his Social Domain also changed. The I-M of other children shifted as they did not feel threatened by Chip anymore and welcomed him into their social groups, easing his anxiety of isolation, and enhancing his Ic as being valuable, respected, and accepted. He began to feel safer, and safer with his own anger and aggression. In therapy, with the dinosaurs, he began to see how his very wish to protect his mother by being strong and powerful had inadvertently hurt the very person he was trying to protect. He could then address his own vulnerability, the terror of being held against his will by his father, a man he loved, feared, emulated, and disdained.

Aggression comes in many forms. The most obvious is external violence, but there is also violence towards oneself, towards property, towards rules and regulations.

As individuals, we can beat ourselves up for not doing as well as we should. We put ourselves down by seeing ourselves as inadequate. Some people go further and physically self-harm, taking the emotional self-abuse and enacting it with violence and aggression on their arms, legs, stomach.

This is not to say that there should be no consequences for one's actions. Of course there should be. Aggression is not to be tolerated. The person will be held responsible because they have influenced someone else's I-M. But the person who is *responding* to that aggression can have a better chance to do so without having their own limbic system activated when they apply the I-M Approach. You can be reflective instead of reflexive. You can wonder instead of worry. The person being aggressive is doing the best they can, given the influence of the domains, but *why* they are aggressive can guide the small change you may need to have an effective influence. Judging that person is, itself, a form of aggression, casting them as bad and untrustworthy, deserving of punishment for their action. But instead of judging them, let's understand why they did what they did and then make an appropriate intervention. Even something as simple as a timeout for a kid or incarceration for a convicted felon can be perceived, by the punished, as an act of aggression.

Sometimes aggression is not that obvious. For example, "passive-aggressive" action. In this case, a person does not overtly or obviously display their aggression, but may do so by being late for work, forgetting to do a task, mistakenly breaking something, or (in psychotherapy sometimes) talking so softly they cannot be heard without enormous effort! It is a desperate attempt to take some control when feeling powerless. In most cases, the aggression is because the person feels inadequate and devalued: in essence, a perception of being disrespected.

I use the word perception purposefully. Sometimes, no disrespect is intended, but is perceived based on the history and influence of the domains on the current I-M. Human beings have brains that intuitively compare sets of information, and sometimes these comparisons lead to an assessment that, while an I-M, may yet be a distortion of reality. The I-M Approach allows one to help the other person assess the veracity of their analysis, while maintaining respect for their interpretation. Applying the I-M Approach, one does not run the risk of exacerbating this misperception and inadvertently reinforcing and activating a further limbic response. When you are disrespectful to me, and I see that as an I-M, I can move away from taking it personally; I won't feel personally threatened and my own limbic system will not activate the fight-flight mechanism. I will not respond in kind with disrespect. Seeing someone else at an I-M decreases *my own* potential for aggression. And when the other person recognizes that I am not going to retaliate with aggression but with a position of respect, their own limbic response is influenced, and they can shift *their* brain to their PFC. The distortion and misperception of threat can be reframed. Using the power of respect, you can decrease the potential for violence and aggression.

Unfortunately, such misperception is not confined to individuals. Sometime rules and regulations themselves are used as an expression of aggression: weapons disguised as laws which suppress the rights of others. Aggression can be physical, emotional, but also economic and political. Entire cultures can oppress another, using laws and rules to justify that oppression.

Entire nations and races can perceive that they have been disrespected, or fear being seen as weak and vulnerable and so preemptively respond with an act of threat or violence to ward off possible aggression. Sometimes the "best" a nation can do is be threatening. I believe that, using the I-M, entire nations can reduce the risk of a "limbic response" to another member of our global community.

The I-M is not confined to an individual but to an *entire* system. A nation has an I-M. The Home Domain is the country, its resources, borders, economic viability, and so on. The Social Domain is its interaction with the global community including trade, tariffs, alliances, conflicts, and the like. Its Ic is the way it sees itself as a nation within the global community, and how it thinks it is seen. And the Biological Domain is its people. And each of them has an I-M. On a global level, it is still the perception of disrespect that drives many of these national interactions, and the potential for dangerous and violent engagements. How will things be different when we see each nation simply at an I-M given the influence of the domains?

And of course, within nations, population segments have an I-M, as well as the perception and often sad reality of being treated with disrespect. From skin color to gender to religious belief, this has been an unfortunate dark side of the Ic, though it must still be seen as an I-M—not necessarily to be liked or condoned, but respected given the context and influence of the domains. This aggression may be hard to see, hidden behind the phenomenon of unconscious bias. For example, while racism can be overt, we may unwittingly be applying our own bias when we treat others certain ways, when we assume something about them based on the color of their skin or the way they talk. We can be biased towards another person because we are judging them as less-than without appreciating them at their I-M. We are all capable of aggression, even if it does not fit with the Ic we want to have of ourselves.

The I-M Approach allows us to really look at ourselves without judgement, without the fear that we will also be less-than because of our biases. If we can't look at ourselves, how are we meant to change? How can you change if you don't know why you do what you do? The I-M Approach reminds us to relax, to wonder, and to move to another I-M if we don't like our current maximum potential.

Prejudice, bigotry, and racism is still an I-M. These forms of aggression must be understood in the context of our deep biological influence on the other three domains. And our own anger and disdain towards those who disdain lead to the activation of our own limbic system.

The I-M Approach recognizes this is happening, but then gives us the roadmap to step back and again-look at why that other person is at *their* I-M. While morally outraged, personally, when I view these behaviors through the lens of an I-M, it changes my understanding of their actions. I can make a small change in myself and become a different *influence* rather than simply reactively judgmental of those who are judgmental. Rather than judge, I can wonder what the reason is that some people are angry with other people. What are the influences of the Four Domains so that the "best" this person can do is something that is anathema to my own perspective? Instead of reflexively judging in reciprocity, I can treat them with respect and thereby decrease the succession to aggression and enhance the chance for conversation and influence.

I do not like or condone these attributes of our human species, but they are all too real. If I respond in the same way—stigmatizing the bigot, chastising the racist, outraged at prejudice—I will do the same to them as they do to the others they have placed in the diminished out-group of their world. When I do this, I should not be surprised that there is no opportunity for discourse, as there is no trust. Respecting a person's perspective is not the same as liking it. But respect will lead to value of the *person*—not the idea. Once a person feels valued, they can share why they have bias, prejudice, bigotry. If we do not try to again-look and understand why that person does what they do, how can we explore this dangerous influence of the domains?

Even as I write this book, the federal government of the United States has just acknowledged one of the great oppressions committed in our nation's past: slavery. The enactment of Juneteenth as a federal holiday is a way of acknowledging that the I-M of a past America is not the I-M of today. Our entire government is attempting to make amends, take responsibility, and acknowledge that we must unify to remain a United States. This is a small change with a big effect—a huge influence on millions of people and their I-Ms.

Once, while on an inpatient psychiatric unit, the staff needed to keep an area safe and asked all the patients to go to their rooms. (This was my unit, so the rooms were not locked!) All but one of the patients cooperated. Staff began to get annoyed; they wanted her behavior to change and for her to go to her room. They started to get more insistent, and the woman became more resistant. Until one of the staff came over to her from the other side of the room and gently said to the patient, "It's OK, it's safe. Let me walk you to your room. It's OK." The patient paused for a moment, looked at the staff member, got up, and allowed herself to be led to her room.

After the event was stabilized, the staff and I were able to process what had happened. What most of them didn't know, but the one staff member did, was that when this woman was a young girl, every time she was sent to her room it meant she was about to be physically and sexually abused by her stepfather. That's what she heard when she was told to go to her room. *Not* that this was a way for her to stay safe from the escalation of another patient.

If we don't know the history and influence of the domains, we, too, will be quick to judge why a person does what they do. It is the same when talking with a person who is racially prejudiced, or misogynistic, or in any form disrespectful to another person. When we apply the I-M Approach, we have a greater chance of finding out how and why that person has that perspective.

We all want to be viewed with respect. It is, indeed, the golden rule of "do unto others." But, as one of my colleagues Dr. Angela Crutchfield notes, there is a *platinum* rule: treat others as they would want you to treat them. I believe this approach is valid in order to make any meaningful shift in moving the I-M from one current potential to another. Understanding the influence of the domains in these unfortunate facets of society paves a road to deeper understanding and appreciation between and among us. This is also the power of respect.

As stated before, respect leads to value, and value leads to trust, and trust is the foundation of potential. I believe the best chance of changing these distortions of a person, or nation, or race, or gender is when one is seen at an I-M. When one truly believes the other sees them as valuable, their limbic response of aggression is muted, and they move into a "thinking" mode. The possibility of correcting the distortion that *led* to the sense of being disrespected has the greatest chance of success. For a long time, many people have felt powerless in changing the mind of a racist. We are not powerless. We can use the I-M Approach to unleash the power of respect.

Chip was not powerless. As he began to recognize this, he became less anxious, and in response, less aggressive. He had unleashed his own true power and ability to get along with other children by treating them with respect. Chip had many hats, but each and every one he wore was still an I-M.

SMALL CHANGES CAN HAVE BIG EFFECTS

Have you ever put yourself down or doubted yourself? In a way, this is a form of aggression towards yourself. You can use the I-M to change this doubt. Why do you see yourself that way? What are the influences of the other three domains that this is your Ic? Just that small change will shift your brain from the limbic to the PFC, and let you think things through so you can take another step towards success.

YOU CONTROL NO ONE BUT INFLUENCE EVERYONE

Have you put someone else down? Not believed in them? Used your disrespect of them as a weapon? Is that the influence you really want to be? Have they become angry and hostile in response? No surprise there! Instead, help them rekindle their sense of value, reframe your doubt of them as an exploration of who they are and why they do what they do. It will take time, as trust will need to be rebuilt. But it can be done. Respect leads to value and value leads to trust. And trust, dramatically, decreases the need for aggression.

CHAPTER 19
NO WAY DID I WANT TO DIE

People who use drugs and alcohol can get medically ill, just like anyone. But when they go to the emergency room, all too often any medical illness is overshadowed by the stigma of addiction. Using drugs is seen and treated as a crime. It is often thought that the people who use do not deserve to be treated with respect. Why should we treat them with respect if they do not respect themselves?

Ben, one of my adult patients, had been in recovery for several years when he had a sudden onset of a new illness. He was found on the kitchen floor by his wife, who quickly called an ambulance to transport him to the local hospital. While giving his history, Ben acknowledged he used to be a drinker.

Everything changed.

The next question asked by the ER doc was, "When was the last drink?" Granted, it is important to know that so the patient does not go into alcohol withdrawal seizures or develop delirium tremens.

"He hasn't had a drink in years, right honey?" his wife affirmed, with the slightest inflection of doubt.

"Seven years, eight months, four days." Ben carried his history not as a scar but as an open, festering wound. Not to himself. But to the cadre of clinicians who shifted their assessment.

"Oh, he's an alcoholic."

Ben's wife paged me from the ER.

"They think he's been drinking."

I spoke with the ER docs, assuring them Ben was not only sober but was in active treatment, attended meetings, and was on medication to assist him in his desire to remain sober. Something else was going on that led to him being on the ground.

Ben was admitted to the medical floor for observation.

That day (and every day), I made sure to redirect the other clinicians. To be sure they knew that this man in front of them was a wonderful, creative person who'd had a challenge with alcohol in the past and carried the memory and a cirrhotic liver.

As Ben began to feel safe enough to tell his story, he admitted falling several days before but that he was too ashamed to seek help after cutting his head. He used to show up at emergency rooms like that before, just another drunk who had injured himself, and was stapled together with no attempt to try to carefully suture the growing gashes of a disrupted life. He did not go to seek help those few days ago, when an infection could have been prevented, perhaps too proud but definitively aware that he would be treated like a pariah, our modern-day leper, labeled as a drunk. Why would he want to seek help?

Repeatedly, I made sure to re-frame the impressions on part of the clinical team as he lay feverish and confused. Something else was driving his current illness. This was not the residua of an alcohol-related injury. He was in heart failure, but just days before, his heart was whole. Just a few days before, he was living and laughing and spending his moments as any of us do every day: cooking a meal, laughing with his family, calling a friend, creating a unique influence on the world around him. But that day, his body failed, and seeking help, he was at risk of the shroud of addiction which hid him like a cowl and blindfolded the eyes of the emergency room team.

He was eventually found to have a bacterial endocarditis, an infection requiring a heart valve replacement, which he received and for which he was grateful. By not seeing him as "just an addict," the clinical team was helping to heal his heart.

* * *

The adolescent is extremely vulnerable to life-long addiction, simply by the way the brain and the Biological Domain develop. The teenage brain wants to feel pleasure, take risks, and be social. An unfortunate set-up for drugs and alcohol. Like a person ready to bungee jump off a suspension bridge into a crevasse, the adolescent limbic system, pleasure seeking and impulsive, is ready to jump, the thrill of the limbic rush propelling them off the bridge. Sometimes, fear can paralyze the jumper, but sometimes that fear is a good thing! Other times, the fear of being seen a particular way overcomes the fear of smashing several hundred feet below on your face, so saving "face" causes you to risk losing your face. We, as prefrontal adults, just have to be sure the bungee cord is tied tight enough to bring the teenager back from the brink of a possible disaster.

Kefi was fifteen years old and in the ninth grade. She had bungee jumped after she overdosed on several dozen pills of Klonopin, Ativan, and Xanax—all highly addictive anti-anxiety prescription medicines—along with a similar amount of Percocet and Vicodin, highly addictive opioid pain killers. The overdose had almost killed her and were it not for a stay in the intensive care unit of a very good hospital, she could easily have died.

She sat across from me in my office, her cropped bangs barely brushing the top of her eyebrows, looking serious and determined. Kefi told me somberly of her experience.

"I'm ready. I really am this time." Insisting she was now ready to stop all drugs forever, Kefi regarded her revival as God's way of giving her a second chance. She was now committed to a sober life, having first been committed to an inpatient psychiatric hospital, where she had been transferred after being deemed medically stable enough to leave the ICU. There, she had spent a week on a locked

213

psychiatric ward, unable to leave, having to ask if she can go to her room, unable to unlock even the bathroom door without permission. The experience was eye-opening as she described other teenagers much, much more impaired than her.

"Some of them were crazy! A bunch had even tried to kill themselves on purpose," she remarked incredulously. "At least I didn't do that."

"No? Taking all those pills wasn't trying to kill yourself?" I asked during our first meeting. "What happened?"

The story I am about to tell you is true, one of many which, after hearing, I wonder *what were these kids thinking*? And then, I realize that in some ways they weren't. Of course, we are always thinking, wondering, but not always planning or anticipating the consequence of our actions. This is especially true in adolescents, a function of the differential maturity of the brain. The question in this regard is less, "What were they thinking?" and more, "What were they *feeling*?"

My patient had planned on sharing. This virtue, taught in preschool, had unfortunately extended to her current set of friends, many of whom were using drugs and alcohol like her. It was Friday, and the weekend beckoned intriguingly. Kefi carried in her pocket the little baggie full of Klonopin, Ativan, and Xanax, along with Percocet and Vicodin, absolutely ready to distribute them freely to her three best friends. The four of them were going to go somewhere after school and get high. In this one event, her teenage brain was going to do the three things it wanted: to feel pleasure, take risks, and be social.

This was new drug territory for Kefi. Even as, a minute before, she had somberly told me of her intent to be sober, the memory of the anticipated moment surrounded her voice with a cadence of exuberance. This is not uncommon when listening to the drug stories of my patients but does not exclude their desire for sobriety. Most of them at that moment are just hours away from having used, and the deep dopamine drive is not yet fully at bay. But in their heart of hearts, they *want* to be sober. Unfortunately, addiction does not happen in the heart. It happens in the brain.

Having no idea of the effects, however, or how long they would take to work, Kefi took two or three pills on her way to school with the intent of sharing the other thirty or so with her friends. She didn't really feel anything for a while, but her teachers seemed to notice a difference. In fact, when she started to fall asleep in class, one of the teachers took Kefi down to the principal's office, fairly sure her student was on drugs.

Kefi sat in the waiting room for the principal. Telling this part of the story, her voice changed from the euphoria of using to the anxiety of being caught. She was about to get in serious trouble. "I started to *think*, Dr. Shrand, I mean really think. If I got caught with drugs on school property, especially like a baggie full, which looked like I was trying to sell the stuff, I was going to get expelled. Poof. There goes college, and I'm a junior and I have a plan to go to like, the West Coast. So, I started to get a little panicked."

And now comes that amazing moment where I listen to a brain caught in the developmental turmoil where impulses emerge before a well-formed thought. Kefi had a baggie full of pills. She had to get rid of them. Having a positive drug screen, if they did one, would perhaps get her a suspension, but more likely a warning. She was a good kid and had never been in drug trouble before. But getting caught with pills would nail her. So Kefi decided to flush them, get them out of sight once and for all.

But instead of flushing them down the toilet, Kefi flushed them down her esophagus. As she sat in the waiting room, with a water fountain just outside the door in the hall, she surreptitiously pulled the baggie out of her pocket, deftly emptied the contents into her hand, threw, like seeds, the pills into her mouth, and as she got up to go to get a drink from the fountain, shoved the barren baggie back into her pocket.

"What were you thinking?" I asked, with a trained inflection in my voice designed to present an image of slapping your forehead with the palm of your own hand as you wonder just that. "You could have died from all of that," I added with all the aplomb of Captain Obvious!

215

"I know, I know," she said in astonishment and agreement, without a shred of impertinence. "But I really wasn't trying to kill myself. I just didn't want to get into trouble."

OK, so this is where I had to stop and scratch my head. Here is such a wonderful example of the immediacy of thought inherent to a teenager. Despite their growing ability to abstract, to write poetry, for example, to explore the nuances of American History, to learn a language—their brains, in part, are still all about here and now. "I don't want to get in trouble *now*," not even considering that taking all those pills could kill her. This absolutely was not a suicide attempt. This was the prefrontal cortex of the brain succumbing yet again to the impulse-driven limbic logic. *Of course* it made sense to take all the pills. She had to get rid of the evidence!

Knowing how the brain works is not an immunization for my constant amazement at how the brain works. Kefi was not a stupid girl. She would get to college. She had the grades she needed to be competitive at very good universities. Taking the pills was not about stupidity. It was about the danger inherent to the three great loves of being a teenager: taking risks, feeling pleasure, and being social. All three were at play with Kefi and the pills episode, but as she said herself, "No way did I want to die."

Kefi was bungee jumping. Any teenager could be a Kefi. Not necessarily by taking an accidental overdose, but by taking any action that may make an adult scratch their head and say, "What were they thinking?" Why on earth would she take such a chance? How did her fear of being caught outweigh the fear of dying from an overdose of pills? Was it fear that gripped her limbic system? The fear of being seen a certain way so intolerable that her only choice was to get rid of the evidence? Now. Immediately.

The adolescent makes decisions based on past experience, which is limited but attributed to the current situation. Unfortunately, how can anyone know their experience is "limited" when they are an omnipotent teenager, intoxicated by the growing awareness of who they are? Perhaps a much younger Kefi was about to be caught by her mom, having taken an unauthorized cookie, and quickly swallowed it to get rid of the evidence. Perhaps, at another time, she had been in a situation where she was scared and hid to avoid a danger rather than run away or try to fight. Perhaps she had been bullied, ostracized, and the only way she could make friends was to take a shortcut and hang out with the cool kids smoking weed. Perhaps she had simply been so overwhelmed with fright of being caught by the principal that her thoughts turned to survival at that moment only, not the moment five minutes from then.

So Kefi swallowed the pills. And almost died as a result. She jumped off the bridge and we, the adults, were the cord that tethered her. It was an adult that recognized she was drugged. An adult who called the ambulance. An adult who drove her to the hospital. An adult who triaged her, lavaged her, intubated her, got her into the ICU, saved her life. Many, many adults were the bungee cord, bringing back this teenager from the precipice of a deathly jump off a bridge from which she need never have propelled herself. Bungee jumping.

To bungee jump and survive, one has to use a cord, which stretches and recoils, pulling you back up to the top of the bridge then relaxing and contracting as you bounce up and down. In many ways, we adults are the cords. We adults are meant to have outgrown the vagaries of development, enjoying the maturation of our ability to curtail that lusty limbic logic with a cortical cognition of consequence: an appreciation that actions do indeed have outcomes. But we have to practice what we preach. We must be cautious not to judge the adolescent, as our actions have consequences as well. How *we* become that bungee cord for our kids will have an influence on the brains of our teens. How they perceive *our* perception of them has incredible impact. Do we want to perpetuate the limbic logic by shouting, by going limbic ourselves? Or model mindfulness and cortical control, helping our kids understand the dilemma they face, through no fault of their own but simply a result of evolution?

Knowledge is power, and our new understanding of the teenage brain has got to be a part of how we develop our appreciation of the teenage mind. Their brains may not be their fault, but they are their responsibility. Kefi was indeed lucky, but how she walks her path of sobriety will take more than luck. It will take careful guidance, a carefully tempered cord. Not too constricting, not too loose, not umbilical, but flexible for her to safely take her next jump and hopefully not recoil into the world of addiction but instead rebound into a commitment to sobriety. No way did she want to die, and perhaps now she was ready to jumpstart her cortical cognition of consequence.

Kefi began to learn about her amazing brain during our group therapies. She learned that one of the great risk factors for first-time substance use is low self-esteem.

"I had been bullied," she admitted in group. Towards the end of middle school, she had decided to hang out with those same bullies, the popular girls, the ones who stank of weed on the school bus at 7:27 in the morning. She had her first hit of weed in the spring of eighth grade.

Kefi also learned that the teenage brain is often an impulsive brain. Over time, the brain matures. Brain maturation is measured by a brain substance called myelin. The brain is made up of brain cells, called neurons. Neurons are like electoral wires, transmitting information from one cell to another, sometimes thousands of other neurons. Like any electrical wire, they work better when insulated. This insulation is called myelin and is produced by glial cells that wrap themselves piece by piece around the neuron. The more myelin, the more mature the brain.[15]

At the base of the brain is the brain stem, responsible for automatic things like heart rate and breathing. The brain stem is fully myelinated at birth, ready to go. Babies born without functioning brain stems die and do not get to have babies of their own. Sitting on top of the brain stem is the limbic system, which we have spoken about a lot in this book. It is only partially mature and myelinated at birth. You already know that the limbic system is responsible for impulses, memory,

---

[15] Your brain is only 10 percent neurons and 90 percent glial cells. For a long time, the glial cell was considered merely a servant of the neuron: not doing much, certainly not "thinking." This now-disproven idea led to the mistaken belief that we only use 10 percent of our brain.

emotions, and pleasure. And you now know that it is also the place where addictions start.

Covering the limbic system is that massive part of the brain we call the neocortex. This part of the brain is also partially myelinated, a complex world responsible for all of our senses, our movement, and our thinking. We have all seen babies squiggle around, but they are not slam-dunking basketballs. The motor cortex responsible for moving arms and legs and everything is only partially myelinated at birth: enough to suck down food, rock around and cry, but not much else.

The brain matures from the bottom up. Which means that, at some point, the limbic system is actually more myelinated and in charge of the brain than the neocortex, in particular the prefrontal cortex responsible for thinking, solving problems, executing a plan, and anticipating what will happen next. The PFC also happens to be where theory of mind is living. This is why teenagers are at such risk for addiction; they may use drugs without being able to think about the future and what will happen next.

Kefi learned that if you start using drugs or alcohol after the age of twenty-one, 1 out of 25 people are at risk for life-long addiction. But if you start using before the age of eighteen—"I did," acknowledged Kefi and every kid in the group—that number goes from 1 in 25 to . . . do you want to guess?

1 in 4.

1 in 4—just because the way the brain is developing.

Kefi absorbed all this knowledge and had an epiphany.

"That happened to me. That's why I swallowed those pills. I wasn't thinking about the future."

Like Kefi. And like Timmy.

Timmy sat across from me, a tall, thin, lanky fellow, more distracted than discouraged or distressed. Most of the time, his eyes wandered away, not impolite, but with a clear message that this meeting was not high on his pleasure list. He was tolerating me. Timmy was seventeen years old, admitted for the second time in six days for smoking weed. His parents had not sent him back to the first rehab.

From their perspective, it clearly had not worked as their son relapsed in less than a week.

Given his relapse so soon after being in treatment, some would wonder about his sincerity and commitment to sobriety. His family was so disappointed that they were contemplating sending him to a much longer-term program, something like Job Corps, as they could not control him. The juvenile courts were involved, he was dropping out of school, and he had relapsed within a week.

I was curious.

"Why six days?" I asked him. "Why not seven, or five? Why six?"

He slowly returned his gaze, with some growing recognition that this was a different kind of question. "I don't know." He succinctly replied.

"Any guesses?"

As an aside, adolescents and kids in general may very often answer "I don't know" to questions. This may, at first, seem a real conversation killer, but it has to be put in context. Kids are in school most of the time and have been conditioned generally to "right" and "wrong" answers. Of course, our "adult" motivations to do things are much more complex, so a kid may truly *not know*. As such, I encourage them to wonder, to guess. Usually this opens the door to ongoing dialogue.

"Anything else happen on day six?"

Without hesitation, he said with more animation in one second than the previous ten minutes combined, "The bike I was working on got smashed."

I found out that Timmy loved to restore antique bikes. He would go to junkyards, pawn shops, and other places where he could buy broken, battered bikes cheap. These he would take into his garage at home, where he had built himself a shop. Vices to hold the bike, tools to delicately take out the bends and crevices with dents and bumps of wear, paint brushes, metal polishers, brake wires, pads, handlebars, seats.

"So, I was restoring this antique bike, a Schwinn 1963 Sting-Ray," (I did not tell him that I was born in 1958!), "I got it from this guy for ten bucks and it was really beaten up. Dr. Shrand—this is a *classic* bike. When I got it fixed, I could have sold it for plenty of money. I saw handlebars on eBay for twelve bucks . . . *just* for the handlebars!

"So, I'm fixing this bike. I love doing this stuff. So, I've just finished painting it. I got it right after I got out of rehab. It was my treat, you know, so I wouldn't smoke weed. I mean, I love doing these bikes. You start off with a piece of junk and you make it into something anyone would want. And I'm moving it real careful, 'cause I don't want to scratch it or mess up the paint, and somehow I bumped into this huge crowbar and it just smashed right down on it and it was crushed. It smashed right through the spokes and bent up the frame. There was no way I could fix it. So, I got so bummed—I just smoked."

"Ah. A blunt just materialized out of the air, right there in front of you? Like poof, 'Hey what's this? A blunt!'"

"Nah, I had to call my buddy and get some money and we went and bought some weed."

"And that took how long?"

"I don't know. An hour?"

"So, if the bike hadn't been smashed?"

"I'd be sober. I love doing bikes."

"And if you could choose between the pleasure of restoring bikes and getting stoned? You could only have one."

"Bikes! I could do it forever." Without hesitation. This guy got more pleasure from restoring antique ("antique"!) bikes than from getting high. The human brain wants to feel pleasure. This is critical to understand addictions and also how to treat them.

Every time you use a drug to avoid a feeling, you begin convincing your brain you are not strong enough to deal with that feeling. (Does the name Pavlov ring a bell?) If you don't think you are strong enough to deal with being angry, anxious, or sad, those feelings don't go away, they get worse. But your brain says, "Hey, what are you waiting for? You know how to get rid of these feelings. Use!" And you begin creating the very feelings you were trying to avoid to begin with.

As Kefi, Timmy, and Ben learned: it's an I-M. But rather than judge or blame themselves, which only increased those feelings, they could use the I-M Approach like a roadmap, step back and look-again, respect themselves and remember, "Of course, I am strong enough to deal with these feelings."

You can't have a trigger without a memory, and those memories live in the limbic system: the ancient, irrational, impulsive part of our reptilian brain where emotions live and addictions start. But the limbic system does not plan. Solving problems, planning, executing the plan, and anticipating the outcome of that execution (anticipating the future), lives in a part of our modern mammalian brain called the prefrontal cortex. That limbic impulse to use has to then harness the prefrontal cortex to make a plan: how to get the substance that your limbic system has been trained and conditioned to use to get rid of those feelings. That's what Timmy did. The metal bar crashed down on his bike, crushing his dream and his pleasure. That small change had a big effect. Kefi could not see much further into the future than the few minutes before she was about to be searched and get in trouble, so she took all the pills. It was still a plan, but that small change had a big effect.

When a person in recovery learns that being triggered is not a defeat but an I-M, that small change can have a big effect. At some point, you will feel angry, anxious, or sad. Normal. Faced with a danger, our limbic system activates survival mode. Having all these feelings is *normal*. There is nothing wrong with a feeling. It's what you do with it that matters. Using the I-M Approach, you can learn to recognize the trigger, and be reflective instead of reflexive. You can shift from the limbic to the prefrontal. You can anticipate what will *really happen* if you use. You know—nothing good. That is your moment to make a different plan. *Make a different plan.*

Timmy and Kefi were just doing what the teenage brain is designed to do: take risks, feel pleasure, and be social. But Timmy was learning that the real pleasure was from feeling successful, being productive, enjoying the pleasure of taking something that others had thrown away and making it valuable again.

Both Kefi and Timmy were beginning to do the same for themselves. Reclaiming their value like a restored bike.

CHAPTER 20
I-M PERSPECTIVE: PLEASURE

We all want to feel pleasure. That's normal. Our brain has several chemicals, or neurotransmitters, that produce that experience. There are many kinds of pleasure. Among the most succinct and sought after is the pleasure of relationships, of connection, of feeling valuable to someone else. Ben experienced that in his marriage. There's the pleasure of doing something you love. Timmy experienced that when repairing and selling bikes. There's pleasure you get when someone reminds you of your value or you remind someone of theirs, and the pleasure of trust. The brain chemical involved in this pleasure is called oxytocin (not *oxycontin*). It is the neurochemical of trust—that feeling you get when someone says, "You are amazing."

Remember that little boy playing baseball with his dad? The kid who couldn't hit, catch, or throw but his dad said to him, "You were amazing out there." The smile on that boy's face was because his brain was being flooded with oxytocin. He trusted his dad and kept trying.

Feeling angry, anxious, or sad is the antithesis of feeling pleasure. Many people start using drugs or alcohol to feel some pleasure and mask their anger, anxiety, or sadness. But this type of pleasure can lead down a very slippery slope. The brain likes it! If the brain is going to choose between fear or anger or sadness or pleasure, it will choose pleasure every time.

Drugs and alcohol activate a different, and actually much more ancient, neurotransmitter: dopamine. Produced in the limbic system, part of our Biological Domain and a more ancient part of our brain than the PFC, the brain chemical dopamine *interferes* with oxytocin. You can get high but the price you pay is trust. Addiction is not about morality, it is about mor*tality*. It's just the way the brain works.

But dopamine can have a ripple effect on all three other domains. A person who uses drugs may be kicked out of their Home Domain, lose their job in the Social Domain, and be seen as a person with less value and morally corrupt in the Ic Domain. They give away the social pleasure of oxytocin to the isolating pleasure of dopamine. It's just the way the brain works. It's an I-M. You make a small change in the Biological Domain with any drug or alcohol, you can have a negative effect throughout the entire system.

I work with kids who are using heroin, alcohol, marijuana, every drug conceivable. Unlike adults, their ability to anticipate the future consequence of using a drug is under-developed. Their limbic systems are more in control of their brains than their PFC. They never could anticipate getting addicted, but they are. Each and every one of the kids now using heroin started by smoking marijuana. Each and every one of them said, "Not me, I'm never going to use heroin. It's just weed. I'm not going to get addicted." But addiction cannot simply be willed away.[16] In their heart of hearts, they want to be sober. But addiction doesn't happen in the heart. It happens in the brain.

Addiction is not about morality; it is about mortality.

There is now compelling evidence that oxytocin can break the loop of addiction.[17] I use this influence of our Biological Domain in my nonprofit group, Drug Story Theater (DST).[18] As a former child actor on the WGBH TV show

---

[16] In my work with people challenged by substance use, I tell them it's not about "will" power—it's about "won't" power. They have plenty of willpower: "I will try that" or "I will try another." What they need is "won't" power: "I won't try that." As I also say to my patients, if you don't have that *first* drink or drug, you don't have to worry about the second one.

[17] Iain S. McGregor and Michael T. Bowen, "Breaking the loop: oxytocin as a potential treatment for drug addiction," *Horm Behav* 61, no.3 (March 2012): 331-39.

[18] www.drugstorytheater.org.

Zoom, and through my work on the stage, I experienced first-hand that rush of hearing an audience applaud, or a stranger coming up and asking for an autograph. That experience of feeling valued is something we can do for each other every day, and I use that to help teenagers in their recovery from drugs and alcohol. When the kids hear that applause, oxytocin flows through their brains, a much better and rewarding social rush than the isolating rush of dopamine.

In Drug Story Theater, my team and I take teenagers in the early stages of recovery and teach them improvisational theater. We then use a therapy technique called "psychodrama" to help the teens create their own shows about the seduction of, addiction to, and recovery from drugs and alcohol. They perform these shows for middle schools and high schools, so the *treatment of one becomes the prevention of many.* In between each scene, the teenagers step out of character and do PowerPoint presentations, teaching the audience about the development of the adolescent brain and why it is at such risk for addiction. The audience takes a pre-show neuroscience quiz, and then the exact same quiz after the show. We are measuring how kids who learn about their brains change their perception about the influence of drugs and alcohol on their relationships and at school. After the show, there is an open discussion between the audience and the DST kids.

The COVID-19 pandemic shut down our ability to have our weekly in-person meetings and rehearsals. My phrase for COVID became: "Adaptation is Innovation." We met every week throughout the pandemic using the video teleconference platform Zoom. COVID-19 shut down our ability to go into the schools. Instead, we responded by sharing a professional video of our middle school show *Second Chances* for schools all over Massachusetts. And we have translated the show into Spanish and Portuguese so we can reach even more teens and their parents. Small changes can have big effects. There may be no "smaller" thing than a virus, but it has had a huge effect on our entire world. Our work had to go on, because COVID-19 is not an immunization against substance use. For some, it may be quite the opposite.

What do teenagers want? To feel pleasure, take risks, and be social. This is a set-up for addiction. But it doesn't have to be. Feeling pleasure, taking risks, and being social sounds like theater to me! Drug Story Theater capitalizes on that impulsivity and spontaneity of the adolescent brain, blending it with the thoughtful planning needed to create a work of art. Improvisational theater is all about trust, value, and respect: everything the I-M Approach supports. Theater is also about planning ahead, waiting for your cue line and responding to it, then giving a cue line to your fellow performer. It begins to connect the impulsive limbic system with the PFC, exercising the latter, shifting our I-M to one that is more thoughtful and reflective: "If I do drugs now, what will happen next."

The kids in DST continue to astonish and amaze me. They are sensitive to the worry that the "seduction" phase of the show will glorify drugs and alcohol, tempting some kids in the audience to want to try it. But they acknowledge that the "addiction" phase is horrible, portraying how much an addict has given away to drugs. We teach the kids that *drugs* did not take anything from the user: they *gave* it away. It was as if the user said, "Here's my brain. I'm not using it. Want it?"

The peer-to-peer power of DST is palpable. The audience of sixth through twelfth graders is always riveted. And every time an audience applauds our DST teens on stage, I know the oxytocin is flowing through the performer's brains just like that little boy playing baseball. It is where the DST kids get their treatment as they try to prevent their peers from ever going down that same path of addiction. That oxytocin high, being valued, is better than any drug or alcohol.

Our DST kids are truly living up to our slogan: The treatment of one becomes the prevention of many. And in so doing, they are living another one of my slogans: Contribute to society to help with your sobriety. When they are helping someone else, they reestablish their value and decrease their sense of sadness, anger, and anxiety.

DST teaches three core concepts:

1. The limbic system of the adolescent is more in control of their brain. DST teaches them how to activate their PFC.
2. Due to this difference, the adolescent brain is more at risk for life-long addiction, presenting a 1 in 4 chance if you use before the age of eighteen as compared with 1 in 25 if over the age of twenty-one.

While we prefer a teen never uses drugs or alcohol, we are asking them to at least use their PFC and wait until they are older, in hopes that, once they get older, their PFC tells them it's not worth it.

3. At any and every moment in time, we can remind someone of their value. We know that one of the greatest risk factors for first-time substance use in kids is low self-esteem. Every time you remind someone of their value, you increase your own value. This brings not just pleasure, but happiness. Using the I-M Approach, we can do that for each other at any and every moment in time. We can remind someone else of their value.

For Timmy, perhaps the highs gained from his bike repairs were the neuro-economic pleasure of money, but more likely the oxytocin accolades from others of a job well-done and the personal pride and accomplishment of taking junk and making it into something "anyone would want." This young man saw beauty hidden beneath the rust and dirt of a discard. With a little effort and care, the splendor was restored, and he felt proud. It was this oxytocin happiness that he would choose over the dopamine and transient pleasure of doing drugs.

For Kefi, she realized that she could still be popular even if she did not do drugs with her current social group. Entering high school and not being popular significantly influenced her Ic. This low self-esteem placed her at risk for first-time substance use, which then quickly progressed to her inadvertent and impulsive overdose.

For Ben, he realized that his substance use had not just affected *his* brain, but the brain of his wife. She still had a hard time trusting him, as the oxytocin in her brain had been influenced by his alcohol use. Until she began using the I-M Approach, she thought he was choosing alcohol over her in their Home Domain. This perception influenced her Ic and then her Biological Domain. As she recognized this was his I-M, the two of them were able to rekindle their oxytocin connection to overcome the selfish seduction of dopamine.

These are amazing kids and people, and it is our mission to help us all remember that. People with addiction are too often seen as the rusted, broken discards of our society, careening out of control and beyond repair. But can we see where others are blind? Where others saw trash, Timmy saw the hidden wonder of a 1963 Schwinn Sting-Ray. The I-M Approach can be a simple tool to reveal, renew, and transform the hidden jewel beneath.

SMALL CHANGES CAN HAVE BIG EFFECTS

Pleasure comes in many forms, not just drugs and alcohol. It is a good thing to experience pleasure, even something as simple as weeding (no pun intended) a garden, creating a piece of art, cooking a tasty meal, exercising, rewarding yourself as being valuable. During COVID, a lot of people began doing something they had been wanting to do for a long time but, with the bustle of life, they just never got around to. It may have been reading a book they never had time to read. Or starting a yoga practice at home. Find something you want to do—and do it!

YOU CONTROL NO ONE BUT INFLUENCE EVERYONE

Finding pleasure in influencing someone else may be a lot easier than you think. When you share something positive with another person, you become a benefactor, which makes our ancient limbic brain just feel safer, calmer, more at ease, and more capable of enjoying the pleasure of being part of a group. When you help someone else feel pleasure, it is amazing how good you will feel yourself.

CHAPTER 21
WHAT DO YOU THINK I AM? CRAZY?

Bobby, a sixteen-year-old boy, had been picked up by the local police while struggling to push eighty-six Walmart shopping carts down a two-lane highway. He insisted he had not stolen them but was taken to the station anyway. His parents were called. They arrived, expecting the worse, and were astonished when the police just released him.

This was not the first time Bobby had been in trouble over shopping carts. He had almost drowned once trying to get one out of the Charles River, where he had seen the shiny metallic glint of an upturned carriage beckoning to him as a siren.

Sitting in my office, Bobby eagerly told me the story. He was lanky, with summer corn-colored hair, breeze-blown and falling jagged over his eyes. His face was turned at a slight angle so his eyes looked over and past me, only rarely making a contact that seemed strained and uncomfortable behind the sharp-toothed jungle of his bangs. His voice sang and snagged with an arrhythmic cadence, although the excitement blossomed with a volume that was slightly too loud and slightly too harsh for the distance between us and the size of the room.

He loved shopping carts. Actually, he explained, not the entire cart but the smooth and elegantly curved base on which the caged container perched, a metal nest waiting to accept the collections of its persuasive guide. The nest he would discard, the wheels he would remove, and he would be left with the graceful steel-shiny flow of the carriage, stripped to its essence.

He loved the flow of the metal, how it curved and snaked in a seamless pattern, each one like the other, each one perfect in its shape and figure. The quest for this object had led him on all sorts of adventures. He had seen the upside-down wheels of one cart forced up in the mud on the banks of the Charles River, waded out into the dirty brown water, lost a sneaker in the gulping sludge, lost his footing, tumbled, drank, sputtered, but grasped to his prize, dragging it to the shore.

In vain. The cart recovered was the wrong kind, an inferior type from a different mega-store. Only Walmart carts had the particular profile that captured his desire. The others had a different style, one which did not provide the sheer pleasure and fascination he sought. He walked home that day disappointed, mud-caked, one sneaker lost forever to the Charles. His solace came at home, a small two-bedroom apartment shared with his parents who had tolerated their son's "hobby" to the tune of twelve cart bases that were stored carefully in the shared confines of the apartment basement, four in their living room, and five in Bobby's bedroom.

The landlord of their previous apartment had objected to the collection. He had threatened to evict them on the grounds that the objects had to be stolen property. They had to get rid of them or they were out.

Bobby calmly told his parents that he would leave and take his prizes with him if they touched his carriages. He did not cry or plead. He simply stated the facts.

His parents found another apartment.

But now they faced another eviction. The collection had, in one swift motion, increased by eighty-six. The local Walmart was relocating. Bobby had approached the store manager and offered to sweep the entire store—acres and acres, football field dimensions—with the enthusiasm of a treasure hunter who had found a long-sunk galleon. He did not want any money. In exchange for his labor, he wanted all the shopping carts.

Eighty-six.

The manager quickly agreed, handed Bobby a whisk, broom, and a large garbage can on wheels, and sent Bobby in an easterly direction, instructing him to go from east to west then north to south as he swept, dusted, broomed his way to his prize.

Over the next several days, Bobby cleaned. He described the experience as would a religious zealot, entranced by the Zen-like meditation and hyper-focus on his mission. He watched as the dust that he collected in Egyptian desert mounds in front of his broom's black bristles collapsed, like a silently falling dune, into the waiting whisk, tipped into the can, from whence a small portion escaped, a wisp of earth-gray powder swirling like a lost and lonely cloud rising like a sandstorm.

His arms grew weak then strong from the methodical back and forth, and he became an automaton, his arm an extension of the broom. He described to me how he thought of nothing else other than the moment he could push the carts that were waiting for him, each carriage with its outer grating raised high to accept the next. And how he would push them, a wagon train of his success, down the road and to his home.

Day after day, into the night, Bobby swept the cornfield-sized superstore. And then it was done. And the manager, good to his word and delighted to both have his store swept and the carriages removed, helped Bobby gather his new family of carts, marshal them together horizontal and stacked, and watched him push his trophies out of the parking lot and into Bobby's world.

The police happened to drive randomly down the road, after Bobby had been pushing for about a mile. They didn't believe him that he had earned the carts, and so took him to the station. The carts were left behind—a choice that Bobby described as much, much more worrisome than going to the police station. It was the driving away, seeing the carts getting smaller and smaller, not knowing if someone was going to steal them. Would they be there when he got back?

The police called his parents, then called the store. Astonished, the police just let Bobby's parents take him home. Down the same small highway, the carts began to appear. Rather than have the insistent Bobby jump out of a moving vehicle, his parents slowed, stopped, and followed their son the 1.5 miles back home, shielding him from the few scattered cars and their drivers rubbernecking past in amazement.

Over our next several sessions, Bobby spoke about nothing other than his shopping cart bases. He told me other adventures experienced during the adventure of collecting. Once, he saw one in a dimly lit alley. It was garnished with old rags, plastic bags hung from its sides and handle. He noticed it was rusty, but the base still held its inexplicable appeal.

He began to wheel it away, out of the alleyway, when filth-caked hands grasped to stop him, hands at the ends of thin but enormously strong arms clothed in the frayed scrap of an old coat. The man, homeless, began to claw at Bobby, pushing him away from the cart and chasing him back out into the street.

Bobby did not give up. He stole a cart from a local grocery store and returned to the alley looking for the vagrant. The Walmart cart was not there. He left the other cart as a hopeful exchange. Bobby told me the story without looking at me, but continued to report his tale to a point just over my shoulder. Although animated, again his voice had a cadence that had erratic rhythm, even as his story approached its climax.

He had been scared by the violence of the man, but his desire for the cart trumped any fear. The next day he returned. Two carts crowded the alley, one with rags and bags and plastic bottles and metal cans, and old blankets, and garbage bags filled with homeless possessions. And next to it was an empty one, the Walmart cart, the sleek beauty of its coveted base newly exposed and waiting.

For the next session, I asked if Bobby could draw a picture of the cart. With the skill of a master craftsman, he brilliantly and methodically created in front of me, line by detailed line, an image emerging in both complexity and simplicity. He only drew the base, describing its features as a lover describes his fresh new love.

"And here is the first curve. See how it wraps right into the next one, right here where the wheels would fit? The frame goes along here, it's straight, really,

really, strong, because it has to hold the whole weight of the cart. Do you know, it can easily carry a hundred and fifty pounds of stuff? But I don't know how anyone would get that much stuff in, unless it was, like, bags of sand or something. I bet it could carry maybe two hundred pounds of sand, or dirt, or stuff."

At first, I thought Bobby had Obsessive Compulsive "Disorder," but he did not describe the anxiety that accompanies the need to perform a behavior to calm the obsessive thought. Instead, he had a clear and soothing fascination, to the exclusion of everything else. He could talk for hours about the carts, never noticing that his audience had long drifted off. To him, the carts were wonderful, exciting, satisfying, complete in their ability to gratify.

He cherished them, lined them up, polished them with Rust-Oleum, became angry and annoyed if they were touched or moved or displaced as his mother tried to clean around them, walk around them, simply live around them. All his extra money earned would go to the care of the carts. He knew the history behind each one: where it had been found, where it had been manufactured, its dimensions to the millimeter, its weight, the composition of the metal.

I asked him if he would bring in pictures and he did. He described, in his arrhythmic intonation, with clear love and awe, the story behind this one, that one, his first one, his latest one, his most cherished, the one that needed the most repair, how he polishes them, how his parents want to get rid of "at least some," but how that would ruin all of them. How is he supposed to choose which one? Which ten? He needs them, wants them, loves them all.

He didn't want to go on any medicine, and neither did his parents want him to. He had no other obsessions, did well in school, although he didn't have any friends, none at all. He had always been the kid on the outside of the playground, with difficulty fitting in, but not really seeming to care. He thought he had plenty of friends. They would do things with him, then laugh. He had no idea why. He would tell them about the carts, invite them over to see the collection, but they never came. He didn't mind. After all, he could understand that perhaps they were jealous because the carts were his, and who wouldn't want one?

But he did not want to give any of them up, not even for his parents. Several sessions were spent helping Bobby to appreciate his parents' point of view. We explored the difference between how the carts made Bobby feel and how his collection impacted his parents, where they lived, how it encroached on their *space* but never on the love they had for their son.

As the sessions progressed, I began to see Bobby as having Asperger's Syndrome (AS), a particular form of autism.[19] He was of normal, perhaps above-normal intelligence, but had difficulty intuitively understanding what other people were thinking or feeling. Very often, these kids are profoundly misunderstood as we all expect someone else to at least *pretend* to appreciate what we think or feel.

Some people with Asperger's have very narrow interests, but an encyclopedic knowledge of the subjects. Bobby was fascinated by shopping carts. He could tell me the weight, the dimensions, the alloys that went into the manufacturing process. While I was fascinated with Bobby's intrigue, as a window into who he was and why he did what he did, I could imagine his friends or teachers, perhaps even his parents, becoming fatigued and annoyed with his ongoing dissertations about the merits of the shopping cart frame.

His single-mindedness also got other people angry at him, as they felt he was being disrespectful. For example, he would not be able to understand what the social expectation was in that moment in time, seen as oppositional and defiant while simply being oblivious to the situation.

Indeed, he talked about little else, which led his social environment to constrict. Bobby could not appreciate or recognize that other people thought him odd, and then boring, and then disturbing because he didn't *get* that other people saw him as odd, boring, and insensitive. Why did he just keep talking when he should know that no one cared? Or worse, they thought he was trying purposefully to aggravate them. And was boring!

---

[19] DSM-5 merged Asperger's into the broad category of Autistic Spectrum "Disorders."

But Bobby seemed not to be influenced by other people's perception of him. Instead, he was happy as he described to me his interest. He had a rich internal emotional life, even if he could not appreciate that of mine or any others. There was not a malicious bone in his body. He never went out of his way to hurt someone else and could be kind and generous. Indeed, he could easily be exploited by other people, as he had no hidden agendas, and did not expect anyone else to have one either. He simply loved to collect shopping carts.

His parents had never heard of Asperger's Syndrome. As I went through the symptoms, their eyes widened, and his mother began to cry softly. "That's him. That's Bobby." She looked over at her husband. "And some of that is you, too!" As his parents became more educated about their son, they could recognize how he had never intended to "hurt" or "disobey" them, but was simply oblivious to their inner wants, needs, desires, thoughts, and feelings. He loved them without doubt, but they always thought he didn't really "care."

Their relief was palpable. And so was Bobby's. He had always known he was a little different than the other kids, and he wanted to get along with them but just didn't know how. So it was easier to just keep away. He wished he had a friend, but didn't know what to do to get, and keep, one.

As he came to understand his own personal AS, he became determined to learn how to recognize the thoughts and feelings of others. He began to realize that facial expressions actually carry meaning about the inner, hidden world of a person's emotions. He realized he could learn what they meant and began to practice like a person practicing a musical instrument.

As a result, Bobby worked first on understanding the emotions of his parents, and the impact on them of his hobby. With this insight, Bobby was able to see that a compromise was needed. He had never intended to burden his parents and had not connected their having to move from place to place with his cart collection. In fact, he thought that if he felt that way about carts, then everyone must feel the same. He was perpetually astonished that other people didn't. Although never a fluid understanding, he began to recognize that his parents had their own thoughts and feelings as well. He became tearful in one of the sessions, perhaps as he began to recognize how much he had missed as he'd grown up.

As Bobby became more aware of his parents' feelings, he also became more flexible and eager to please them. Bobby agreed to let his parents explain his AS to their landlord. They were fortunate to have a landlord who listened and appeared to understand.

As a result, his parents were able to work something out with the current landlord. There was a large storage area in the apartment complex, and it was agreed that if Bobby helped mow the lawns and keep up the grounds for a few hours a week, he could keep his carts in that area. He and his parents agreed that he could keep three carts in his room, and he would rotate them from the shed where the others were stored once a week.

This arrangement was acceptable to Bobby.

The therapy began to draw to a close. At the last session, reviewing the drawings, looking again at the pictures, it occurred to me there was a question I had never asked. Here was this boy stricken by these carts, a fascination that had led him to risk in the extreme, and I had never asked him one simple but revealing question.

He looked past me as he usually did when we spoke, and I found myself wondering how he would respond to my inquiry. "Bobby, we've worked together for a couple of months now, and I realize I never asked you this: You talk about the shopping carts, where you found them how you take care of them, what they look like, and I wonder—given how much they mean to you, how much trouble you go to polish them and keep them neat and organized—have you given them names? Like, 'this one from the river is Sally,' or 'the one from the playground is Jeff,' or 'this one's Timmy and this one's Sheila.'"

Bobby moved his eyes from behind me, from that fixed point on the wall. For the first time in the *entire* time we had met, his eyes looked straight into mine. They grew wide in amazement, as if I had finally stumbled on a most important, undisguised component of his passion. I felt that feeling a psychiatrist gets right before an enormous insight, anticipating a revelation that would break open the mystery of his absorption.

His eyes riveted to mine, his voice was clear and with a beat and measure I had not heard before. Bobby spoke.

"Give them names? What do you think I am? Crazy?"

It was our last session.

CHAPTER 22
I-M PERSPECTIVE: HAPPINESS

Bobby loved shopping carts. They made him happy. In previous chapters, I have explored the I-M in the context of crime, aggression, diagnosis, and other aspects to suggest that at any moment in time we are all at an I-M. So why not happiness as an I-M? Why not contentment, self-esteem, value? For Bobby, shopping carts made him feel complete.

Bobby likely had a form of autism called Asperger's Syndrome. Autism has a wide variation of presentations, from the most severely challenged to this high functioning but somewhat idiosyncratic form called Asperger's Syndrome or AS.[20] In AS, the core "deficit" is difficulty understanding the thoughts and feelings of other people. It is a developmental delay of theory of mind, the Ic Domain. Bobby had no idea that his fervent desire to obtain shopping carts had an enormous impact on his family. He had no idea that he had been exploited by the Walmart manager who paid Bobby in shopping carts to clean a store the size of three football fields. Bobby was oblivious, but happy. Bobby respected himself and took pride in his passion for his shopping carts. This presented an interesting window into the Ic Domain.

---

[20] While the term *Asperger's* was subsumed under the broader term *Autistic Spectrum*, it is still a distinguishable condition, and is towards the more "functional" side of the spectrum. Famous Aspergian's include Bill Gates and Elon Musk.

But theory of mind develops in two parts: The second part, the part most studied, is the ability to take someone else's perspective. But the *first* part is wondering what perspective another person has of you. That part was intact in Bobby, who clearly demonstrated this when he challenged me in the last session saying, "What do you think I am? Crazy?" Bobby had an interest in what I was thinking about him at that time.

I look back on those sessions with Bobby and wonder if my last question to him was perceived as disrespectful. Here was a young man perfectly content in his fascination and love of his cart collection. He was happy, and how others thought or felt about his impact on them had no inroad into his self-contentment.

This insight into AS suggests that individuals on the autistic spectrum may be unable to fluidly apply empathy but are still aware of how they are being treated; they just may not know why. Without an intuitive ability to apply theory of mind, they may find that another person is angry with them but will have no idea how that person got there. Despite Bobby's AS, he could still appreciate when other people were angry at him, proud of him, liked him, but was not always sure *why* they were experiencing these emotions.

The I-M is just as applicable here as anywhere. Bobby was happy. In his world, he was successful, capable, competent, an expert in Walmart shopping carts. The way he saw himself, his Ic, was certainly not as "crazy."

When we first met, Bobby was less concerned about how his collection impacted on his parents, how they felt about having to move from place to place to accommodate him, and he had little empathic response at their distress. He could see they were upset, but had no clue as to why; how could his passion be the root of their discomfort? Without meaning to, Bobby may have activated the fight-flight limbic response in people around him because they *perceived* his actions as disrespectful.

This happens frequently to people with AS and other conditions who only have the first part of theory of mind. We explored this in "The Two Gifts," as Brenda shut down her ability to appreciate the thoughts and feelings of others and was deemed "borderline" as a result. When we believe that our thoughts and feelings don't matter to someone else, we get angry, and feel disrespected. AS offers a window into not only the world of a person who is challenged in empathy, but also into each of us who has ever felt disrespected, or at least *perceived* we are being disrespected.

The I-M Approach removes all of this potential for misunderstanding. It is a roadmap to communication between each other, and in that lies the potential power of respect. The I-M leads to an unleashing of this power, promoting a mutual respect.

My traditional approach to Bobby in therapy was relatively unsuccessful despite exploring with him and joining in his excitement about shopping carts. However, as his I-M became more evident, it allowed a shift in the family therapy component, educating both Bobby and his parents about AS. With this small change of shared awareness, they could find a compromise so Bobby could still have his collection, but in a way that did not jeopardize their living situation.

Today I have the honor and privilege of working as medical director of Road to Responsibility, a remarkable organization of people dedicated to and passionate about caring for adults with profound developmental challenges. Some are so challenged that they startle when they see their reflection in a mirror, unable to recognize that it is themselves that they see. This is their I-M. None of these people may have any insight into how I think or feel. But every one of them knows how *they* are treated. Every one of them knows I see them as valuable.

One of the women I work with, I'll call her "Jamie," now in her early sixties, has profound autism. She speaks with no words, just a series of guttural noises to communicate her myriad of experiences. I would meet with her and a staff member every month. Her staff would drive her to one of the group homes, this one in a lovely neighborhood in a suburb outside of Boston. Jamie would sit in the passenger seat, strapped in, a bicycle helmet on her head to protect her from the multiple times a day when she would throw herself to the floor. Each month, I would say hello to her, ask her how her month had been, always tell her about any changes I was going to make in the medicine based on the staff's observations. She made no eye contact, rarely glancing over at me as my arm rested on the open window of the car door. Once a month, the second Tuesday, for over a year.

On one visit, Jamie sat as always, helmeted, strapped in, no eye contact. Her staff told me that Jamie's mother had died since I had seen her last. Without hesitation, I told Jamie how sorry I was for her loss and asked how she was doing. This woman—who had never *looked* at me—then reached out, touched and patted my arm, made eye contact, a sound, a moment. That was one of the total highlights of my entire career. Now, each month, Jamie and I touch hands as I lean in through the car window. She is much more verbal, no words but rumbles a melody of sounds as she glances briefly into my eyes, her own I-M of connection as she responds to my questions. Just the memory of that moment makes me feel *happy*.

In other words, *one does not need to always appreciate someone else's point of view to still afford them respect.* Indeed, we don't always understand each other's motivation right away, and can fall into the trap of fear, anger, and mistrust. When we adopt the I-M Approach of simply seeing that person as doing the best they can, we can then spend the next moments wondering why they do what they do and try to understand the influence of the domains on their current choices. I think this is more likely to lead to a mutual discussion and eventual understanding, without the moral overlay and defensiveness that only serves to activate more resistance and mistrust in each other.

Bobby and his parents are a great example, as is the landlord, who's I-M was willing to compromise and understand Bobby's behaviors in the context of AS. Unfortunately, many children and adults who are like Bobby continue to be misunderstood. Many children are misdiagnosed as troublemakers. Schools and teachers consider their behaviors as oppositional and defiant. Teachers can feel disrespected and challenged, perceiving the student's actions as purposefully trying to undermine and disrupt their authority. Until the lens of AS is understood, until the core difficulty in theory of mind is recognized and appreciated, these kids grow up ostracized, misunderstood, and isolated by others. As they grow older, and their Ic component becomes more active, they begin to recognize that they are being treated differently, often devalued, and can become depressed and isolate themselves. Some become convinced that they truly are useless, worthless, and inadequate. They are more and more aware how others see them, and it is usually with judgment and without respect. This barrage of disrespect, for reasons they have difficulty understanding due to their I-M, is no different than for anyone else who has felt overlooked, misunderstood, or believed they were inadequate in the eyes of others. Even as the I-M Approach hopes to unleash the power of respect, the power of disrespect remains all too evident in our society.

The *power* of respect, however, is in the ability to feel happier, more capable, competent, caring, compassionate, and uniting around the common cause of enhancing ourselves while also enhancing our families, communities, and society. Bobby was not crazy. He had found a passion that gave him pleasure. Despite his not having the second part of theory of mind, when he realized his actions were perceived as being disrespectful, he was able to change. As he recognized how much he influenced other people's thoughts and feelings, he was able to compromise with his family for the common good. Despite his challenge in not having an intuitive sense of empathy, he overcame this by learning that his collection did have an impact on his parents and became willing to modify his own wishes for the collective good. The shopping carts still provided pleasure, but he also experienced happiness as he began to feel respected and understood, and as he began to respect and understand his parents.

Our brain does not get angry when it perceives being treated with respect. This Ic Domain perception then extends into the Biological Domain of our limbic system: we feel good about ourselves when we feel respected by someone else. But Bobby teaches us another remarkable aspect: we can simply respect *ourselves* and feel happiness. When we see ourselves at an I-M, we can respect who we are and why we do what we do without the often depressing overlay of judgement. Seeing ourselves at an I-M is a path to happiness. This is a small change with a powerful effect.

Pleasure is not the same as happiness. Pleasure may be fleeting and transient, sometimes the result of doing drugs, more often the reward of doing something productive for yourself and society. *Happiness is that feeling you get when you feel valued.*

Having practiced psychiatry for more than two decades, I have distilled my understanding of who we all are down to this: In our heart of hearts, a human being simply wants to be valued by another human being. That's what we want, and it is so simple to do. Human beings are very good at helping someone else feel valuable, but we are just as good at devaluing someone. I think that all of my patients have felt devalued at some point, and that is part of why they come to see someone like me, a psychiatrist. All I am trying to do is remind them of their value. Just as my patient was restoring antique bikes, I think we in this profession can restore a sense of value and meaning, and a reminder that no one, *no one* is "broken." But reminding someone of their value is not confined to psychiatry. It is not confined at all. Reminding someone of their value can permeate every Home and Social Domain on our planet and in our universe.

Bobby's story illustrates the power of the I-M even in a person with an Ic Domain that cannot always appreciate and understand what someone else is thinking or feeling. Bobby felt respected by me. Asking if I thought he was crazy was a huge step for a person with Autism. Bobby was truly wondering what I was thinking or feeling. That was a small change with an enormous effect. Bobby was happy. And so were his parents. They had truly unleashed the power of respect, a direct result of recognizing that they had all been, and were still, at an I-M.

SMALL CHANGES CAN HAVE BIG EFFECTS

The vast majority of us are interested in what other people think or feel, but we are especially interested in what *you* are thinking or feeling about *me*. Imagine what happens to a person when they believe that you see them at an I-M, as doing the best they can at this moment in time. This is a small change we can do today, right now.

YOU CONTROL NO ONE BUT INFLUENCE EVERYONE

You can choose to be an influencer who reminds someone else of their value. This unleashes the power or respect. Happiness is deeper and longer lasting than pleasure. It is a state of being that increases the more you share it with others.

CHAPTER 23
RATS!

"I know people think I'm crazy, but I saw it. Hiding under the Coke machine."

Frank had been committed to the locked inpatient psychiatric ward after he was found screaming "Rats! Rats!" while running naked up and down the hallway of a cheap motel. Loping his fifty-two-year-old raw-boned body up and down the hallway, he had drawn some attention to himself as guest after guest, with the chains still attached to the interior of their motel room door, cracked open their entryway just enough to catch the glimpse of a naked man streaking past.

Someone had called the front desk. The front desk had called the police. The police called an ambulance. All of them descended on the motel. Frank was wrapped in a blanket and taken to a local emergency room. There, he repeated his story about seeing rats under the Coke machine where no one else had seen anything but the grime and gelid dust collected by the not-to-be-told memories of this "no-tell" motel.

Insisting that he was not crazy, Frank became more agitated when told he would have to go to a psychiatric hospital for evaluation. He became enraged, tried to leave wrapped only in his blanket, was held, injected, sedated, and then sent anyway.

Now he lay in his bed, drowsy, under the covers, trying to tell me his story. He did not dismiss me despite his sleepiness and my offer to return when he felt more alert. There was a grim determination to have his story heard, believed, to dispel his own personal myth of mental illness.

Delusions are, by definition, a fixed false belief. Frank truly believed he had seen a rat under the Coke machine, even if no one else had seen it. The mind and brain can become fixed and concrete in such beliefs, and a challenge to them by an observer may serve only to have that other person incorporated into the delusion. If a person believes they are being followed and monitored by the FBI, *you* may become part of that monitoring system—another FBI agent, planted, posing as a psychiatrist.

Or the entire hospital may be a façade, other patients no more than actors pretending to be insane so as to draw you into a complacency, or to truly drive *you* insane. "I know there are cameras in the mirrors." "I know the air conditioner is really emitting a poisonous gas." "I won't eat the food because it has medicines hidden in it." "Nurses come and beat me up in the night." "I know—I know—I know. . ."

During the initial stages of treatment, it can be extremely harmful to challenge these beliefs. There are no entry points, no chinks in the armor of the delusion as it permeates the mind of the patient, each event interpreted, incorporated, adding sustenance to the terrifying belief that one is being controlled or observed, manipulated for a reason insidious and malevolent. Those who suffer are often terrified and accept little consolation.

Frank believed there was a rat under the Coke machine. Evaluated in the emergency room, he had appeared psychotic, out of touch with reality.

And he was going to try to convince me otherwise—that he was not insane.

So I listened.

I am a psychiatrist, not a judge. I am simply interested in why people do what they do. While I have to make a "diagnosis," people are much more than the label with which we attribute. Frank had been seen as psychotic, but despite his drowsiness, he was determined to tell his story. He had not incorporated me into whatever process his mind was experiencing. But the medicines he had received were strong, leaving him sleepy and drowsy. As he lay in his hospital bed, eyes lidded, he struggled for wakefulness. His story could wait a few more hours.

"I'll be back in a few hours, and we'll talk. Go back to bed."

"It's not in my head."

"I'll be back." Frank accepted this with a disgruntled flick of his head, tipping up his jaw, settling his head back on the pillow. He closed his eyes, and I left the room.

By the next morning, Frank was clear-headed and ready to talk.

"I don't appreciate your saying it is all in my head," he started. He was terse and tense, angry at me before we exchanged a word. I had come to get him from his room, inviting him for a chat. Walking down the hallway, he would glance around, perhaps responding to voices and sounds that only he could hear. Passing the dayroom where other patients sat and talked, he paused briefly to say hello. The other patients waved, and seemed to shout his name, louder, with more volume than the distance seemed to warrant.

Frank waved back, smiling and with a voice calm and full of animation said hello to each by name, gently locking his eyes to theirs without distress. He then continued to walk after me, his tension and resolve returning with determination.

"It's not in my head," he repeated.

"When did I say that?" I responded, confused. Such a phrase is not in my repertoire, as it reeks of disrespect. And it would push me firmly into his psychotic paranoid process if one did indeed drive his current state of mind.

"Yesterday. And then you left."

"When I left? Yesterday?"

"'It's in your head.'"

"I said, 'Go back to bed.'"

"You did?" Frank looked genuinely astonished, and then abashed.

"'Go back to bed.' You were exhausted, and medicated. This chat could wait."

"Not, 'In your head?'"

I motioned my head gently to say no. "So what's the story?"

"My hearing is not so good."

251

"Just do your best."

"It is a lot of stress."

I went with it. "Go on." And Frank began to open up.

"I run a business degreasing the kitchens of high-end restaurants. I'm going through a divorce and living with my mother. My kid is meant to be in college. I've got huge bills. My shoulder is injured from the degreasing machine. And the noise of it has hurt my hearing."

"That's a lot."

"What have I got? My shoulder is so bad I need pain meds, and I have to go to a doc to get a hearing aid but I haven't had time because I can't leave work because I've got tuition to pay and a mortgage, as well as giving my mom some money for food and rent."

"So what happened?"

"Of course I'm not happy! Are you joking?"

"I said—"

"Drop dead yourself!" Frank got up to leave, infuriated with such a stupid shrink. He paused and turned back. "Did you say 'drop dead?'"

I shook my head no and gestured him to sit back down. He did, and I leaned into him. With a volume to match the patients in the dayroom I said, "Let's start over. I just want to know what happened that got you into the hospital. Just the facts."

"That's right—rats!"

Inside I sighed. I said nothing but gestured for Frank to go with his story. I was just going to listen until he was done.

"So, here's what happened," he started. I gestured for him to go on and he continued. "The other day, I'm at my mom's and I feel like getting a little—you know. So I can't do that at my mom's because it wouldn't be right. So I rent a motel room and make a call. I'm on some Percocet for pain, so I decide to take a little extra and also get a bottle of rum. I'm in my room, waiting for the girl, and I figure I've got to get some ice. So I wrap a towel around me and I'm going to go out into the hallway and get some ice. I'm in the doorway and I look across the hall. There's a Coke machine next to the ice machine, OK? So I'm about to go and get the ice when I see something moving under the Coke machine.

"I work with this big degreasing machine, right, and when I degrease the stoves and those vents, you know, in the restaurants, sometimes I'm blowing all this water—high pressure water—into the nest of some kitchen rat. Have you seen one of those things? They are huge. And fast. So, I've been bitten a bunch of times by these buggers, and sometimes I can't hear them coming, you know, because of my hearing from this damn machine. So I'm really on edge about these rats, right, and keep my eyes out for them, because I can't hear them coming, right, because of my ears.

"So there I am in this hallway, and I see a bugger under the Coke machine. Not one of those mother kitchen rats, but it's still a rat. I mean, it's not like I booked a room at the Ritz, you know. I just wanted some and I couldn't do that at my mom's right? So I'm a little high already from the Percs and the rum, I won't lie to ya doc, and I see this rat. So I lunge at it, because that's what you do when you see one. Lunge at it and it's going to run away, and scream at it, 'RAT!'

"So I do this, right, and my towel gets caught in the door and I'm butt naked and the door closes and I'm locked out and the rat is still there so I keep screaming and the other doors in the hallway open a bit, you know, on their chains, and I'm screaming, 'Look at the rat! It's a rat!' and then I realize I'm butt naked, and I try to get back into my room and I can't, so I start running up and down the hallway and the next thing I know the police are there and the manager and they're carting me away and here I am and—Doc, you gotta believe me, I really don't need to be here. There really was a rat."

Every now and then, a person is seen as psychotic but they're not.

I thanked Frank for his story.

"Gory? What part?"

I discharged him home.

CHAPTER 24
I-M PERSPECTIVE: YOU AND THE I-M

Frank was not psychotic. His behavior was the direct result of the convergence of his Four Domains. He needed to make money to support the family in his Home Domain. To do this, he worked in the Social Domain, but this had an impact on his Biological Domain resulting in hearing loss. His Ic was influenced as he began to feel inadequate to support his Home Domain. And then he entered the Social Domain of a motel, where the I-Ms of the other guests were influenced by his small change of shouting "Rat!" Then the system responded by interpreting the behavior as a danger to society. Frank reacted in response, becoming combative in the ER. He thought I, too, was disrespectful, in this case a distortion of reality not based on a mental "illness" but the biological influence of diminished hearing—the result of the loud cleaning machine he used at work.

It is unlikely we will always be able to immediately understand why someone else is doing what they are doing. Indeed, it may take the individual themselves a long time to understand. But by seeing the behavior as an I-M, it reduces the chances of seeing each other through the dark side of the Ic. Wondering why the other person does what they do is an invitation to a dialogue, a discussion, with the shared goal of understanding. Mutual respect, a direct result of the I-M Approach, is a potentially more productive path to mediation.

I have treated people with disrespect, and I always get the same response: they get angry. Same for you? Has anyone ever had any different response when treated with disrespect? Yes! When you utilize the I-M Approach you can appreciate that even being treated with disrespect is an I-M. You don't have to like it or condone it, but you have to respect it. Then what will happen differently? You will break the potential feedback loop that leads to both parties going limbic.

Have kids? Imagine using this as a technique: when your kid is being disrespectful, you can step back and wonder why this is their current maximum potential. Have parents? Co-workers? Respect leads to value, and it is the foundation of trust. Trust is the foundation of potential. Instead of shouting *at* each other, we can talk *with* each other.

This is not just a "feel good" approach to life. It has deep roots in our Biological Domain—our brain and our body. You *know* that you have a visceral response when feeling disrespected. Sometimes we disrespect ourselves, devalue ourselves, mistrust ourselves. When we feel we have not lived up to our own expectations, we can feel sad, guilty, and angry with ourselves. We can worry we will never be good enough, and will remain inadequate, at risk of being kicked out of our protective group.

While still an I-M, you have to choose which motivates you more: beating up on yourself because you are not doing the best you can, or recognizing that this is not the best you may ever do but that every moment is a current maximum potential based on the Four Domains. With this approach as a roadmap, you can target in which domain you want to make a small change to move yourself to a different I-M. Just forgiving yourself may be the place to start.

This is not about encouraging "bad habits" or enabling yourself to, for example, stay overweight, keep drinking, not go back to school, or not pursue any number of "self-help" things that so many of us value. You are at an I-M, but by exploring the domains, by understanding why you do what you do, you then have choices: you can stay at this I-M or make changes to move to another, one that you like more and are able to condone.

This book has grown out of a belief that when we treat ourselves and one another with respect, we can look at ourselves honestly without fear of finding we are less-than and apply the same to others. When we apply the I-M Approach, we can make a small change that can lead us closer to our own definition of success. That definition will change with every success we achieve. Treating each other and yourself with respect can have positive outcomes. We can all benefit from this simple approach.

A nurse colleague of mine, who was cut off by another driver coming to work, told me about her experience applying it. "At first, I was so mad—that whole road rage thing. But then I thought, 'Well, he's at an I-M,' and I felt my anger going away. He was at an I-M!"

Another friend of mine was recently diagnosed with Type 2 Diabetes. A significant change in his Biological Domain, but still an I-M. He began to make small changes in the other domains. He stopped putting sugar in his coffee and began walking at least fifteen minutes a day. A passionate pizza lover, he used this pleasure to add motivation, indulging in a pizza every Friday night as a reward. He actively responded to the shift in his Biological Domain with purposeful choices in his environment. And as his Ic shifted to seeing himself with diabetes— not *judging* himself—he responded to this shift in I-M by seeing his "diagnosis" as a component of his I-M. As such, he was able to treat himself with respect and make a commitment to his health.

My friend with diabetes and my nursing colleague had both applied the I-M to themselves. Not only do we get calmer when seeing that someone else is at an I-M, we get calmer when we appreciate that *we* are also at an I-M. And when we apply the I-M Approach and treat other people with respect, it unleashes the potential of that person. Nobody can ever truly change anyone else. But they will always have an influence. Because we are always in a low-grade state of vigilance— an ability needed for survival born from the fight-flight response—we are always influencing and influenced *by* every person with whom we come in contact.

Many years ago, I had an experience that highlighted the I-M Approach. I had bought a second-hand car from my local mechanic who I have gone to for years. A few days after purchase, my car's battery light went on. I am not a mechanic, but I knew this was not a good thing. I took it to the shop to have it fixed. I drove away a few hours later, the battery light off and a hundred or so well-spent dollars poorer. Two days later, the battery light went on again. In frustration, I emailed the following to my mechanic, which I cringe today when I re-read:

I am writing relatively annoyed as the engine light came on again after just a few miles of driving. Surely you are not going to tell me you sold me a car that does not work in the rain!

As your phones do not accept messages on the weekend, I am sending you this email. I am going to bring the car in Monday, and this time it is on your dime. I will need a rental car to get to work, which I will also ask you to pay for.

We have been good and loyal customers for many years, spending thousands of dollars in your shop. This is a critical turning point for me, as I need to be able to rely on my mechanic to get the job done, and get it done right the first time. I simply do not have the time or money to waste on multiple visits.

If there is a problem with this, I would like to sit down with you and Paul [the shop owner], so we can come to some resolution. I remind you that we have a similar problem with my wife's car, which we brought in three times. We spent thousands of dollars, perhaps on things that were not needed, as you tried to make a diagnosis. The car *still* has the same problem for which we initially brought it in, all this time and money later. While you are not the mechanic, your shop still holds responsibility for the work.

I know you "don't make them," as someone from your shop said to me, but I rely on you to fix them! And I know you can't predict the future, as someone also said to me, but I expect your shop to provide the best chance that an immediate recreation of the same problem does not occur. I assume this is not an unreasonable expectation from a customer.

Hoping you won't let me down and see you on Monday.

I received this email from him in response:

Dear Dr. Shrand,

You are correct, you have been very good and loyal customers and we truly appreciate this fact. However, I do not feel that your email demands and tone are justified given the facts of this situation and, quite frankly, I'm taken back by your tone.

I would be glad to discuss the recent repair (singular) and diagnose why the car is exhibiting the same symptom for no charge. I feel that you are commingling recent issues of your wife's van and your Lincoln, and you are projecting that in this email. We are here to help and I trust that you feel that we have always been and will continue to be fair to each of our customers.

You are more than welcome to bring your car in today to be looked at.

My letter of frustration had been perceived as disrespectful, and my mechanic responded defensively, referring to my "tone." Of course, I responded with another email:

An unfortunate side effect of email is the ability for the reader to impart a tone on the communication. You also know me from over the years and I have and remain respectful and polite. I am not sure what tone you read but let me be crystal clear it is no more than remarkable frustration.

I have been on holiday for two weeks.

Today is my first day back to work.

What is meant to be the routine un-bumpy road of simply getting into my car and driving to work has now become a complicated travail of either borrowing my wife's car, having the Lincoln towed, or finding some solution to what was already meant to be a problem resolved. You can imagine my frustration!

I will see you later on this morning. Perhaps the engine light has gone out and the ghosts of Lincoln mechanics have deftly repaired the problem. Hope springs eternal.

When I brought the car in, my mechanic and I had a chance to talk. He had felt disrespected, angry, and criticized. We talked about how resistant he and most people become when asked to do something for a person who has such an attitude. There is much greater reluctance to do anything for a person who is not asking "nicely," or with respect.

This interaction happened years ago, but I talk about it now as I write this book on unleashing the power of respect. My real-life experience reminded me of how easy it is to be disrespectful. The results always seem to be the same. When my mechanic and I cleared the air, and I explained respectfully that I was frustrated and why, the relationship moved forward. I knew he was doing his best, but I was still annoyed at the inconvenience.

With this clarification, he not only calmed down but wanted to help solve the problem. He was more committed to helping than to being defensive, as I was perceived again as treating him with respect. He checked the car right there, made it his priority, and fixed the problem. I drove away more convinced than ever that seeing each other at an I-M is a powerful path to success. In my interaction with my mechanic, we had resolved our differences through respecting each other. When I acknowledged he was doing the best he could, he calmed down and was able to help meet my goal of repairing my car.

This is unleashing the power of respect. My anger had activated his, and he got angry and defensive. At that point, I had a choice: I could have continued to escalate, perhaps find another mechanic, or I could respect what had happened, and the influence we had on each other's I-M. We've all done the same, become angry at someone and then treated them disrespectfully. We all have then been astonished that our disrespect resulted in a return of disrespect. But now you know why—and can make a small change with a big effect.

For example, how many times have you had to deal with a salesperson or cashier that just seemed rude? How would your response change if you kept the I-M Approach in the back of your mind as you were dealing with him or her? If you react with rudeness yourself, you know what happens: escalation. If you stop and think, *this individual is doing the best they can*, perhaps your approach would change, and with your newly engaged and operating compassion you send a different message to the person on the receiving end. Your I-M is impacted by the initial rudeness, you then check in with your Ic and alter your approach in the Social Domain.

How many times has a customer or client been frustrated and rude to you? If you respond rudely, it only escalates the situation. But as soon as you say you're sorry and that you want to help, that position of respect almost immediately calms the customer's angry brain.

Imagine how an employer can use the I-M to truly maximize the potential of their workforce. Even the word work*force* has the unfortunate connotation that the people who work for you are not doing it out of pride or desire, but because of the power differential inherent to any hierarchy. In physics (still awake?), force equals mass multiplied by acceleration. In the workplace, too much force causes the masses to have an inverse acceleration and slow down! How can you use the I-M Approach to help? If an employee is not being as productive as you would like, ask why. To the extent that they feel comfortable discussing, try to discover what is happening in their domains that influences their current I-M? Are they having difficulty at home? Do they feel criticized or are having conflict in the Social Domain of work? Are they being asked to perform a task that taps into their Ic Domain and self-esteem, fearing they are not up to the task and will then be seen as a failure? Do they have anything medically compromised in their Biological Domain? Using I-M to help formulate these questions, an employer has an opportunity to truly get the most out of their major resource: their people. If an entire workplace is aware of the I-M, then the employee will begin to ask *themselves* why their current potential is what it is. If a human resources employee is available, they will ask, and ultimately the boss will have a better handle on their employees and in a much more meaningful and productive way. Ask yourself for whom have you done your best work? For a boss who motivated you with sincerity and respect, or one who tried to intimidate you to perform out of fear? From a biological point of view, we perform better when under less stress. We have less cortisol (the stress hormone) flowing through our bloodstream and are able to be more productive. The work environment component of the Social Domain critically impacts on productivity and an individual's I-M. Ultimately, we want a person to love going to work and love going home—when they do, it means they feel valued in both the Home and Social Domains.

In the I-M Approach, deference is given to the influence of the Home Domain and its influence on our I-M. One intuitively appreciates how even a small experience in *early childhood* can influence the I-M during adulthood. In fact, a major field of study right now is called ACEs: Adverse Childhood Experiences. These early experiences have an enormous influence on how a person develops, their risk for psychiatric and substance use conditions, violence and being a victim of violence, and long-term work productivity. But if you have had a home in which you felt productive, and you developed an Ic of competence, you are likely to be able to live up to the challenges posed by your boss and life in general. Indeed, those with such self-confidence may seek out challenge, with an I-M that *expects* to succeed.[21]

How many times has your child been disrespectful to you? If you ground them, you may temporarily be exerting your power, but what are you modelling? When you say, "Let me understand what you just said," you model that you are not judging them for being rude but are seeing the behavior as an I-M. You don't have to like it nor condone it. You hold them responsible. But you want to understand why they just did what they did. This builds the foundation a parent

---

[21] I suggest to parents that they change the word "chore" to "contribution." A chore sounds onerous, an external pressure and demand that is resisted. A contribution is how you add to the Home Domain and thereby increase the value of others and yourself.

really wants with their child: one of respect and value and trust. It is critical for your child to be able to come to you with anything. They are not going to do that if they think they are going to be judged.

If a child has grown up in a home where they feel inferior and not industrious, they may shy away from challenge, as their Ic is in a very different place. For a person like this, an employer has an opportunity to help their employee build self-confidence, and ultimately become an even more productive member of the work community. The Ic is not just about how the person perceives themselves, but, equally important, how they believe the world sees them—profoundly influencing one's self-image. Feeling valued is one of the greatest predictors of a child's resilience in the face of traumas like ACEs.

I see myself, in part, the way I think other people see me. Do they see me as capable or incompetent? As a loser or a winner? A person who is working in your office may secretly believe they really are the incompetent worthless person their parents or siblings perceived, or at least showed them that they perceived. From the Ic perspective, a secret is not a secret because of what we have *done*. A secret is a secret because we wonder, *how will someone view me differently if they know my secret*? This Ic is carried into the Social Domain and can interfere with work. An employer who recognizes this can, for example, create a series of jobs that lead to success, and a fundamental shift in the Ic and then I-M of their employee.

The I-M Approach has broad application to our daily lives, our interactions with each other, and larger systems such as towns, governments, ethnicities, and on and on. Imagine how these systems would be impacted by everyone truly recognizing that we are *all* simply doing the best we can at this moment in time, and by truly treating each other with respect.

The I-M Approach then generates a much simpler statement: Respect = Respect. We may not like what someone else does, or condone it, but we have to respect that it is an I-M. When I see that you are treating me the same way, then we can have some frank discussion about our likes and dislikes.

For example, when you vote for a political candidate I don't agree with, or cut me off in traffic, your choices—the best you can do at that moment in time—have an impact on my I-M. When you think about it, it is pretty obvious. But unless we utilize the position of respect, we can get overwhelmed by the "not liking" and "not condoning" aspects of our differences and divisions.

You can apply this discussing politics. I was talking with a person who watches a different news station than me. She has different opinions on what is happening in our country and world, and is angry. At first, she was angry because I did not share her views. But when I explained that just because I didn't share her perspective did not mean I felt she had less value, she literally immediately calmed. We both realized that the anger was not about our different perspectives, but that a different perspective implies the other person is less valuable. That's why she was really angry.

Anger is an emotion designed to change something. My initial thought was, *she wants me to change the way I think about the situation*. But then I realized that was not it. She interpreted my disagreement as a lack of respect. As soon as I said, "Just because I don't agree with you doesn't mean I don't value you," she immediately calmed down. When we can all recognize that someone else's opinion is their I-M, then a disagreement does not mean that person is less valuable. It is not always about seeing eye to eye. It is about seeing Ic to Ic.

Continuing to tap into the human capacity to appreciate someone else's point of view, we can then begin to appreciate their inner experience and perhaps how similar it is to our own. We all want the same thing: to simply feel valued by someone else. That shared perspective can be the foundation of discussion and exploration. When is the last time you got angry at someone treating you with respect?

CONCLUSION

In society today, I think we have moved far away from the simple approach of reminding even a person of an opposite political persuasion of their value. And I believe the current worldwide anger and anxiety is a result. We don't trust each other. We restrict our trust to our in-group, our own tribe, at the exclusion of a multitude of out-groups. Earlier, I discussed the evolutionary pressure on this behavior. We cannot afford to follow this strategy; it has become counterproductive.

My wife and I often reflect on how different the world was when we were growing up. For her, the most dramatic comparison is letting our kids go and play outside. She grew up in a town with beaches and forests. Her parents would open the door, and out she went with her brothers and sisters. At night they would come home. And there was never an expectation of anything else.

But today, with the fear of kidnappers, drugs, malevolence—kids don't just go out to play without some underlying anxiety. Many years ago, a close friend who I trust completely had bought a new red convertible. He offered to drive my then twelve-year-old daughter and two of her friends up the hill to the little country store. It was closed when they got there, so my friend asked where else they would like to go. As they lingered in the parking lot, they were noticed by a policeman in his cruiser. And when they left the parking lot, the policeman followed them all the way back to our driveway down the hill. While grateful, on one hand, that the police are so vigilant, it is a sad example of how much we worry and how so very mistrustful we have become.

As a nation, our Social Domain has shifted to one of mistrust. With this shift, the impact on our Ic is that we see the world as more dangerous than it was when we were growing up. Respect leads to value and value leads to trust. But disrespect leads to feeling devalued, which results in mistrust. We live in a world where there is an enormous amount of disrespect. It is no surprise, then, that we have so much mistrust.

I write this during a time of global economic depression, pandemic, and a world of anger and fear. For many, money is short, and the distribution of resources is being actively discussed domestically and internationally. Health care reform, climate change, the undercurrents of religious wars, political divisions bordering on civil war. A mutual fear of each other. Anger towards one another. Far . . . *far* from trust.

How does this I-M shift to another? What do we need to do, one person at a time, to shift the mistrust between nations, between neighbors, between strangers? You have an enormous influence on everyone around you. Perhaps in the face of so much anger and danger, invisibility, or the freeze response, being uninvolved and without influence, a person with no agency and no power, who does not matter is safer.

But you do matter. And even the choice of doing nothing, you have an influence.

Adopting and applying the I-M Approach will make you a more active participant, helping us all recognize how we are very much involved, that even passivity has an influence as much as aggression; and that the choices *you* make have an impact on *my* I-M! This helps us all to realize that I am less likely to get angry when treated with respect; less likely to get angry and more likely to be able to shift from my fight-flight-freeze response to family-friendship-fellowship; able to listen, understand, and mutually respect. Respect leads to value and value leads to trust. And trust is the foundation of unlimited potential.

The first perspective in this book was about the I-M and the stigma of mental illness. I built on the idea that the foundation of stigma is about mistrust. I suggest it is this mistrust that leads, for example, my wife to worry about the kids going out, or whether I am getting the best deal on a car. I think that, without meaning to, we have created this mistrust when we began to become so self-focused—in part with all those self-help books!

Our world is full of prejudice and judgment. Prejudice towards mental illness is one of the more obvious, and one that I deal with a lot in my profession. But there are others that permeate our globe. Racial discrimination, sexism, gender and sexuality bias, ageism, political bias, religious prejudice. All of these are based on mistrust and used and exploited to separate people into groups. It should be no surprise that the profound disrespect born out of this leads to profound mistrust and anger.

But anger is an emotion designed to change something. So rather than run from anger, or get angry ourselves, let's use the I-M Approach and respect that most angry people simply want to see something different. And, more likely than not, the thing they want to see different is how *they* are seen: not as less-than but as valuable. Just like all of us. Rather than separate into groups—the anger we all experience, the fear we all experience, and the joy and happiness we all experience prove that we are one group, humanity.

We can start the I-M Approach by seeing ourselves as doing the best we can, without judging but respecting. We can only look at ourselves honestly when we do not fear that we will find ourselves as less valuable, lacking, and at risk of being kicked out of our protective group. When we stop worrying, and instead wonder, who we are and why we do what we do. When we realize that even if someone else is judging us, that is their I-M. We don't have to like it or condone it, and we can hold that person responsible, but rather than judge them back, we can use the I-M Approach to again-look at why they do what they do. What has happened within any of their Four Domains that the best they can do is try to make me feel less valuable? I don't have to take it personally and can consciously approach that person with respect.

It is time to move from the "me" generation to the "we" generation. Our lives are intrinsically interwoven. We cannot escape each other, nor should there be reason to. Each of us has a rich inner emotional life, driving our behaviors, fluidly assessing the thoughts and feelings of others. We look to each other to assess ourselves. Wouldn't it be so much better to find respect in the eyes of others, rather than disdain? We can do that by seeing other people at an I-M.

SMALL CHANGES CAN HAVE BIG EFFECTS

When we adopt the I-M Approach, several things begin to happen:

➢ We recognize that our I-M is influenced by the Four Domains.

➢ We can look at each domain and see how they influence each other.

➢ We can look at the influences on our I-M as a roadmap to understanding why we do what we do.

➢ We recognize that life can be a challenge, influenced by so many things outside and inside our brains and bodies, but that our response is always the best we can do at that moment in time.

➢ We may not like or condone our I-M.

➢ We will hold ourselves responsible rather than *blaming* ourselves for our I-M.

➢ We can then again-look and respect our I-M.

➢ And if we do not like or condone our current I-M, then we have the ability to change it to an I-M that we feel we can like and condone.

➢ We recognize that a small change in one domain can have a huge and amplified effect throughout the system.

➢ We can then change our Ic and the way we see ourselves to empower us to move to a different I-M.

➢ We can begin to move towards how we *want* to be seen, and how we want to *see ourselves*.

YOU CONTROL NO ONE BUT INFLUENCE EVERYONE

➢ When we really see ourselves as at an I-M, it is easier to see other people that way as well.

➢ We recognize that we control no one but influence everyone.

➢ We get to choose the kind of influence we want to be.

➢ We recognize that the changes that happen in our I-M have influence on everyone else's I-M.

➢ When we see others at their I-M, they feel more valuable, and that increases our own value.

➢ Respect for others influences the "quality" of our choice. We recognize we are not powerless.

➢ We see that we are more in control of our lives than we thought.

➢ We take responsibility and don't blame ourselves.

➢ We begin to respect ourselves and can then make choices on how we want to treat ourselves.

➢ We forgive ourselves.

➢ We hold each of us responsible for our I-Ms without blame or shame.

➢ We wonder about another's I-M without judgment.

➢ When another person feels respected, they do not get angry.

➢ As such, we become less anxious, and can approach life without the overlay of the number of things that induce anxiety.

➢ We feel safer.

➢ We feel safer with others when they treat us also with respect and at an I-M.

➢ We *unleash* the power of respect.

The I-M Approach is not just about "self-help." Even the term self-help implies you should be doing better. It is an approach that says you are *already* doing the best you can, but if you don't like it, you can change it. The I-M Approach is powerful because when I see you at an I-M, I communicate respect. When you feel respected, you know that I am seeing you as valuable. When you feel valuable, you are more likely to treat me the same way—also with respect, which increases my own value. We no longer need to increase our value at the expense of someone else's. Just the opposite: the more we value others, the more valuable we become.

As we begin to value each other, we can give each other the gift of trust. Respect leads to value and value leads to trust. And trust is the foundation of unlimited potential. We can regain trust, but the only way is by treating each other with respect, to again-look at who we are and why we do what we do. It is the only way we can, together, defuse the anger in the world. It is the only way we can truly remind ourselves and each other that we are one group called *humanity*. Impossible starts with an I-M.

We are all at our I-M. When we truly see others and ourselves as being at an I-M, we will not become stuck, head-to-head, on a one-lane road unwilling to back down and inevitably drowned in an unrelenting tide. When we use the I-M Approach, we can drive in concert from the island of isolation to the mainland of a shared community.

This is who I-M, this Is Me, and I Matter. And so do you, and all of us. We are each and every one of us a remarkable human being. When we see each other as such—we unleash the power of respect.

CPSIA information can be obtained
at www.ICGtesting.com
Printed in the USA
LVHW052311070722
722996LV00001B/60